Coventry

14th/15th November

Casualties, Awards and Accounts

Trevor Harkin

War Memorial Park Publications

2010

Coventry

14th/15th November 1940

Casualties, Awards and Accounts

First Edition 2010

Published by War Memorial Park Publications

For a copy of this publication e-mail trevorharkin@btinternet.com

This book is dedicated to
those who died as a result of enemy action
14th/15th November 1940

Contents

Preface

Having researched my own family tree, in 2005 I began a project to research the Memorial Plaques in Coventry's War Memorial Park. The plaques gave few details about those commemorated, purely initials, surname, rank and regiment. A web page was started www.warmemorialpark.co.uk and local appeals were made, with relatives of the Fallen coming forward. This project led onto several more projects and this is now my tenth book.

Seventy years after the air raid of the night of the 14th/15th November 1940 this book has been released.

Trevor Harkin

Acknowledgments

This book would not have been possible without the assistance of the following:

Peter Adams
Richard Aldridge
Gladys Codling
Walter Cooper
Sheila Duffy
Tony Duffy
Glyn Edwards
Scott Fensom
Dennis Field
Kenneth Gamble
Neil Golby
John Goodwin
Muriel Green
Mike Griffiths
Alan Hartley
Chris Hawthorne
Arthur Ince
Joan Ince
Harry James
John Jeavons
Brian Kelsey

Albert Lindon
Mary Maginnis
Ron Miles
Selina Miles
Gordon Moyes
Les Neale
Gerald Patterson
Sadie Perry
Bert Rawlins
John Roberts
Dennis Sadler
Ron Suddens
Vic Terry
Sheila Thornett
Roy Vernon
Marjorie Viner
Eunice Wale
Ellen Whitwood
Joan Willoughby
Beryl Worswick

Researching and compiling this book would not have been possible without the support of my wife, Emma and children Molly and Toby allowing me to indulge in this passion. The Commonwealth War Grave Commission (CWGC) Head Office in particular Maureen Annetts, was fundamental in helping with the complex searches and background information.

On a local level thanks to Tim Parsons work on the Fires Fighters Memorial, Dave Lewis from Culture and Leisure, Coventry City Council, Terry Patchett from Bablake School, Jane Hewitt from www.familyresearcher.co.uk, Mike Trueman (Birmingham Fire Services Memorial) and Bill McGonville (Coventry Fire Services Memorial) and Tony Rae (Coventry Police Station). The records maintained by Coventry Local Studies Library and the City Archives have been essential in adding information to the details of the fallen and their permission to use pictures and photographs is gratefully acknowledged. Pictures have also come from The Midland Daily Telegraph' and 'The Coventry Telegraph' with permission of MirrorPix and David Scripps.

In some cases I have been contacted directly by the families and friends of the Fallen and I thank them for permission to use photographs and information: Jane Hewitt (Louis Daly), Jackie Gough (John Eaves), Janet Harrison (Stanley David Endersby), Jenny Coates and Ellen Whitwood (Ethel and Leonard Frost), Arthur Ince and Joan Ince (Agnes Harriett Ince), Jo Vernon (Horace Lapworth), M. Smith (Audrey Annie and Audrey Patricia Roberts), Neil Golby (Leonard Golby), J. Blagburn (James Blagburn) and Andy Cox (Arthur Henry Warner) .

Margaret Barber, Crematorium Clerk, Southend. Deidrie Sweeney Local History Dundee, Andrew Bennett Brighton and Hove Archivist. Sue Taylor Stratford Upon Avon Council, Jackie Blackburn Cemeteries, Community History Department, Blackburn, Christine Greer, Rugby Council. Edinburgh Crematorium. Terry Northamptonshire Family History Society, Linda Rhodes, Local Studies Librarian, London Borough Barking and Dagenham,

On a more local level thanks to the following for publicity and promotion; Sheila Adams from *The Earlsdon Echo*';

Finally to those who remain anonymous but were cajoled into helping by those mentioned above, I also express my thanks.

The Evidence

Throughout this book various resources have been compiled to build a database of those that fell. The original *'City of Coventry: Roll of the Fallen'* was fundamental to the project. Compiled in 1947, this included the names of 2,017 members of the Armed Forces, Merchant Navy, Civil Defence and Civilians who fell and were either born, employed or resided in Coventry. Detail on each entry varies but typically covers name, rank, regiment, former regiment, address, birth details, occupation and in some cases employer. Being educated in Coventry did not qualify for inclusion in the *'Roll of the Fallen'*.

Additional information was obtained from the Commonwealth War Grave Commission. The casualties included are those who were classified as death due to 'War Operations'.

The CWGC provided a download from their database with any of the following key words in the next of kin detail: Allesley, Ash Green, Binley, Canley, Coundon, Coventry, Earlsdon, Exhall, Foleshill, Keresley and Tile Hill. It should be noted, however that about a third of the records hold no next of kin detail. In addition, information was provided on the following cemeteries within the Coventry boundary: London Road, Windmill Road, Canley Garden and Crematorium, St. Paul's, Walsgrave on Sowe, Keresley (St. Thomas) Churchyard, Exhall (St. Gile's) Churchyard, Allesley (All Saint's) Churchyard, Radford (St. Nicholas) Churchyard, Binley (St. Bartholomew's) Churchyard), Stoke (St. Michael's) Churchyard, Foleshill Congregational Burial Ground, Wyken (St. Mary) Magdalene Churchyard, Baginton (St. John the Baptist) Churchyard, Bedworth Cemetery, Longford (Salem) Baptist Churchyard, Styvechale (St. Jame's) Churchyard, Kenilworth Cemetery, Stoneleigh (St. Mary's) Churchyard and Baginton (St. John the Baptist) Churchyard.

Those that died are associated with the following districts: Atherstone Rural District, Bedworth Urban District, Birmingham County Borough, Bromsgrove Urban District, Coventry County Borough, Evesham Municipal Borough, Hinckley Urban District, Kenilworth Urban District, Leamington Municipal Borough, Meriden Rural District, , Nuneaton Municipal Borough, , Rugby Municipal Borough, Solihull Urban District, , Stafford Rural District, Stratford Upon Avon Municipal Borough and Warwick Municipal Borough.

A final download established all registered deaths between the 14th and 15th November, 1940 this was then used to determined if any of these were linked to the air raids in Coventry. Photographs have been used from the Alfred Herbert News, the Bablake School *'Roll of Honour'*, supplied by the relatives of the Fallen or from the local newspaper with permission.

From the Local Archives, the *'World War 2 Plaque Applications'*, (War Memorial Park, Windmill Road Cemetery, Hearsall Common, St. Paul's Cemetery, Stoke Heath, London Road Cemetery, War Memorial Park and Walsgrave Common) and the *'List of Deaths Due to War Operations in Coventry'* providing a useful insight. Researching War Memorials throughout Coventry also provided a useful list and those that were examined included St. John's Church, St. Mary's Guild Hall Fire Services Memorial, Radford Fire Station Memorial, Coventry Preparatory School, Walsgrave Memorial, British Thompson Houston Memorial, Post Office Memorial, Coventry Corporation Memorial in the Council House, Earlsdon Working Men's Club, Barras Heath Working Mens Club, St. Paul's Memorial, Baginton War Memorial, Wolston War Memorial and the London Road Memorial at the Communal Grave. Rolls of Honour were used from Bablake School, King Henry VIII School, Barr's Hill School, Alfred Herbert (excluding employees from outside Coventry) and Coventry Tool and Gauge Roll.

It is likely that a number of Citizens from Coventry died at home some time after the war owing to longer term illnesses such as the effects of wounds received and regrettably the full list of these men and women is not known. During the war, a number of local employee magazines ceased publication, local papers were used although the obituaries did not offer conclusive evidence for individuals. In Memoriam has been used from 1942 to correlate with the list of casualties.

If further details can be supplied or amendments required for future editions please contact me. It is important to note, however, that the cross- referencing of material has raised anomalies, in particular order of forenames, middle names, rank, spelling, address etc. In these cases I have gone with the majority. Searching *'The London Gazette'* provided citations but not all were found. Citations did not just appear in the months following the air raid but for sometime afterwards, they also do not mention the date so these have been supported by local articles printed at the time.

The Outbreak of War

On Sunday September 3rd 1939 headlines declared 'Britain at War ' and a dramatic announcement was made by the Prime Minister on the wireless at 11.15am "*I am speaking to you from the Cabinet Room at 10 Downing Street. This morning the British Ambassador in Berlin handed the German Government a final note stating that, unless we hear from them by 11 o'clock that they were prepared at once to withdraw their troops from Poland, a state of war would exist between us. I have to tell you now that no such undertaking has been received, and that consequently this country is at war with Germany.*"

By the 14th September 1939, fireman were putting the final touches to a blast and splinter proof shelter they had manually constructed at Westhill, Radford. The shelter could accommodated 200 people and a declaration made locally that 500 men were efficient enough in fire fighting skills to assist the Auxiliary Fire Services. The following day with blackouts imposed, the fifth casualty was encountered when 71 year old Elizabeth Villiers of Leicester Causeway was knocked down and killed by a van. The figure would rise to double figures by the end of October and one of Coventry's blind men was urging people do use their sense of hearing more and the city's buses were fitted with blackout curtains.

'Alfred Herbert News' pointed out the black-out must stay, that it is one of the principals of Home Defence. The Ministry of Transport suggested it is hard to prove you were in the right, if you wake up in hospital. Traffic was restricted to 20mph in build up areas and those who walk in the darkness were asked to play fair with the man who went about his business on wheels!

Lighting offenders who failed to observe the full requirements of the blackout and showing light from their premises were being fined up to a £1 by the Coventry City Police Court. The difficulties with allocating air raid shelters in the dark was quickly recognized and the Corporation along with the Chief Constable experimented with street lamps that displayed the letters ARP, to those walking along the pavement. A number of authorities would soon copy the idea.

News headline were full of the details of courtcase of the IRA Broadgate Explosion that had taken place on the 25th August 1939, with those being found guilty being executed. In November 1939, local papers reported that stained glass from the cathedral was being moved to a place of safety and the City's population was 230,541 citizens. On November 7th,1939 fatality thirteen occurred due to the blackout when a victim was knocked by a tram shortly after he left hospital with a poisoned finger. On the 27th December 1939, the loss of Coventry's first RAF man, Norman Frederick Lines was reported.

In January 1940, 200 allotments were being cultivated in the 'Dig for Victory' campaign with land valued in the City Shopping Centre at £50 a yard with Woolworths being estimated at £100. In February 1940 warnings were being published about the unauthorized collectors of scrap metal that was due to start on the 1st March 1940, estimates were that Coventry had enough metal for two battleships!

Large scale ARP exercises were being planned with every Coventry ARP unit in the city but also stressing the mutual assistance between Coventry and other towns. One of the big points in the manoeuvres is the lessons that can be learned from any set of circumstances and it was hoped by frequent exercising all conditions can become known. Coventry Authorities insisted that the scheme laid down by the Ministry for Home Security in the events of an air raid could be improved upon. An event held on the 1st April 1940 included 1,500 Civil Defence workers in Birmingham and 300 vehicles from five counties. A houses and mock streets were laid out and the event was described as the finest Civil Defence demonstration yet given.

In March 1940 the ARP at Alfred Herbert carried out a successful evacuation. The whole of the staff about 1, 260 people were evacuated to the back of the offices. The time taken from start to finish was less then five minutes. Being proactive Alfred Herbert also made provision for a building for a first aid centre to give contamination and for the treatment of casualties from both sexes.

Entering the Trenches

Alfred Herbert's First Aid Centre

April the 21st 1940, the whole of Coventry's ARP was engaged in a large scale combined exercise with the staging of 94 incidents. Over 2,000 wardens, auxiliary firemen and repair gangs were on duty. On May 6th 1940 lessons of a Clacton disaster were communicated and the citizens of Coventry warned that falling glass comes inwards and that 136 people were injured as a result at Clacton by watching out of the window when an unknown plane was overhead. A week later, the public were assured that

Coventry was prepared for parachutists and that the public should be confident if any additional steps are necessary they will be promptly taken. The public were reminded *'It is of course the duty of the citizens to watch out for enemy parachutists, where any are observed the police should be immediately notified'*.

On the 14th May 1940 the headline read *'If Coventry were bombed, 10'000 ARP Workers would be ready'*, the article continued; *'there are nearly 10,000 men and women excluding the 5,000 women in the auxiliary services who could be mobilized in a very short time if Coventry was bombed '* stated Mr C. T. Bonham, ARP Officer for the city. This was supported by *'We are ready for any eventuality'* said Dr. a. Massey Medical Officer of Health he continued *'first line posts and ambulance and first aid depots have been manned day and night since war broke out'*. By this point 1,000 Coventry men had enrolled as Local Defence Volunteers (later the Home Guard).

By June 1940 thousands of shelters wherein demand as they were a new type of brick and concrete ARP surface domestic shelters with the Women's Volunteer Service canvassing the streets of Coventry establishing requirements. By the end of June 1940 it was confirmed that Air Raid Shelters would be built in the streets of Coventry and on the carriageway and further notes that *'this scheme will not be confined to any particular district of the city'*.

Decisions to have shelters were governed by two considerations:
1) Number of persons in a street qualified to have a brick and concrete shelter for free
2) Width of the carriageway.

A number of reasons led to this decisions being taken by the authorities. Among them was the
1) Big saving in time that can be effected in the provision of shelter accommodation for a number of families living in the same street
2) A saving in cost by providing communal shelters; general convenience of access
3) Additional opportunity offered for those who may be in the streets when an air raid warning is given

Further detail explained; if there was land available to accommodate communal shelters, whether in private ownership or not, it was taken over for this purpose. In streets where no land is available and the carriage way is wide enough to carry two lines of traffic the communal shelters will be erected in the carriageway.

Work returns showed that worked has been completed on communal domestic shelters for 1,744 persons and that work on similar shelters for 2,493 persons was in hand. Individual domestic shelters to accommodate 519 persons have been completed and work in hand to provide another 2,121 persons. Altogether upwards of 60 buildings are engaged in providing shelters of this type on about 600 different sites.

Sir William Wyley a benefactor and a well-known citizen died in August 1940 and was cremated at Perry Barr Crematorium with his ashes interred in the crypt at Coventry Cathedral by the side of his wife who died in 1931. William was aged 88. On his death Charterhouse and the associated grounds were passed into the possession of the City.

Also in August on the 20th members of the public were given demonstrations in the use of a stirrup pump. Chief Officer W. H. Cartwright appealed for the maximum of public co-operation when the city might have 'visitations'. Experience of recent raids had shown that incendiaries posed little or no real difficulty providing they were dealt with quickly and citizens were reminded that; *'those that fell on open ground could be dealt with by putting soil on them and in residential area fireman should be helped by leaving out buckets and spades and obeying instructions. For those who owned premises inspection were required after an air raid in the roof and night watchmen should be used to make inspections'.*

On the 4th September 4th 1940 it was reported that demand for the free domestic air raid shelter has now reached the highest demand since they were first offered to the public. Everyday hundreds of applications are being received, registration has been open for a number of years but demands are high during periods of tension. It was rumoured that shelters are stocked piled and can be paid for, the Council stated this was not true.

The Council also stated that in isolated cases where people live near a communal shelter they have been secretly sold. Communal shelters that were being built in the streets were meeting high percentage of demands but they were receiving complaints as they are being misused. The shelters have been erected for specific use by where they were placed. The Council stated that *'People from entirely different districts consider that they can use these shelters if there is a raid and taking bedding to sleep in there. Although the legitimate users of shelters are expected to give every assistance to be who might be caught in the streets, other people should not enter the shelters'.* A brick shelter placed on the Holyhead Road, caused annoyance as it had little room for pedestrian passing and they squeezed by the traffic rather then cross over the road.

Coventry National Emergency Committee on the 24th September 24th 1940, were forced to justify why they had asked householders who were allocated responsibility for shelters to erect doors and lock them because they had been improperly used. The Council had replied that expected cleaning costs were £5000 per year. Councillor Weston at a Committee meeting questioned about a child unable to get in a locked shelter on his way home from school, a further Councillor questioned the location on St. Patrick's Road on the pavement instead of in nearby open space.

Four days later on the 28th September 1940 it was reported *'Housewives to act as ARP helpers'*; by receiving and putting on display a special card in the window it would show ARP wardens that a bucket of sand and spade were available and maybe a cup of tea! The idea was when the housewife is out they remove the card, the response to this scheme was not subsequently reported, although cards were printed.

Twelve fixed points (churches, halls and institutions) were identified by the 4th October 1940 that could assist 3,000 people immediately in the event of a raid, if whole families lost everything clothing, shelter and incidentals would be available. A War Damage Advice Centre was to be set up in Hertford Street where people who had suffered bomb damage could obtain all the necessary information. The Corporation would run the Bureau on behalf of The Ministry of Health who would pay the expenses and fifty corporation house would be set aside for the re-housing off those made homeless.

On the same day, news came that Coventry was to prepare scheme for deep shelters, the issue was raised by Alderman G. E. Hodgkinson and Coventry's National Emergency Committee were on agreement on the subject. The City Engineer, Mr. Ford was asked to submit without delay to Government technical experts. Throughout August, September and October news was published of undisclosed towns in the West Midlands that had suffered air raids.

A further scheme stated *'ARP want your names on gateposts'; After two months off bombing, a rescue worker who has spent two months digging suggested names on gateposts. The worker explained that even though the house was destroyed by a bomb the front gate and post remained standing. They should add if individuals sleep in the house or shelter so they know where to start. The list should be up to date and a note made on visitors.* Another suggestions said that First Aid Workers should make themselves more widely known, so the walking wounded could be treated within a distance of 500 to 1,000 yards.

The following day an announcement that steps were being taken to secure empty houses for re-housing families. Town Clerk (Mr. Frederick Smith) examined using compulsory requisitioning powers to take over houses in the hands of estate agents, auctioneers and the like. It was believed that enough accommodation exists in the city with friends and families for victims who have lost houses. The Charterhouse left by Colonel Wyley may be used for accommodation and those who have Corporation houses bigger then they need would be grateful if a swap could be arranged.

Reported on the 14th November 1940 was the Duchess of Gloucester tours Coventry's bombed areas. The Chief Constable described how thirteen people had lost their lives in a house in front of the completely shattered remains of which the party was standing. She met Mrs. Oldfield who lost seven relatives, his mother, brother, sister and a niece. Mrs. Oldfield told how she had been trapped for an one hour and a half by heavy timbers as she was in a shelter in the garden and did not know that her husband had been trapped and people killed. Severe damage to the Cathedral was also reported when an incendiary dropped through lead roof of the nave and lodged between that and a subsidiary roof.

Meeting the relatives

Circular 1779

In Circular No. 1179 issued at the end of February 1939 the Ministry of Health made reference to the arrangements to be made for the disposal of the bodies who might be killed as a result of War Operations in this country. In May 1939 in 'The Municipal Review' in the preparations for the scheme for the City of Westminster a number of points of detail arose from the Town Clerk and a questionnaire prepared for which the Ministry could offer their observations. The eighteen questions were replied to by the Ministry.

Various parts of form CWD (Civilian War Death) were to completed by various people in authority and triplicate copies of the form to be filed with the Town Clerk, Police and for file. Subsequent memorandums were issued to Town Clerks throughout the country and one Memorandum 222 covered points on 'Identification, Records and Registration'.

Dated the 12th April 1940 a copy of the following was given to Coventry Corporation as an example from Ilford Borough Council, Cemeteries Department.

Disposal of Civilian War Dead

On arrival at the mortuary the body will be numbered, a numbered shroud, a numbered large canvas bag and a numbered small canvas bag will be allocated for that particular body. (Large bag for clothing and a small bag for personal effects). This number will definitely be identified with that body throughout.

Part A of Ford CWD is to be filled in at once and signed by the officer or person who brought the body to the mortuary. If the name and address are known they will be entered in Part C. Where identity cannot readily be established Part D of the Form is to be filled in. Inventory of valuables to be completed, checked by officer bring in body, and placed in small canvas bag. Clothing particulars will be taken later as time permits.

At the close of the day a completed list of all the bodies (including unidentified, male, female, child etc) brought to the mortuary will be made. Three copies, 1. Town Clerk 2. Collection by Police 3. File. Should it be practicable in the case of identified body the letter (Form 1) will be sent out direct from the mortuary. If possible by hand. The next step is to await identification and decision of relatives as to whether the burial is to be undertaken privately or by the council.

IF BURIED BY THE COUNCI, and the body has been identified Form CWD. Part C will be completed in full, signed by the Mortuary Superintendent, and two copies forwarded to the Town Clerk.

IF BURIED PRIVATELY, Form CWD Part B will be completed in full and form No. 5 handed to person signing item No. 1. Any temporary entries made in Part C will be deleted. Two copies will then be forwarded to the Town Clerk.

UNIDENTIFIED BODIES Form CWD Part D to be completed in full and signed by the Mortuary Superintendent. Two copies will then be forwarded to the Town Clerk.

Should a National Registration Card be found on the body, the Mortuary Superintendent must forward such card, attached to the CWD forms, to the Town Clerk for transmission to the Registration General.

Likewise should any food cards be found, the Mortuary Superintendent must forward such cards, attached to the CWD forms to the Town Clerk for transmission to the Food Controller. The Food controller to be advised direct by the Mortuary Superintendent of all cards so forwarded (Forms Attached).

REFERENCE TO CORONERS Where the Mortuary Superintendent has reasons to believe that death was not due to War Operations he must report the death to the Coroner. If the Coroner is satisfied that death was in fact due to War Operations he must endorse Form CWD to that effect and return it to the Mortuary Superintendent. The Mortuary Superintendent will then insert any additional particulars in the form and transmit it to the Town Clerk. If the Coroner is not satisfied, the provisions of the ordinary law apply.

ACTION TO BE TAKEN BY TOWN CLERK ON RECEIPT OF FORMS CWD

If Part B is completed, one copy to be forwarded to the Registrar for the appropriate sub-district i.e. the place of death, to assist him in securing registration of death by the relatives or friends, but the form is NOT to be certified on behalf of the Town Clerk.
In the case of bodies which are to be buried by the Council, and if the body has been identified that is, if Part C is completed in full, Form CWD is to be certified by the Town Clerk and one copy sent to the registrar for the appropriate sub-district.

Make out Certificate of Disposal (Form 7A)
If the body has not been identified Form CWD is to be retained by the Town Clerk. Should identification subsequently established the form is to be appropriately completed and a copy send to the registrar.

Make out Certificate of Disposal (Form 7a)
CASES WHERE FORM CWD HAS BEEN SIGNED BY THE MORTUARY
SUPERINTENDENT; ARRANGEMENTS MADE FOR BURIAL BY COUNCIL BUT
NOT COMPLETED, AND RELATIVES DESIRE TO ARRANGE PRIVATE BURIAL.

The Town Clerk is to give the applicant a certificate that death was due to War Operations, and written authority to remove and dispose of the body (Form 7A).

In such a case the death is NOT to be registered by the relatives or friends, and they should be so informed. (Form 6 to be handed to them). For the purpose of burial and registration the body in such cases is to be deemed to be buried by the Council.

A written note is to be obtained by the Town Clerk informing him of the place where the body is to be interred (Form 7C). Form 7B also to be completed. A note indicating that the body has been buried by relatives is to be inserted by the Town Clerk on Form CWD which is to be forwarded to the Registrar.

ARRANGEMENTS FOR BURIAL

The Town Clerk will collate the certificates of disposal he has made out and still in his possession. These will be forwarded to the Borough Engineer, together with Form 3. The Borough Engineer will arrange for the van to pick the bodies up at the Mortuary – the driver to be supplied with the Disposal Certificates, for examination at the Mortuary and retention at the cemetery, and deliver them to the cemetery.

The Town Clerk to complete Form 2 and deliver to the Mortuary Superintendent

----

Should the number of bodies to be buried by the Council be only small, I shall endeavour to arrange with local undertakers for the burials to take place in the cheapest coffins. If the number is large, then burial will have to be in shrouds of which I have nearly a 1,000 in stock.

As far as the cemetery is concerned, I have already two trenches excavated. One for the burial of HM Forces and the other for civilians in general, the civilian trench will accommodate about 400 bodies.

Should the number of burials at any one time be large, the bodies will be laid in the trench in the early morning, covered and the ceremony arranged a little later. I have spoken to clergymen of all denominations, and they are all prepared to give a short service. The Roman Catholic ceremony to be a very short time after the others. In this connection, I would very respectfully suggest that it would be a token of respect if it were possible for the Mayor to be represented.

Form IB will be forwarded where practicable, or Form IC when this applies.

The conveyance from the mortuary to the cemetery are converted dust carts, and as these would not be quite 'de riguer' I would suggest that all transport be carried out early in the morning, even though the number of burials was small.

Records of the exact position of all bodies in the trench will be kept at the cemetery.

EFFECTS Application for the effects of the deceased person must be made to the Town Clerk. If he considers the applicant to be the rightful owner, authority on Form IA will be handed to him for production to the storekeeper.

On the 5th June 1940 a Memorandum notes The form referred to is now superseded by the form supplied by the Ministry in Circulation 2024 dated 21st May 1940, and the two forms supplied with their Circular 2009 on the 24th April 1940.

Circular 2177 from the Ministry of Health was send to County Councils and hospitals on the Emergency Scheme on the 16th October 1940 and received by the Town Clerk on the 18th October and referenced *'Burial of Emergency Medical Service Cases Dying in Hospital'*. Subsequent correspondence passed from the Town Clerks office to Coventry and Warwickshire Hospital.

On the 4th November 1940 further correspondence was received by the Ministry of Health with eight specific points. Point 1 referred to the death in HM Forces whilst points 2 to 7 referred to civilians and are stated below.

2. Experiences so far has been that in the majority of cases the bodies are claimed by relatives or friends for burial at their own expense in the customary way. In many cases, however e.g. Where the body has not been identified or where the relatives cannot be traced or else do not wish to claim it, it will be for the local authority to arrange for burial, the cost being borne by public funds.

3. Funeral arranged by local authorities should invariably be carried out in a seemly fashion and whilst avoiding any unnecessary display or expense should be of the most dignified kind that circumstances may permit. Burial of civilians by a local authority should be regarded as no less honourable than burial of a soldier by his comrades. The Ministry feels sure that it should be the wish of local authorities generally to arrange, where practicable, particularly in the case of funerals of civil defence volunteers who are killed in the execution of their duty, for official representation of the local authority at the funeral as a mark of respect.

4. It is recognised that where heavy casualties have occurred in a district it may not always be practicable to arrange for burials to be carried out in the customary manner. The local authority is not in a position to predict the scale of future casualties, or when they will occur, and it will under the necessity of making such emergency modifications in the normal burial arrangements as the situation requires in order that there may not be a breakdown of the burial organisation to the detriment not only of public health but of moral. The authorities of all districts in which there are substantial aggregations of population would be well advised to draw up plans, if they have not already done so, to meet such a contingency. Attention should be directed inter alia to the arrangements for the preparations of graves, for the conveyance of bodies to the burial ground and for the

use if necessary of substitutes for wooden coffins. The Senior Regional Officer should informed of the arrangements proposed.

5. In the event of heavy and frequent casualties a severe strain will be imposed upon the cemetery authorities and others concerned in the burial of the dead. While the Minister would deprecate any attempt by local authorities to prohibit private internments – and indeed the fullest opportunity which circumstances permit should be given to relatives to claim the body where it is clear that private burial is not only desired by the relatives but is also practicable – he would agree that multiplicity of funerals might in some circumstances be obviously undesirable and that the local authority might in such cases properly discuss the position with the relatives, drawing attention as they think fit to the conditions set out in Paragraph 3 and 4 above.

6. The Imperial War Graves Commission have intimated that where special plots have been set aside for the burial of military personnel these plots will be available, if circumstances permit, for the burial by the local authority of civil defence volunteers who are killed while on duty or who die of a war service injury. It is the intention of the commission permanently to record the names of those buried in these plots and to consider other possible means of commemorating them.

7. In the view of His Majesty's Government the use of the Union Jack as a pall at the funeral of any civilian, whether a civil defence volunteer or not, whose death is due to enemy action is appropriate and would be a fitting tribute and those responsible for the funeral arrangements should consider themselves as fully at liberty to use the flag in this manner as in the case of military funerals.

8. Local authorities should ensure the mortuary superintendents and other responsible officers are fully aware of the terms of Paragraph 2 of Circular 2165 (intimating that a grant of £7.10s.0d is payable by the authority in the case of a civil defence volunteer who is killed on duty or dies from a war service injury and is buried privately by relatives or friends) in order that they may be able to explain the position quite clearly to relatives and friends. It is obviously desirable that their should be no misapprehension on this matter, and that in case where a grant is payable those entitled should be aware of it, and conversely, that where a grant is not payable the relatives and friends should realise that, if they wish to make their own arrangements, they must do so at their own expense.

After the raid with the number of casualties mounting and with reference to Circular 1779 the Corporation had to advise people of the situation with this notice.

TO THE RELATIVES OF THE FALLEN

2ND Notice Sunday   17th November, 1940

Since the issue of the first notice of Saturday, the 16th November 1940 steps have been taken to obtain help from neighbouring cities, and there is a strong hope that by Wednesday, the 20th November (the time appointed for funerals) it will be possible to provide a coffin for everyone of the fallen.

While the National Emergency Committee feel that their decision of the 16th November 1940 as to the whole of the burials being undertaken by the City Council was in general the right one a collective basis, the Committee (who wish to the utmost extent that the emergency conditions permit to meet the desires of the relatives) have decided to amend their decision of the 16th November 1940, to the following extent:-

a)   Relatives who prove that they are able at their own expense and under arrangements to be made by themselves to bury their fallen in a cemetery or burial ground **outside the municipal boundary of the City of Coventry** may do so. The Town Clerk has been authorised in such cases to issue the necessary certificate to enable relatives to obtain registration and the necessary authority to the outside burial authorities to effect the burial.

b)   As regards other burials the National Emergency Committee are satisfied that the only practicable and fitting course is for the fallen to be buried by the Council together on Wednesday in the reserved area of Coventry Cemetery, so that those who side by side died for their country may lay side by side in the Garden of Rest.

BYDIRECTION OF THE NATIONAL EMERGENCY COMMITTEE

Casualties prior to the 14th/15th November 1940

28th August 1940

Swanswell Street

ASHMAN, Iris Jane. Injured as a result of enemy action, 28th August, 1940 at Swanswell Street, died at Coventry and Warwickshire Hospital. Age 20. Daughter of Wallace and Jane Ashman, of Moira, Coventry Road, Bulkington. Born 16th April, 1920 at Bedworth. Employed British Thompson Houston Ltd. Grave Ref. Bedworth Cemetery.

CLARIDGE, Charles Henry. Age 20. Son of William and Florence Claridge, of 32, Heath Crescent, Stoke Heath. Born 13th April, 1920 at Coventry. Employed Morris Motors Ltd. Grave Ref. A. 1/2. Communal Grave, Coventry (London Road) Cemetery.

COATES, Evelyn. Age 17. Daughter of William Coates, of 28, Church Street. Born 20th May, 1923 at Coventry. Grave Ref. Coventry (London Road) Cemetery.

FORSTER, Robert. Injured as a result of enemy action, 28th August, 1940 died at Coventry and Warwickshire Hospital. Age 26. Resided at 16, Edmund Road. Son of Thomas and Frances Forster, of 15, Dale Street, Crawerook, Ryton, Co. Durham. Born 24th July, 1914 at Crawcrook, Co. Durham. Employed Parkside Garage Ltd. Grave Ref. Ryton Cemetery, Ryton-on-Tyne, Co. Durham.

HARVEY, Daniel. Age 25. Resided at 75, Harnall Lane West. Grave Ref. A. 3/1. Communal Grave, Coventry (London Road) Cemetery

LEES, Thomas. Age 45. Resided at 60, Owenford Road. Husband of A. Lees. Grave Ref. Coventry (London Road) Cemetery.

LITCHFIELD, Harry Leonard. Age 21. Son of Harry and Edith Litchfield, of 16, Vincent Street. Grave Ref. Coventry (London Road) Cemetery.

MULHALL, Richard. Age 25. Resided at 19, Lincoln Street. Grave Ref. A. 3/2. Communal Grave, Coventry, (London Road) Cemetery.

WEBB, Kenneth Ernest. Age 23. Resided at 212, Earlsdon Avenue. Son of Ernest Edward Webb. Born 19th March, 1917 at Portsmouth. Employed British Thompson Houston Ltd. Grave Ref. A. 1/1. Communal Grave, Coventry (London Road) Cemetery.

EWING, Annie. Died at 62, Swanswell Street. Age 84. Resided at 62, Swanswell Street. Wife of George Ewing. Born 1859, at Baddesley, Nr Atherstone. Housewife. Grave Ref. Communal Grave, Coventry (London Road) Cemetery.

EWING, George. Died at 62, Swanswell Street. Age 87. Resided at 62, Swanswell Street. Husband of Annie Ewing. Born 1857 at Norwich. Employed Coventry Corporation Highways Department. Grave Ref. Communal Grave, Coventry (London Road) Cemetery.

Cambridge Street
CALLAGHAN, Desmond Paterson John. Died at 38, Cambridge Street. Age 15. Resided at 38, Cambridge Street. Son of John and Edith Callaghan. Born 23rd February, 1925 at 9 Court, 2 House, Well Street. Employed Pattison & Hoburn Ltd. Grave Ref. A. 3/3. Communal Grave, Coventry (London Road) Cemetery.

Wright Street
GREEN, John Sidney. Died at 51, Wright Street. Age 5. Resided at 45, Wright Street. Son of Sidney Green. Born 6th November, 1934 at Coventry. Attended Frederick Bird School. Grave Ref. Coventry (London Road) Cemetery.

Hartlepool Road
WILKINS, Mary Elizabeth. Died at Hartlepool Road. Age 61. Resided at 4, Hartlepool Road, Wife of William Henry Wilkins. Born at Foleshill. Housewife. Grave Ref. Communal Grave, Coventry (London Road) Cemetery.

WILKINS, William Henry. Died at Hartlepool Road. Age 61. Resided at 4, Hartlepool Road. Husband of Mary Elizabeth Wilkins. Born at 4, Hartlepool Road. Employed Humber Ltd. Grave Ref. Coventry (London Road) Cemetery.

29th August 1940

CASE, Emily Louise. Died at Coventry and Warwickshire Hospital. Age 79. Resided at 25, Harnall Lane East. Widow of Henry Case. Grave Ref. Coventry (London Road) Cemetery.

30th August 1940

GALSWORTHY, Thomas John. Died at Coventry and Warwickshire Hospital. Age 64. Son of William Galsworthy. Resided at 66, Foleshill Road. Husband of Leonora L. Galsworthy, of 4, West Avenue, Stoke Park. Born 21st February, 1876 at Radford, Coventry. Employed by Clarke & Sons. Grave Ref. Coventry (Stoke, St Michael's) Cemetery.

16th September 1940

Wallace Road

BACON, Abraham. Died at 67, Wallace Road. Age 65. Husband of Clara Bacon. Born 24th July, 1876 at Haverhill, Suffolk. Resided 67, Wallace Road. Husband of Clara Bacon. Storesman at Renold and Coventry Chain Company Limited. Grave Ref. Keresley (St. Thomas) Churchyard.

BACON, Clara. Died at 67, Wallace Road. Age 67. Wife of Abraham Bacon. Resided 67, Wallace Road. Born 7th December, 1874 at Haverhill, Suffolk. Housewife. Grave Ref. Keresley (St. Thomas) Churchyard.

BACON, Kitty Irene. Died at 67, Wallace Road. Age 38. Daughter of Abraham and Clara Bacon. Resided at 67, Wallace Road. Born 7th March, 1907 at Haverhill, Suffolk. Supervisor, Renold and Coventry Chain Company Limited. Grave Ref. Keresley (St. Thomas) Churchyard.

ELKINGTON, David Thomas. Died, 16th September, 1940 at 74 , Wallace Road. Aged 23 months. Resided at 17, Miles Meadow. Son of Private Thomas Jesse Elkington, Royal Army Ordnance Corps, and Gladys Elkington. Born 3rd October, 1938 at Coventry. Grave Ref. Coventry (Radford, St. Nicholas) Churchyard.

KLETZENBAUER, Joanna. Died, at 74, Wallace Road. Age 25. Daughter of Carl Franz and Leopoldina Kletzenbauer, of 25, St. Paul's Road. Born 25th March, 1916 at Coventry. Educated Barr's Hill School. Comptometer Operator. Grave Ref. Coventry (Radford, St Nicholas) Churchyard.

CLARKE, Arthur Joseph. Died, at 76, Wallace Road. Age 33. Home Guard. Resided at 76, Wallace Road. Son of Joseph William and Alice Elizabeth Clarke, of 105, Gulson Road. Husband of Ida Vera Clarke. Born 6th February, 1907 at Coventry, Employed Sir W. G. Armstrong Whitworth Aircraft Ltd. Grave Ref. Coventry (London Road) Cemetery.

CLARKE, Ida Vera. Died, 40 at 76, Wallace Road. Age 34. Resided at 76, Wallace Road. Daughter of Mr. and Mrs. Genge, of Birtley, Manby Road, Great Malvern, Worcestershire. Wife of Arthur Joseph Clarke. Born 2nd April, 1906 at Coventry. Housewife. Grave Ref. Coventry, (London Road) Cemetery

CLARKE, Maurice. Died, at 76, Wallace Road. Aged 5 months. Resided 76, Wallace Road. Son of Arthur Joseph and Ida Vera Clarke. Born 8th May, 1940 at Coventry. Grave Ref. Coventry (London Road) Cemetery.

ALLSOPP, Charles. Died as a result of enemy air action at 78, Wallace Road. Age 67. Resided at 80, Wallace Road also of Emberton, near Olney, Buckinghamshire. Husband of Laura Allsopp. Born 4th December, 1872, at Ozleworth, Gloucestershire. Grave Ref. Emberton Church.

POWLEY, Harold. Died, at 78, Wallace Road. Age 20. Resided at 78, Wallace Road. Son of William and Phyllis Powley. Born 1920 at Coventry. Employed Daimler Co. Ltd. Grave Ref. Coventry (London Road) Cemetery.

POWLEY, Phyllis. Died, at 78, Wallace Road. Age 40. Resided at 78, Wallace Road. Daughter of Mr. Mrs. Bailey, of 52, Nunts Lane, Keresley. Wife of William Powley. Born 1894 at Lancaster, Lancashire. Grave Ref. Coventry (London Road) Cemetery.

POWLEY, William. Died, at 78, Wallace Road. Age 45. Resided at 78, Wallace Road. Son of R. and Margaret Ann Powley, of 48, Holmesdale Road, Foleshill. Husband of Phyllis Powley. Born 1895 at Ulverston, Lancashire. Employed Daimler Co. Ltd. Grave Ref. Coventry (London Road) Cemetery.

Stevenson Road

BARNES, Ellen. Died, at 58, Stevenson Road. Age 35. Resided at 58, Stevenson Road, Radford. Wife of Arthur Barnes. Housewife. Mother of Rosalie Barnes. Born 17th July, 1906 at Salford. Grave Ref. Coventry (London Road) Cemetery.

BARNES, Rosalie. Died, at 58, Stevenson Road. Aged 1. Resided at 58, Stevenson Road, Radford. Daughter of Arthur Barnes, and of Ellen Barnes. Born 25th August, 1939 at 58, Stevenson Road. Grave Ref. Coventry (London Road) Cemetery.

NICHOL, Ann. Died, at 60, Stevenson Road. Age 73. Resided at 60, Stevenson Road. Wife of John Nichol. Born 24th July, 1867 at Hauxley, Northumberland. Resided at 60, Stevenson Road. Housewife, Grave Ref. Keresley Cemetery.

NICHOL, John. Died, at 60, Stevenson Road. Age 73. Resided at 60, Stevenson Road. Husband of Ann Nichol. Born 13th December, 1866 at Bellingham, Northumberland. Grave Ref. Keresley Cemetery.

MASON, Ann. Died, at 62, Stevenson Road. Aged 3 months. Resided at 62, Stevenson Road, Radford. Daughter of Ernest James Mason, and of Vera Mary Mason. Born 7th June, 1940 at Coventry. Grave Ref. a. 2/1. Communal Grave, Coventry (London Road) Cemetery.

MASON, Vera Mary. Died, at 62, Stevenson Road. Age 26. Resided at 62, Stevenson Road, Radford. Daughter of Mrs. V. M. Warner, of 114, Grangemouth Road. Wife of Ernest James Mason. Born 17th July, 1914 at Coventry. Grave Ref. A. 2/1. Communal Grave, Coventry (London Road) Cemetery.

26th September 1940

MORGAN, Douglas Hazel. Died, at 1, Parliament Hill Mansions. St. Pancras, London. Age 31. Resided at Parliament Hill Mansions, Lissenden Gardens. Son of Charles and Eleanor L. Morgan, of 36, Broadway, Earlsdon, Coventry. Husband of Elsie May Morgan. Grave Ref. St. Pancras, London.

12th October 1940

Aldbourne Road

NEVENS, Alexandra. Died, at Aldbourne Road. Age 40. Albanian National. Resided at 64, Aldbourne Road. Born Greece. Employed Daimler Company Limited. Grave Ref. Coventry (Radford, St. Nicholas) Churchyard.

MAGUIRE, Elizabeth. Died, at 58, Aldbourne Road. Age 30. Resided at 58, Aldbourne Road. Daughter of James and Elizabeth Laverty, of 180, Falls Road, Belfast, Northern Ireland. Wife of John Vincent Maguire. Born at Belfast. Grave Ref. Communal Grave, Coventry (London Road) Cemetery.

MAGUIRE, John Vincent. Died, at 58, Aldbourne Road. Age 31. Resided at 58, Aldbourne Road. Son of John and Mary Maguire, of 24, Hugo Street, Belfast, Northern Ireland. Husband of Elizabeth Maguire. Born at Belfast. Grave Ref. Communal Grave, Coventry (London Road) Cemetery.

TURVEY, Beatrice Battenburg. Died, at 68, Aldbourne Road. Age 53. Resided at 68, Aldbourne Road. Widow of Alfred Turvey. Born 15th November, 1886. Employed Royal Air Force Depot, Sandy Lane. Grave Ref. Coventry (London Road) Cemetery.

ALLEN, Hilda Mary. Died, at 85, Aldbourne Road. Age 46. Resided at 85, Aldbourne Road, Radford. Wife of George William Allen. Grave Ref. Coventry (Radford, St. Nicholas) Churchyard.

ALLEN, Hubert Reginald. Died as a result of enemy air action, 12th October, 1940 at 85, Aldbourne Road. Age 15. Resided at 85, Aldbourne Road, Radford. Son of George William Allen, and of Hilda May Allen. Grave Ref. Coventry (Radford, St. Nicholas) Churchyard.

ALLEN, Ivy Gwendoline. Died as a result of enemy air action, 12th October, 1940 at 85, Aldbourne Road. Age 11. Resided at 85, Aldbourne Road, Radford. Daughter of George William Allen, and of Hilda May Allen. Grave Ref. Coventry (Radford, St. Nicholas) Churchyard.

Foleshill Road

ARNOLD, Thomas Henry. Injured as a result of enemy action, at Foleshill Road, died at Coventry and Warwickshire Hospital, 13th October, 1940. Age 44. Resided at 97, Foleshill Road, Coventry. Born 21st December, 1898 at Stockingford, Nuneaton. Director and General Manager, The Hogarth Warehouses Ltd. Grave Ref. Westwood Church, Coventry.

KELSEY, Matilda. Injured as a result of enemy action, 12th October, 1940, at 96, Foleshill Road, died at Coventry and Warwickshire Hospital, 22nd October, 1940. Age 77. Resided at 96, Foleshill Road. Widow of John Kelsey. Grave Ref. Coventry (London Road) Cemetery.

TOOBY, Charles Frederick. Injured as a result of enemy action, at Corporation Gas Works, Foleshill, died at Coton Hill Hospital, Stafford, 26th January, 1942. Age 55. M. Inst. GasE., A.M.I.Mech. E. Resided Elm Cottage, Foleshill Road, Coventry. Husband of Winifred F. Tooby, of 48, Smirrells Road, Hall Green, Birmingham. Grave Ref. Stafford Rural District, Staffordshire.

Bishop Street

BLAKEMAN, Stephen Thomas. Died, 12th October, 1940 at Bishop Street, Coventry. Age 39. Son of Stephen and Clara Blakeman, of 250, Longford Road. Husband of Ada Elizabeth Blakeman. Resided at 49, Howard Street. Grave Ref. Coventry, County Borough.

FOX, James Arthur. Died, by the Cranes Hotel , Bishop Street. Age 37. Sergeant, Coventry City Police, Coventry Corporation. Son of John William and Julia Sophia Fox, of Outwoods, Coleorton, Leicestershire. Husband of Gladys Mabel Fox, of 22, Lammas Road, Radford. Born 4th April, 1902 at Coleorton, Leicestershire. Grave Ref. Worthington Parish Cemetery, Worthington, Leicestershire.

GOUGH, Philip. Died, at Bishop Street. Age 41. Resided at 2, Leicester Row. Son of Thomas Gough, of Carrigarea, Kilrossanty, Co. Waterford, Irish Republic. Grave Ref. B. 3/1. Communal Grave, Coventry (London Road) Cemetery.

LEEDHAM, William Henry. Died, whilst on duty by the Cranes Hotel at the top of Bishop Street. Age 36. Police Constable, Coventry City Police. Resided at 26, Beaumont Crescent, Radford. Son of Harry and Elizabeth Shakespeare Leedham, of Manor House, Netherseale, Burton-on-Trent, Staffordshire. Husband of Effie May Leedham. Born 2nd November, 1903 at Netherseale. Grave Ref. Netherseale Baptist Church.

Mowbray Street

BRADLEY, Alice. Injured as a result of enemy action, at 14, Mowbray Street 1940, died, 13th October, 1940 at Gulson Road Hospital. Age 43. Resided at 14, Mowbray Street. Wife of Ernest Bradley. Grave Ref. Coventry (London Road) Cemetery.

BRADLEY, Ernest. Died, at 14, Mowbray Street. Age 44. Resided at 14, Mowbray Street. Husband of Alice Bradley. Employed A. C. Wickman Ltd. Grave Ref. Coventry (London Road) Cemetery.

Walsgrave Road
CURRIE, Gavin. Died, at 131, Walsgrave Road. Age 42. Member of St John's Ambulance Brigade. Resided at 131, Walsgrave Road. Husband of Marion Currie. Surgery Attendant, Humber Ltd. Grave Ref. Coventry (Stoke, St. Michael's) Churchyard.

Henry Street
McCREA, Mrs. Died, at 3, Henry Street. Age 27. Resided at 3, Henry Street. Grave Ref. E. 1/1. Communal Grave, Coventry (London Road) Cemetery.

McCREA, Noel. Died, at 3, Henry Street. Aged 22 months. Resided at 3, Henry Street. Grave Ref. E. 1/2. Communal Grave, Coventry (London Road) Cemetery.

LOGAN, Florrie. Injured as a result of enemy action, , at 9, Henry Street, died at Coventry and Warwickshire Hospital, 13th October, 1940. Age 31. Resided at 9, Henry Street. Wife of Michael Logan. Grave Ref. B. 3/3. Communal Grave, Coventry (London Road) Cemetery.

LOGAN, Michael. Died, at 9, Henry Street. Age 42. Resided at 9, Henry Street. Husband of Florrie Logan. Grave Ref. B. 3/2. Communal Grave, Coventry (London Road) Cemetery.

LOGAN, Frank. Died, at 9, Henry Street. Age 5. Resided at 9, Henry Street. Son of Michael and Florrie Logan. Grave Ref. B. 3/4. Communal Grave, Coventry (London Road) Cemetery.

ROBERTS, James Henry. Died, at 30, Henry Street. Age 8. Resided at 30, Henry Street. Son of Mr. G. E. Roberts. Grave Ref. Coventry (London Road) Cemetery.

ROBERTS, Pamela Ruth. Died, at 30, Henry Street. Age 4. Resided at 30, Henry Street. Daughter of Mr. G. E. Roberts. Grave Ref. Coventry (London Road) Cemetery.

ROBINSON, Peter. Died, 12th October, 1940 at 31, Henry Street. Age 8. Resided at 31, Henry Street. Grave Ref. B. 1/2. Communal Grave, Coventry (London Road) Cemetery.

HOOPER, Alice Elizabeth. Died, at 31, Henry Street. Age 32. Resided at 31, Henry Street. Daughter of Harriett Butler, of 204, Saxton Road, Abingdon, Berkshire. Wife of Cecil Hooper. Grave Ref. B. 1/1. Communal Grave, Coventry (London Road) Cemetery.

HUMPHREYS, Susetta. Died, at 34, Henry Street. Age 52. Resided at 34, Henry Street. Widow of W. Humphreys. Born 1888. Shopkeeper. Grave Ref. Coventry (Longford, Windmill Road) Cemetery

KIRKMAN, Alfred Ernest. Died, at rear of 37, Henry Street. Age 33. Resided at 2, Henry Street. Husband of Hilda Kate Kirkman. Grave Ref. Coventry (London Road) Cemetery.

KIRKMAN, Hilda Kate. Died, at rear of 37, Henry Street. Age 29. Resided at 2, Henry Street. Daughter of Mr. and Mrs. Povey, of 39, Henry Street. Wife of Alfred Ernest Kirkman. Born 8th June, 1911 at Coventry. Housewife. Grave Ref. Coventry (London Road) Cemetery.

KIRKMAN, Jean Ann. Died, at rear of 37, Henry Street. Age 2. Resided at 2, Henry Street. Daughter of Alfred Ernest and Hilda Kate Kirkman. Grave Ref. Coventry (London Road) Cemetery.

Stamford Avenue

PHILLIPS, John Alan. Died, at Stamford Avenue whilst on duty. Age 39. Air Raid Warden. Husband of Ethel Phillips, of 38, Dillotford Avenue. Born 21st July, 1908 at Leamington. Employed Alfred Herbert Ltd. Grave Ref. Coventry (Styvechale, St. James) Churchyard.

WILLIAMS, David John. Died, at Stamford Avenue. Age 31. Senior Warden. Son of Gwilym and Alice Williams, of 58, Seymour Street, Aberdare, Glamorgan, Wales. Husband of Nan Williams, of 7, Stamford Avenue. Born 2nd August, 1909 at Aberdare. Employed as an assistant Schoolmaster. Grave Ref. Coventry (Styechale, St. Jame's) Churchyard.

Bablake Fire Station

WILLOUGHBY, Herbert Frank. Injured as a result of enemy action at Bablake Fire Station, died at Coventry and Warwickshire Hospital, 13th October, 1940. Age 43. Messenger, Auxiliary Fire Service. Resided at 21, Lavender Avenue, Coundon. Son of Thomas and Mary Willoughby. Husband of Adelaide Martha Willoughby. Born 11th June, 1897 at Daventry. Employed Thomas Bushill & Son Ltd. Grave Ref. Coventry (London Road) Cemetery.

Cambridge Street

MAGSON, Ethel Mary. Died at 60, Cambridge Street. Age 52. Resided at 60, Cambridge Street. Wife of Reginald Silver Magson. Grave Ref. Coventry, (London Road) Cemetery.

MAGSON, Reginald Silver. Died, at 60, Cambridge Street. Age 55. Resided at 60, Cambridge Street. Husband of Ethel Mary Magson. Grave Ref. Coventry (London Road) Cemetery.

CARPENTER, Harriet Elizabeth. Died, at 62, Cambridge Street. Age 60. Resided at 62, Cambridge Street. Daughter of Mr. and Mrs. Charles Judd. Wife of William Carpenter. Born 27th November, 1881 at Little Park Street. Housewife. Grave Ref. Coventry (London Road) Cemetery.

LARNER, Phillip Edward. Injured as a result of enemy action, at 62, Cambridge Street, died at Gulson Road Hospital, 16th October, 1940. Age 24. Resided at 62, Cambridge Street. Son of Mr. and Mrs. Larner, of 54, Heathcote Street, Radford. Husband of W. Larner. Born 5th May, 1916 at Coventry. Employed Daimler Co. Ltd. Grave Ref. Coventry (London Road) Cemetery

St. Lawrence's Road

WRIGHT, Glennis. Injured as a result of enemy action, 14th October, 1940 at St. Lawrence Road, Foleshill, died at Coventry and Warwickshire Hospital, 15th October, 1940. Age 15. Resided at 20, Benthall Road, Foleshill. Daughter of Mr. L. and Mrs. E. Wright (formerly Williams). Born at Coventry. Employed Messrs. Laird. Grave Ref. Coventry (Longford, Windmill Road) Cemetery.

LESTER, Hannah. Died, at 4, St. Lawrence's Road. Age 56. Resided at 4, St. Lawrence's Road, Foleshill. Wife of W. H. Lester. Grave Ref. Attleborough Cemetery

WILKINSON, Doris Mary. Injured as a result of enemy action, 14th October, 1940, at 8, St. Lawrence's Road, died at Coventry and Warwickshire Hospital, 15th October, 1940. Age 32. Resided at 8, St. Lawrence's Road, Foleshill. Wife of A. Wilkinson. Born at Myther, South Wales. Housewife. Grave Ref. Coventry (Longford, Windmill Road) Cemetery.

Albert Street

MALONEY, Cornelius. Died, at 11, Albert Street. Resided at 11, Albert Street. Son of George and Bridget Maloney, of Chute Hall, Tralee, Co. Kerry, Irish Republic. Born 17th October, 1915 at Abbey Donney, County Kerry. Labourer employed by Building Contractors. Grave Ref. C. 3/8. Communal Grave, Coventry (London Road) Cemetery.

SCANNELL, John. Died, at 11, Albert Street. Age 22. Resided at 11, Albert Street. Son of Andrew and Catherine Carey Scannell, of Tulligmore, Killorglin, Co. Kerry, Irish Republic. Grave Ref. C. 3/1. Communal Grave, Coventry (London Road) Cemetery.

LOBY, Michael Thomas. Died, at 11, Albert Street. Resided at 11, Albert Street. Son of Mrs. M. Luby. Grave Ref. C. 3/2. Communal Grave, Coventry (London Road) Cemetery.

Ford's Hospital, Greyfriars Lane

After the Raid

TOWNSEND, Elizabeth. Died, at. Age 82. Widow of A. Townsend. Resided Ford's Hospital. Born 13th August, 1858 at Coventry. Grave Ref. Coventry (London Road) Cemetery.

WOOD, Elizabeth. Died, at Ford's Hospital, Greyfriars Lane. Age 75. Daughter of Abraham and Mary Beal. Widow of James Wood. Born at Coventry. Resided at Ford's Hospital. Grave Ref. Coventry (London Road) Cemetery.

BEARSLEY, Sarah Ann. Died, at Ford's Hospital, Greyfriars Lane. Age 78. Resided Ford's Hospital. Grave Ref. Coventry (London Road) Cemetery.

CHAMBERS, Helen. Died, 14th October, 1940 at Ford's Hospital, Greyfriars Lane. Age 60. Widow of A. E. Chambers. Resided at Ford's Hospital. Grave Ref. Coventry (London Road) Cemetery.

HUTT, Clara Euvinia. Died, 15th October, 1940 at Ford's Hospital , Greyfriars Lane. Age 82. Widow of W. Hutt. Born 7th November, 1858 at Coventry. Resided at Ford's Hospital. Grave Ref. Coventry (London Road) Cemetery.

LEECH, Martha. Died, 16th October, 1940 at Ford's Hospital, Greyfriars Lane. Resided at Ford's Hospital. Age 74. Grave Ref. Coventry (London Road) Cemetery.

YATES, Florence. Died, 16th October, 1940 at Ford's Hospital, Greyfriars Lane, crushed by falling masonry at Fords Hospital. Matron of Fords Hospital. Age 65. Daughter of William and Eliza Hall. Widow of Charles Yates. Grave Ref. Coventry (London Road) Cemetery.

LEWIS, Sarah Ann. Age 77. Wife of Terence Lewis. Born 1863. Resided at Ford's Hospital. Grave Ref. Coventry, (London Road) Cemetery

Lythalls Lane
WARREN, Herbert Sydney. Died, at 333, Lythalls Lane. Age 60. Resided at 333, Lythalls Lane. Son of Alfred and Hannah Warren, of Lockhurst Lane. Husband of Emma Warren. Born 19th March, 1880 at Coventry. Employed Courtaulds Ltd. Grave Ref. Coventry (St. Paul's) Cemetery.

Treherne Road
NELSON, Unknown. Died, at 29, Treherne Road. Grave Ref. Coventry Borough.

Charterhouse Road
STEANE, Annie. Died, at 16, Charterhouse Road. Age 60. Resided at 16, Charterhouse Road. Wife of Thomas E. Steane. Born 1880 at Coventry. Housewife. Grave Ref. Coventry (London Road) Cemetery.

CAMPBELL, Second Lieutenant, Alexander Fraser GC. M.I.Mar.E. 135004, 9 Bomb Disposal Coy., Royal Engineers. Age 42. Son of Archibald and Mary Campbell, of Dalmellington, Ayrshire. Husband of Agnes Sharp Campbell, of Dalmellington.

The following details are given in the London Gazette of 22nd January, 1941: The King has been graciously pleased to approve the award of the George Cross, for most conspicuous gallantry in carrying out hazardous work in a very brave manner, to Second Lieutenant A. F. Campbell, Royal Engineers. (since deceased). Second Lieutenant Campbell was called upon to deal with an unexploded bomb in the Triumph Engineering Company's works in Coventry. This bomb had halted war production in two factories involving over 1,000 workers and evacuation of local residents. He found it to be fitted with a delayed action fuse which was impossible to remove. He decided to remove the bomb to a safe place. This was done by lorry with Second Lieutenant Campbell lying alongside the bomb to enable him to hear if it started ticking so he could warn the driver to escape. Having got it to a safe place he successfully disposed of it. Unfortunately, he was killed the next day whilst dealing with another unexploded bomb. Grave Ref. Square 348. Coll. Grave 46. Coventry (London Road) Cemetery.

GIBSON, Sergeant, Michael, GC. 4445289, 9 Bomb Disposal Coy., Royal Engineers. Age 34. Grave Ref. Square 348. Coll. Grave 46. Coventry (London Road) Cemetery.

The following details are given in the London Gazette of 22nd January, 1941: The King has been graciously pleased to approve the award of the George Cross, for most conspicuous gallantry in carrying out hazardous work in a very brave manner, to Sergeant M. Gibson, R.E. (since deceased). Sergeant Gibson supervised the excavation of a large unexploded bomb which fell upon an factory on 14th September, 1940. Whilst working on this another nearby bomb exploded. Gibson continued to work on his bomb and eventually it was uncovered. It was then that an unusual hissing noise was heard to be coming from the bomb. Gibson sent his men away and defused the bomb alone. His actions saved a dangerous situation.

GIBSON, Sapper, William. 1890139, 9 Bomb Disposal Coy., Royal Engineers. Age 22. Son of William and Eleanor Gibson, of Burnage, Lancashire. Grave Ref. Square 348. Coll. Grave 46. Coventry (London Road) Cemetery.

GILCHREST, Sapper, Richard. 2000532, 9 Bomb Disposal Coy., Royal Engineers. Age 23. Son of James and Annie Hilda Gilchrest, of Gorton, Manchester. Grave Ref. Square 348. Coll. Grave 46. Coventry (London Road) Cemetery.

PLUMB, Sapper, Jack. 1942443, 9 Bomb Disposal Coy., Royal Engineers. Age 25. Grave Ref. Square 348. Coll. Grave 46. Coventry (London Road) Cemetery.

SKELTON, Sapper, Ronald William. 2073635, 9 Bomb Disposal Coy., Royal Engineers. Age 20. Son of James and Edith Emma Skelton, of Grange Town, Cardiff. Grave Ref. Square 348. Coll. Grave 46. Coventry (London Road) Cemetery.

19th October 1940

Castle Street
COOK,   Daisy. Died, at Castle Street. Age 45. Resided at 79, St. George's Road. Daughter of Mrs. E. Harris, of 74, Albert Street, Hillfields. Wife of Joseph John Cook. Grave Ref. Coventry (London Road) Cemetery.

COOK, Joseph John. Died, at Castle Street. Age 49. Resided at 79, St. George's Road. Son of Joseph Walter Cook, of 44, East Street. Husband of Daisy Cook. Grave Ref. Coventry (London Road) Cemetery.

BASKETTS, William Henry. Died, at Castle Street. Age 42. Resided at 60, Adelaide Street. Husband of Evangeline Mary Basketts. Born 13th January, 1896. Employed Renold and Coventry Chain Co. Ltd. Grave Ref. Coventry (London Road) Cemetery.

ADAMS, Annie Maria. Died, at 49, Castle Street. Age 53. Resided at 49, Castle Street. Wife of A. Adams and Mother of Hilda Adams. Born 26th January, 1889, at Coventry. Housewife. Grave Ref. Coventry (London Road) Cemetery.

ADAMS, Hilda. Died, at 49, Castle Street. Age 24. Resided at 49, Castle Street. Daughter of A. Adams, and of Annie Maria Adams. Born 31st December, 1918, at Coventry. Employed Armstrong Siddeley Motors Ltd. Grave Ref. Coventry (London Road) Cemetery.

HORTON,   Derek Suvla. Died, at 49, Castle Street. Age 24. Son of Charles and Ada May Horton, of 375, Swan Lane. Born 6th November, 1915 at Coventry. Resided 375, Swan Lane. Employed Humber Limited. Grave Ref. Coventry (London Road) Cemetery.

OLDFIELD,   Edward. Died, at 49, Castle Street. Age 52. Resided at 46, Wright Street. Son of Edward Harriett Oldfield. Husband of Louie Oldfield. Employed Rootes Securities Ltd. Grave Ref. Coventry (London Road) Cemetery.

OLDFIELD,   George. Died, at 49, Castle Street. Age 48. Resided at 56, Hartlepool Road. Son of Edward and Harriett Oldfield. Husband of Mabel Oldfield. Employed Rootes Securities Ltd. Grave Ref. Coventry (London Road) Cemetery.

OLDFIELD, Harriett. Died, at 49, Castle Street. Age 75. Resided at 49, Castle Street. Widow of Edward Oldfield. Housewife. Grave Ref. Coventry, (London Road) Cemetery.

OLDFIELD, Louie. Died, at 49, Castle Street. Age 51. Resided at 46, Wright Street. Daughter of Mr. and Mrs. Ensor, of Bishopsgate Green. Wife of Edward Oldfield. Housewife. Grave Ref. Coventry (London Road) Cemetery.

OLDFIELD, Mabel. Died, at 49, Castle Street. Age 44. Resided at 56, Hartlepool Road. Daughter of Mr. and Mrs. Haines, of Godiva Street. Wife of George Oldfield. Housewife. Grave Ref. Coventry (London Road) Cemetery.

SPARROW, Alfred. Died, at 51, Castle Street. Age 56. Resided at 51, Castle Street, Hillfields. Husband of G. Sparrow. Born 24th April, 1884 at Coventry. Employed as a Storekeeper, Armstrong Siddeley Motors Ltd. Grave Ref. Coventry (London Road) Cemetery

Armstrong-Siddeley

DAVIES, John. Died, at Armstrong-Siddeley Works, Parkside. Age 18. First Aid Post member. Resided at 235, Humber Avenue. Son of Mr. and Mrs. F. L. Davies. Grave Ref. Coventry (London Road) Cemetery.

GATFORD, Fred Charles. Died, at Armstrong-Siddeley Works, First Aid Surgery, Parkside. Age 39. Member of the St .John's Ambulance Brigade. Son of Mr. Fred Gatford Mrs. Adeline Gatford, of 95, Raglan Street. Husband of Ethel Gatford, of 19, Max Road. Born 22nd February, 1901 at Brighton. Employed Armstrong Siddeley Motors Limited. Grave Ref. Cremated and ashes buried in Coventry (London Road) Cemetery Coventry.

STEPHEN, Jessie Helen. Died, at Armstrong-Siddeley Works, Parkside, Coventry whilst on duty. Age 53. Works Nurse, Siddeley Armstrong. Resided at 28, Westbury Road. Daughter of Alexander and Jean Stephen, of Gardenston Street, Laurencekirk, Kincardineshire, Scotland. Born 18th November, 1887 in Scotland. Grave Ref. Allesley Churchyard.

STONES, George Henry. Injured as a result of enemy action, 19th October, 1940, at Armstrong-Siddeley Works, Parkside whilst on Red Cross duty, died at Gulson Road Hospital, 20th October, 1940. Age 27. First Aid Post Member. Resided at 23, St. Christian's Road, Cheylesmore. Husband of Marjorie Eveline Stones. Born 6th December, 1912 at Goldthorpe, Yorkshire. Employed as a Capstan Tool Setter, Armstrong Siddeley Motors Ltd. Grave Ref. Communal Grave, Coventry (London Road) Cemetery.

Foleshill Road

HANDS, Elsie Annie. Injured as a result of enemy action, at 45, Foleshill Road, died same day at Coventry and Warwickshire Hospital. Age 57. Resided at 45, Foleshill Road. Daughter of William Henry and Anne Hands. Born 4th September, 1886 at Coventry. Employed at 'Mercer Arms'. Grave Ref. Keresley, St. Thomas Churchyard.

HANDS, Evelyn Hetty. Injured as a result of enemy action, at 45, Foleshill Road, died same day at Coventry and Warwickshire Hospital. Age 46. L.R.A.M. Resided at 45, Foleshill Road. Daughter of William Henry and Anne Hands. Born 16th May, 1893 at Coventry. Music Teacher. Grave Ref. Keresley, St. Thomas Churchyard.

Dymond Road

OVEREND, Lillian Louisa. Injured a result of enemy action, 20th October, 1940, at 50, Dymond Road, died at Gulson Road Hospital, 26th October, 1940. Age 56. Resided at 50, Dymond Road. Wife of Thomas Henry Overend. Born 12th June, 1884 in London. Housewife. Grave Ref. Coventry (St. Paul's) Cemetery.

OVEREND, Thomas Henry. Died, at 50, Dymond Road. Age 56. Resided at 50, Dymond Road. Husband of Lillian Louisa Overend. Born 8th February, 1882 in London. Employed as Master Plumber. Grave Ref. Coventry (St. Paul's) Cemetery

WORTHINGTON, Harold. Died, at 50, Dymond Road. Age 38. Resided at 50, Dymond Road. Son of William and Mary Ann Worthington, of 92, East Street, Hillfields. Husband of Lillian Amy Worthington. Born 12th January, 1903 at Coventry. Employed as a Machinist, Dunlop and Rim Wheel Co. Ltd. Grave Ref. Foleshill Cemetery.

WORTHINGTON, Joan, A. Died, at 50, Dymond Road. Age 17. Resided at 50, Dymond Road. Daughter of Harold and Lillian Amy Worthington. Born March, 1923 at Ramsgate. Employed as a Weaver, Messrs. J & J Cash Ltd. Grave Ref. Coventry (St. Paul's) Cemetery.

WORTHINGTON, Lillian Amy. Died, at 50, Dymond Road. Age 36. Resided at 50, Dymond Road. Daughter of Mr. and Mrs. Shaw, of Ramsgate, Kent. Wife of Harold Worthington. Born 28th June, 1903 at London. Grave Ref. Coventry (St. Paul's) Cemetery.

WORTHINGTON, Mary Ann. Died, at 50, Dymond Road. Age 73. Resided at 92, East Street, Hillfields. Daughter of William and Louisa Smallwood, of Corley Moor. Widow of William Worthington. Born 8th July, 1868 at Corley Moor. Housewife. Grave Ref. Coventry (St. Paul's) Cemetery.

Unknown Address

ORTON, Derrick. Died,. Plaque Application.

20th October 1940

Hen Lane

BUCKNALL, Harry. Died, at 50, Hen Lane. Age 53. Son of Thomas and Martha Bucknall. Husband of Winifred Bucknall, of 50, Hen Lane. Grave Ref. Bedworth Cemetery.

Knight Avenue

GILLESPIE, Daniel. Died, at 1, Knight Avenue. Age 39. Resided at 1, Knight Avenue, Stoke. Grave Ref. E. 1/3. Communal Grave, Coventry (London Road) Cemetery.

Cambridge Street

HUGHES, Ann. Died, at 18, Cambridge Street. Age 75. Resided at 18, Cambridge Street. Daughter of Wilson Hughes, of Sutton Coldfield. Grave Ref. Communal Grave, Coventry (London Road) Cemetery.

DEELEY, Mary. Injured as a result of enemy action, 20th October, 1940, at 18, Cambridge Street, died 24th October, 1940 at Coventry and Warwickshire Hospital. Age 73. Resided at 18, Cambridge Street. Daughter of Wilson Hughes, of Sutton Coldfield. Widow of B. Deeley. Grave Ref. Coventry (London Road) Cemetery.

Vecqueray Street

LOGAN, James Frederick Clement. Injured as a result of enemy action, 20th October, 1940, at Burbridge Timber Yard, Vecqueray Street, died at Coventry and Warwickshire Hospital, 22nd October, 1940. Age 32. Resided at 30, Maycock Road. Son of James and Mary H. Logan, of 2, Cuthbert Avenue, Horsley Hill Estate, South Shields, Co. Durham. Born 1st August, 1908 at South Shields. Employed Burgess Saw Mill. Grave Ref. Harton Cemetery, South Shields.

Stockton Road

PHILLIPS, Wynford James. Died, at 7, Stockton Road. Age 25. Resided at 7, Stockton Road. Son of William and Katharine Phillips, of 36, Brook Street, Blaenrhondda, Rhondda Valley, South Wales. Born 24th August, 1914 at Blaenrhondda. Employed Bretts Stampings Ltd. Grave Ref. Treordy Cemetery, Rhonda Valley, South Wales.

Victoria Street

PIGGOTT, Arthur Percy. Died, at 25, Victoria Street. Age 47. Resided at 25, Victoria Street. Husband of Minnie Matilda Piggott. Employed Coventry Corporation, Gas Department. Grave Ref. Coventry (London Road) Cemetery.

PIGGOTT, Minnie Matilda. Died, at 25, Victoria Street. Age 51. Resided at 25, Victoria Street. Wife of Arthur Percy Piggott. Housewife. Grave Ref. Coventry (London Road) Cemetery.

All Saints Lane
ROLLASON, Thomas. Injured as a result of enemy action, 20th October, 1940, in All Saints Lane Shelter, died at Coventry and Warwickshire Hospital, 10th March, 1941. Age 62. Husband of Jenny B. Rollason, of 40, Oxford Street. Grave Ref. Communal Grave, Coventry (London Road) Cemetery

21st October 1940

Bridgman Road
ASHMAN, William Allan. Died, at 105, Bridgman Road. Age 32. Son of Joseph and Sarah Susannah Ashman, of 60, Broad Lane. Husband of Hetty Ashman. Resided 107, Bridgman Road. Accountant. Grave Ref. Coventry (London Road) Cemetery.

Coundon Street
BARFOOT, Mary Ann. Died at 12, Coundon Street. Age 80. Resided 12, Coundon Street. Born September 1859. Grave Ref. Berkswell Cemetery.

SOUTER, Lillian Lucy. Died, 40 at 12, Coundon Street. Age 37. Resided at 12, Coundon Street. Daughter of John Edward and Lavinia E. Shaw (formerly Cawley). Wife of John Souter. Born 15th July, 1901 at Coventry. Grave Ref. Coventry (London Road) Cemetery.

KIBBLER, Louie Mildred. Injured as a result of enemy action, 21st October, 1940, at 12, Coundon Street, died at Coventry and Warwickshire Hospital, 22nd October 1940. Age 64. Resided at 12, Coundon Street. Daughter of John Kibbler. Grave Ref. Communal Grave, Coventry (London Road) Cemetery.

Princess Street
COOK, Lily Louise. Died, between 107 - 109, Princess Street. Age 55. Resided at 111, Princess Street. Widow of J. Cook. Born 27th April, 1883 at Cheltenham. Housewife. Grave Ref. Coventry (St. Paul's) Cemetery.

REEVES, Jean. Died, at 107, Princes Street. Age 7. Resided at 107, Princes Street. Daughter of William Thomas Reeves, and of Lily Bessie Reeves. Born 9th April, 1933 at Coventry. Attended Paradise Council School. Grave Ref. Coventry (St. Paul's) Cemetery.

REEVES, Lily Bessie. Died at 107, Princes Street. Age 52. Resided at 107, Princes Street. Wife of William Thomas Reeves. Born 5th June, 1888 at Moreton Morrell. Housewife. Grave Ref. Coventry (St. Paul 's) Cemetery.

Birchfield Road
DONY, James Matthew. Died, at 34, Birchfield Road. Age 2. Resided at 34, Birchfield Road. Son of James Henry and K. Dony. Grave Ref. A. 8/6. Communal Grave, Coventry (London Road) Cemetery.

Percy Street

EADES, Emily. Died, at 4, Percy Street. Age 73. Resided at 4, Percy Street. Daughter of Arthur and Sarah Lawrence, of Redditch, Worcestershire. Wife of John William Eades. Born 18th July, 1868 at Redditch, Worcestershire. Housewife. Grave Ref. Coventry (London Road) Cemetery.

EADES, John William. Died, at 4, Percy Street, Coventry. Age 73. Resided at 4, Percy Street. Son of William and Emma Eades, of Redditch, Worcestershire. Husband of Emily Eades. Born 10th August, 1868 at Redditch, Worcestershire. Trimmings, Manufacturer. Grave Ref. Coventry (London Road) Cemetery.

HOLROYD, John. Died, at 4, Percy Street. Age 14. Resided at 4, Percy Street. Son of Mervyn and Ivy Emily Holroyd. Born 26th August, 1926 at Coventry. Attended King Henry the VIII School. Grave Ref. Coventry (London Road) Cemetery.

YOUNG, Alfred. Died, 21st October, 1940 at 4, Percy Street. Age 41. Husband of Freida Beatrice Young. Born February, 1900 at Redditch. Resided at 6, Bond Street. In Business on own account as Fish Caterer, 6, Bond Street. Grave Ref. Coventry (London Road) Cemetery.

YOUNG, Freida Beatrice. Died, 21st October, 1940 at 4, Percy Street. Age 41. Resided at 6, Bond Street. Daughter of John William and Emily Eades. Wife of Alfred Young. Born 31st August, 1900 at Redditch. Housewife. Grave Ref. Coventry (London Road) Cemetery.

READER, Elsie Kate. Died, at 9, Percy Street. Age 39. Resided at 9, Percy Street. Wife of William Henry Reader. Born 15th April, 1900 at Salisbury. Housewife. Grave Ref. Coventry (London Road) Cemetery.

READER, William Henry. Died at 9, Percy Street. Age 41. Resided at 9, Percy Street. Son of Thomas James Reader, of 105, Torrington Avenue. Husband of Elsie Kate Reader. Born 17th March, 1899 at Coventry. Employed Armstrong Siddeley Motors Ltd. Grave Ref. Coventry (London Road) Cemetery.

READER, William Norris. Died, at 9, Percy Street. Age 13. Resided at 9, Percy Street. Son of William Henry and Elsie Kate Reader. Born 27th January, 1927 at Coventry. Attended John Gulson School. Grave Ref. Coventry (London Road) Cemetery.

Clay Lane

FROWEN, Albert George. Injured as a result of enemy action, 21st October, 1940, at 94, Clay Lane, Stoke, died at Queen Elizabeth Hospital. Birmingham, 2nd February, 1941. Age 22. Son of Mr. and Mrs. Ernest Frowen, of 59, Milton Street, Stoke, Coventry. Resided at 59, Milton Street. Grave Ref. Birmingham Cemetery.

FROWEN, Ernest Henry. Died, 21st October, 1940 at 94, Clay Lane. Age 33. Resided at 59, Milton Street, Stoke. Son of Mr. and Mrs. Ernest Frowen, of the same address. Husband of Audrey Edna Frowen. Grave Ref. Coventry (Wyken, St. Mary Magdalene) Churchyard.

WALTON, Albert Harding. Died, 21st October, 1940 at Clay Lane. Age 34. Air Raid Warden. Resided at 19, Clay Lane. Son of Mr. A. T. Walton. Grave Ref. Stoke (St. Michael's) Cemetery.

WICKHAM, Reginald Alfred. Died, 21st October, 1940 at Clay Lane. Age 41. Air Raid Warden. Resided at 11, Clay Lane, Stoke. Husband of Lily F. Wickham. Born 26th June, 1899 at Bournemouth. Retailer at 11, Clay Lane. Grave Ref. Coventry (Stoke, St. Michael's) Churchyard.

Brownshill Green Road
HORTON, Eileen. Died, at 208, Brownshill Green Road. Age 22. Resided at 208, Brownshill Green Road. Daughter of James Brown, of 7, King George Avenue. Wife of Ernest Horace Horton. Born 28th December, 1918 at Coventry. Employed Dunlop Rim and Wheel Co. Ltd. Grave Ref. Coventry (St. Paul's) Cemetery.

HORTON, Ernest Horace. Died, at 208, Brownshill Green Road. Age 30. Resided at 208, Brownshill Green Road. Husband of Eileen Horton. Born 16th April, 1910 at Walthamstow, London. Employed Webster & Bennett Limited. Grave Ref. Coventry (St. Paul's) Cemetery.

Hastings Road
MAYER, Harold. Died, at 18, Hastings Road. Age 27. Resided at 18, Hastings Road. Son of Mrs. Mayer, of 7, Bignall End Road, Bignall End, Stoke-on-Trent, Staffordshire. Husband of Maud Mayer. Born 3rd July, 1912 at Stoke-on-Trent. Employed by British Thomson-Houston. Grave Ref. Coventry (Stoke, St. Michael's) Churchyard.

MAYER, Maud. Died, at 18, Hastings Road. Age 27. Resided at 18, Hastings Road. Daughter of Mrs. Walton, of 62, Heath Road. Wife of Harold Mayer. Born 4th March, 1912 at Stoke-on-Trent. Housewife. Grave Ref. Coventry (Stoke, St. Michael's) Churchyard.

MAYER, Patricia Carol. Died, at 18, Hastings Road. Aged 9 months. Resided at 18, Hastings Road. Daughter of Harold and Maud Mayer. Born 25th January, 1940 at Coventry. Grave Ref. Coventry (Stoke, St. Michael's) Churchyard.

The Remains of 60 – 64 Heath Road

Dalton Road

MOTT, William. Died at 3, Dalton Road. Age 56. Resided at 3, Dalton Road. Husband of Grace Emma Mott. Son of John and Mary Ann Mott of Wisbech. Grave Ref. Wisbech Cemetery.

TOMLINSON, George. Died, at 3, Dalton Road. Age 22. Resided at 3, Dalton Road. Son of Harry and Eleanor R. Tomlinson, of Drove Farm, Osbournby, Sleaford, Lincolnshire. Born 19th May, 1918 at Osbournby, Sleaford. Employed as an Assistant Chemist. Grave Ref. Osbournby Cemetery.

WRIGHT, Francis Charles. Died, 21st October, 1940 at 3, Dalton Road. Age 16. Resided at 3, Dalton Road. Son of Mr. C. Wright. Grave Ref. A. 1/3. Communal Grave, Coventry (London Road) Cemetery

GIBSON, Bernard. Injured as a result of enemy action, 20th October, 1940 at 3, Dalton Road, died at Coventry and Warwickshire Hospital, 24th October, 1940. Age 31. Resided at 3, Dalton Road. Son of Edward and Ada Gibson, of 53, Wilthorpe Avenue, Barnsley, Yorkshire. Born 14th January, 1909 at Barnsley. Employed Standard Motor Co. Ltd. Grave Ref. Barnsley Cemetery.

3 Dalton Road

Alfred Road

PENN, Arthur. Died, 21st October, 1940 at 6, Alfred Road. Age 60. Resided at 6, Alfred Road. Husband of Charlotte Penn. Born 1886. Employed Morris Motors Ltd. Grave Ref. Coventry (London Road) Cemetery.

PENN, Charlotte. Died, 21st October, 1940 at 6, Alfred Road. Age 59. Resided at 6, Alfred Road. Wife of Arthur Penn. Born 1888. Housewife. Grave Ref. Coventry, (London Road) Cemetery

MILLERCHIP, Mary Jane. Died, 23rd October, 1940 at Coventry and Warwickshire Hospital. Age 58. Resided at 10, Alfred Road. Daughter of Alfred Hewitt, of Albert Street. Widow of John Millerchip. Born 17th June, 1884 at Coventry. Housewife. Grave Ref. Coventry (London Road) Cemetery.

Dane Road

SINCLAIR, William Matson. Died, at 32, Dane Road. Age 33. Special Constable. Son of William and Eliza Sinclair, of 55, Kingsley Road, Birmingham. Husband of Sadie Sinclair, of 32, Dane Road. Grave Ref. Cremated, Coventry, County Borough.

WATERER, Frederick George. Died, 21st October, 1940 at 5, Dane Road. Age 37. Senior Warden. Son of Mr. and Mrs. G. Waterer, of 39, Glencoe Road. Husband of Amelia May Waterer, of 5, Dane Road, Stoke. Grave Ref. Coventry, (London Road) Cemetery

34

Lower Ford Street

SMITH, Joseph Wilson. Died, at 72, Lower Ford Street. Age 40. Resided at 72, Lower Ford Street. Grave Ref. Coventry (London Road) Cemetery.

Colchester Street

WALTERS, Lizzetta. Died, 21st October, 1940 at 39, Colchester Street. Age 52. Resided at 39, Colchester Street, Hillfields. Daughter of Mr. and Mrs. Bubb, of Wellsbourne. Wife of Henry Walters. Born 26th August, 1889 at Wellsbourne. Housewife. Grave Ref. Coventry (London Road) Cemetery.

WALTERS, Norman Thomas. Died, 21st October, 1940 at 39, Colchester Street. Age 24. Resided at 39, Colchester Street, Hillfields. Son of Henry Walters, and of Lizzetta Walters. Born 23rd August, 1916 at Coventry. Employed A. C. Wickman Ltd. Grave Ref. Coventry (London Road) Cemetery.

22nd October 1940

Queens Hotel

AUSTIN, Ethel. Died at Queen's Hotel Vaults, Greyfriars Lane. Age 45. Resided at 22, Union Street. Grave Ref. A. 3/5. Communal Grave, Coventry (London Road) Cemetery.

HOLLIDAY, Charles. Died, 22nd October, 1940 at Queen's Hotel Vaults, Greyfriars Lane. Age 26. Son of Mr. and Mrs. Charles Holliday, of 62, Gospel Farm Road, Acocks Green, Birmingham. Born 18th November, 1913 at Birmingham. Son of Mr. & Mrs. Charles Holliday. Resided at 62, Gospel Farm Road, Acocks Green, Birmingham. Employed at Birmingham Small Arms Limited. Grave Ref. Yardley Cemetery, Birmingham.

KIMBERLEY, Walter. Died, 22nd October, 1940 at Queen's Hotel Vaults, Greyfriars Lane. Age 57. Resided at 24, Carter Road, Stoke Aldermoor. Born at Coventry. Employed Mr. Perkins, Florist. Grave Ref. A. 1/4. Communal Grave, Coventry (London Road) Cemetery.

SCANDLON, Mary Caroline. Died, 22nd October, 1940 at Queen's Hotel Vaults, Greyfriars Lane. Age 49. Resided at 6 Court, 1 House, Greyfriars Lane. Daughter of Mrs. Freeman (formerly Scandlon). Grave Ref. Coventry (London Road) Cemetery.

TEBBUTT, John. Died, 22nd October, 1940 at Queen's Hotel Vaults, Greyfriars Lane. Age 65. Son of John and Martha Tebbutt, of Foleshill Road. Husband of Margaret Tebbutt, of 4, Union Street. Grave Ref Coventry (London Road) Cemetery.

TOWNSON, Richard. Died, 22nd October, 1940 at Queen's Hotel Vaults, Greyfriars Lane. Age 56. Resided at 6 Court, 2 House, Greyfriars Lane. Grave Ref. Coventry, (London Road) Cemetery.

Mapleton Road

BOLTON, Thomas. Died, at 2, Mapleton Road. Age 42. Home Guard. Resided 2, Mapleton Road, Radford. Son of Thomas and Ada Bolton, of 99, Windmill Road. Husband of Lillian Bolton. Born 17th September, 1898, at Windmill Road, Foleshill. Employed Sterling Metals Ltd. Grave Ref. Coventry (Longford, Windmill Road) Cemetery.

Vecqueray Street

BROUGHTON, Thomas Bernard. Injured as a result of enemy action, at Vecqueray Street. Died same day at Coventry and Warwickshire Hospital. Age 21. First Aid Post, member. Son of Thomas Rowlatt and Frances Anne Broughton, of 54 St. Paul's Road. Employed Water Department, Coventry Corporation. Grave Ref. Coventry, County Borough.

DONOVAN, John James. Died, at Birds Shop, Vecqueray Street. Age 62. Resided at 6, Chambers Yard, Gosford Street. Born 16th July, 1878 at Coventry. Resided at 13 Court, 3 House, Gosford Street. Employed J. Bird. Grave Ref. Coventry (London Road) Cemetery.

HOLLIDAY, Henry. Injured as a result of enemy action, 22nd October 1940 at H. Burbidge & Son, Vecqueray Street, died at Gulson Road Hospital, 23rd October, 1940. Aged 72. Born 1870 at Coventry. Resided 24, Roundhouse Road. Employed at H. Burbidge & Son, Timber Merchants. Grave Ref. Coventry (London Road) Cemetery.

Greyfriars Green

GARRY, Patrick. Died, 22nd October, 1940 at Greyfriars Green. Age 29. Resided at 5, Starley Road. Son of Patrick and Mary Garry, of Co. Armagh, Northern Ireland. Born 6th March, 1908 at Oldcastle, Meath, Ireland, Resided at Oldcastle. Employed Garlicks Ltd., Builders. Grave Ref. A. 3/ 4. Communal Grave, Coventry (London Road) Cemetery.

Unknown Address

NOON, John Thomas William Edwards. Injured as a result of enemy action, 22nd October, 1940, at Coventry, died at Gulson Road Hospital, 24th October, 1940. Age 37. Husband of Betty Noon, of 1, Whitwell Road, Saffron Lane, Leicester. Born 1903 at Leicester. Employed at Leicester Gas Works. Grave Ref. Saffron Hill Cemetery, Leicester.

Eaton Road

SNELL, Ernest Hugh M.D, D.P.H. Died, 22nd October, 1940 at 3, Eaton Road. Age 76. Resided at 3, Eaton Road. Grave Ref. Cremated. Coventry, County Borough.

28th October 1940

Broomfield Road
BALDOCK, Albert MC. Died at 97, Broomfield Road, 28th October, 1940. Age 64. Resided at 97, Broomfield Road. Husband of Emma Baldock. Grave Ref. Coventry Borough.

Wyken Way
PARISH, Harry. Died, 28th October, 1940 at 36, Wyken Way. Age 39. Resided at 25, Sackville Street. Son of Mr. and Mrs. Parish, of 7, Duke Street, Banbury, Oxfordshire. Husband of Sarah Lizzie Parish. Employed Daimler Co. Ltd. Grave Ref. Coventry (Stoke, St. Michael's) Churchyard.

PARISH, Sarah Lizzie. Died, 28th October, 1940 at 36, Wyken Way. Age 40. Resided at 25, Sackville Street. Daughter of Robert and Ellen Mellor, of 6 ,Watersmeet Grove. Wife of Harry Parish. Born 25th December, 1899. Housewife. Grave Ref. Coventry (Stoke, St. Michael's) Churchyard.

PARISH, Sybil Julia. Died, 28th October, 1940 at 36,Wyken Way. Age 2. Resided at 25, Sackville Street. Daughter of Harry and Sarah Lizzie Parish. Born 2nd October, 1938. Grave Ref. Coventry (Stoke, St. Michael's) Churchyard.

LOVELL, Kenneth Roy. Died, 28th October, 1940 at 38, Wyken Way. Age 13. Resided at 38, Wyken Way, Stoke Heath. Son of Albert William and Winifred Grace Lovell. Born 28th May, 1927 at Coventry. Attended Stoke Council School Grave Ref. Coventry (St. Paul's) Cemetery.

29th October 1940

Greenfields
HARTLEY, Bernard Anthony. Died, 29th October, 1940 at 48, Greenfields. Age 15. Resided at 48, Greenfields. Son of Jonas and Emily Hartley. Grave Ref. Burnley Cemetery.

HARTLEY, Emily. Died, 29th October, 1940 at 48, Greenfields. Age 39. Resided at 48, Greenfields. Wife of Jonas Hartley. Grave Ref. Burnley Cemetery.

HARTLEY, Jonas. Died, 29th October, 1940 at 48, Greenfields. Age 39. Resided at 48, Greenfields. Husband of Emily Hartley. Grave Ref. Burnley Cemetery.

BURT, Agnes Bridget. Died at as a result of enemy action, 29th October, 1940 at 54, Greenfields. Age 52. Resided at 54, Greenfields. Wife of Lawrence L. F. Burt. Grave Ref. Coventry (London Road) Cemetery.

Wycliffe Road

SPRATT, George. Died, 29th October, 1940 at 32, Wycliffe Road. Age 52. Resided at 32, Wycliffe Road, Wyken. Son of Thomas and Alice Spratt, of Hillfarrance, Taunton, Somerset. Husband of Florence Spratt. Born 16th April, 1888 at Ealing Middlesex. Employed at Humber Limited as a Body Maker. Grave Ref. Wyken Parish Church Coventry.

31st October 1940

The Farmstead

GRANT, Florence Mary. Died, 31st October, 1940 at 13, The Farmstead. Age 55. Resided at 1, The Farmstead. Wife of E. Grant. Grave Ref. Coventry, County Borough.

1st November 1940

Stephen Street

EDKINS, George Edwin. Died, 1st November, 1940 at 25, Stephen Street. Age 32. Husband of D. Edkins, of 56, Villiers Street. Born 23rd October, 1908 at Coventry. Employed Standard Motor Co. Ltd. Grave Ref. Coventry (London Road) Cemetery.

Gas Street

ELDEN, Geoffrey James. Died, 1st November, 1940 at Clarke and Cluley's Yard, Gas Street. Aged 9 months. Son of W. J. Elden, of 28, Leyland Road, and of Jessie Louise Elden. Grave Ref. Coventry (London Road) Cemetery.

ELDEN, Jessie Louise. Died, 1st November, 1940 at Clarke and Cluley's Yard, Gas Street. Age 25. Wife of W. J. Elden, of 28, Leyland Road. Grave Ref. Coventry (London Road) Cemetery.

TAYLOR, Margaret. Died, 1st November, 1940 at Clarke and Cluley's Yard, Gas Street. Age 23. Resided at 1 Court, 4 House, Abbotts Lane. Wife of Private Lawrence Taylor, The Royal Warwickshire Regiment. Grave Ref. Coventry (London Road) Cemetery.

McKEAVENEY, Robert Michael. Died, 1st November, 1940 at Gas Street Shelter. Age 2. Resided at 6, Gas Street. Son of James McKeaveney. Grave Ref. B. 2/4. Communal Grave, Coventry (London Road) Cemetery.

Alfred Road

GARVEY, Mary Ellen. Died, 1st November, 1940 at 14, Alfred Road. Age 25. B.R.C.S. Resided at 1, Craners Road. Daughter of Patrick Harry and Ellen Garvey, of Rhynn, Kilkelly, Co. Mayo, Irish Republic. Born 5th April, 1915 at Kilkelly, Co. Mayo, Ireland. Employed Armstrong Siddeley Motors Ltd. Grave Ref. B. 3/1. Communal Grave, Coventry (London Road) Cemetery.

PICKERING, Lily. Died, 1st November, 1940 at 14, Alfred Road. Age 18. Resided at 14, Alfred Road. Daughter of William Henry Pickering, and of Lily Pickering. Born 10th July, 1922 at Coventry. Employed Middlemores Ltd. Grave Ref. Coventry (London Road) Cemetery.

PICKERING, Lily. Died, 1st November, 1940 at 14, Alfred Road. Age 48. Resided at 14, Alfred Road. Wife of William Henry Pickering. Born 2nd October, 1893 at Coventry. Housewife. Grave Ref. Coventry (London Road) Cemetery.

PICKERING, Patricia Mary. Died, 1st November, 1940 at 14, Alfred Road. Age 2. Resided at 14, Alfred Road. Daughter of Mr. and Mrs. William Dennis Pickering. Born 25th December, 1937 at Coventry. Grave Ref. Coventry (London Road) Cemetery.

Bishop Street
HENRY, Charles. Injured as a result of enemy action, 1st November, 1940 at Bishop Street, died at Coventry and Warwickshire Hospital, 3rd November, 1940. Age 53. Resided at 52, Glendower Avenue. Husband of Anne Henry. Born 4th July, 1887 at Barrow-in-Furness. Employed Daimler Co. Ltd. Grave Ref. Barrow-in-Furness Cemetery, Lancashire.

St. Lawrence's Road
WILKINSON, Ennis Jean. Died, 1st November, 1940 at 8, St. Lawrence's Road. Age 11. Resided at 8, St. Lawrence's Road, Foleshill. Daughter of A. Wilkinson, and of Doris Mary Wilkinson. Born at Coventry. Scholar at Broad Street. Grave Ref. Coventry (Longford, Windmill Road) Cemetery.

2nd November 1940

Silver Street
BEHAN, Thomas, MM and Croix de Guerre. Died, 2nd November, 1940 at Silver Street. Age 56. Resided 55, Hill Street. Son of Patrick and Mary Behan, of Derrymullen, Robertstown, Naas, Co. Kildare, Irish Republic. Born 20th February, 1884, Co. Kildare. Grave Ref. D3. 3/5. Communal Grave, Coventry (London Road) Cemetery.

Bishop Street
CLAPP, Alfred Victor. Injured as a result of enemy action, 2nd November, 1940 at Bishop Street, died same day at Coventry and Warwickshire Hospital. Age 37. Resided at 102, Lavender Avenue. Son of Thomas and Amy Clapp, of 9, Arden Road, Smethwick, Staffordshire. Grave Ref. Coventry (London Road) Cemetery.

Unknown Address
KIRBY, Alfred Edgar. Died, 2nd November 1940 at Coventry and Warwickshire Hospital. Age 50. Resided at 102, Lavender Avenue. Husband of E. I. Kirby. Grave Ref. B. 1/4. Communal Grave, Coventry (London Road) Cemetery.

Cook Street

LITTLEWOOD, Eliza Annie. Died, 2nd November, 1940 at 45, Cook Street. Age 55. Resided at 45, Cook Street. Daughter of Mrs. W. Pymm, of Kirby Bellars, Melton Mowbray, Leicestershire. Born 12th August, 1885 at Melton Mowbray. Housekeeper. Grave Ref. Kirby Bellars, Melton Mowbray.

5th November 1940

Foleshill Road

GRENSILL, Violet. Died, 5th November, 1940 at Foleshill Road. Age 22. Daughter of John Howard, of 294, Goodyers End, Exhall. Wife of J. Grensill, of the same address. Born 2nd November, 1918 at Exhall. Employed Armstrong Siddeley Motors Limited. Grave Ref. Exhall, St. Gile's Cemetery.

Coventry City Centre

Bert Bradford, died at Coventry Corporation, Transport Office, Market Place, Coventry carrying out his duties with the Transport Department, Coventry Corporation. Aged 43, he resided at 263, Stoney Stanton Road and married to Mrs H. Bradford. Bert is buried in Southend Cemetery. Bertram Bradford aged 44 years was interred in Grave 3899 at Sutton Road Cemetery on the 7th December 1940. Also interred in the grave are: Frederick Russell Smith aged 32 years, Charles Lovatt aged 60 years and Marguerite Elizabeth Emma Rose Bradford aged 58 years who was interned on the 11th May 1950.

The inscription on Bert's headstone reads *'In loving memory of Bert Bradford Killed by enemy action while on duty at Coventry Nov. 14th 1940 'Life's work well done now comes rest. Always with you Rita'.*

Five citizens are recorded with Gulson Road Hospital as the place of death, with several of these succumbing to their wounds in the days following the air raid.

Age 72, **Annie Louisa Burton** died on the night of the 14th November on admission to hospital. She resided at 159, Foleshill Road and was married to William James Burton. Annie was born on the 19th August, 1868 at Coventry and buried on the 20th November 1940. Records show **a** family member was injured and detained at Stratford-on-Avon Emergency Hospital. Annie is buried in grave reference E21/2 at the Communal Grave.

Injured as a result of enemy action, on the 14th November, 1940, at Whitley, **Brenda Alice Green** died at Gulson Road Hospital the following day, aged 18. Two family members were treated for wounds, one at Evesham Emergency Hospital. Brenda was born on the 8th September, 1922 at Coventry and resided with her mother, Mrs. E. Green, at 212, Harnall Lane East being employed at Triumph Motor Co. Ltd.

GREEN – Treasured memories of our dear, Brenda. From her loving Daddy and Evesham-Grandma.

John Eaves, died as a result of enemy action age 38 on the 15th November 1940 at Gulson Road Hospital, he was fatally injured on the night of the 14th November. John was born in 1902 and named after his father, his mother was Mabel Eaves.

He resided at Queen Mary's Road with his wife, Edith and two children, John and Patricia. An employee of British Thomson-Houston Company Limited (BTH) his name is commemorated on the war memorial and his death featured in the works newsletter; *'Mr. J. Eaves, who received fatal injuries during the air raid, was the only member of the various services on duty that night at the works to be killed. He had been one of a trailer pump crew which had been assisting the city fire service, and was on his way back to the works during the raid, to procure some further piece of equipment, when the bomb which caused his death fell nearby. Mr. Eaves, who leaves a widow and two children, had been an employee of the firm for fourteen years, and was a cheerful and competent worker; he was very popular among his colleagues in the fire brigade, and fearless in carrying out his duty. The British Thomson-Houston Company were represented at this funeral by a party of twelve firemen in charge of 3rd Officer Kendrick'.* John is buried in the Communal Grave and has a plaque in the War Memorial Park.

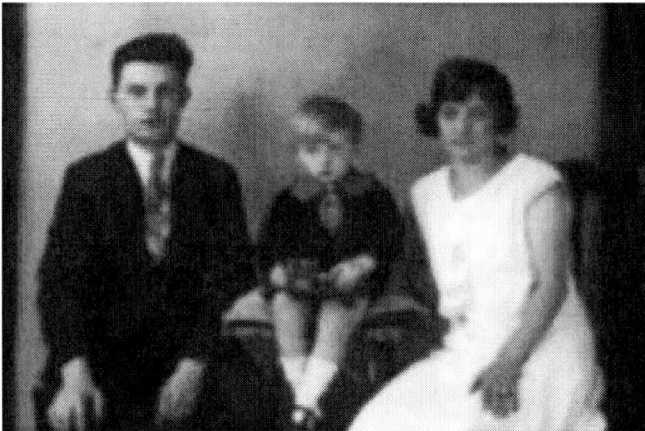

John, John and Flo

John

War Memorial Park Plaque

William Henry Bowers, died as a result of his wounds on the 17th November, 1940 at Gulson Road Hospital, aged 35. He resided at 33, Caludon Road and is buried in Silverdale Cemetery.

Ten days after the raid, Private **James Page**, 2758955, Pioneer Corps, formerly of Black Watch (Royal Highlanders) died as a result of enemy action at Coventry Municipal Hospital, Gulson Road. His parents were Patrick and Jane S. Page of Dundee and James was born on the 23rd March, 1918 at 38, Bridge Street, Leith, Edinburgh. James enlisted in January, 1940 and his official residence and occupation, both refer to Dundee as he resided at 13, King's Cross Road, Dundee. In Dundee he was formerly employed as a Jute worker. Aged 22, he was given a burial in Dundee and lies in Section. XE. Grave 1C. at Dundee Eastern Cemetery, Dundee. A resident and civilian of Dundee he is one of those named in the City of Dundee Roll of Honour.

The following article appeared in *'The Peoples Journal'* on the 30th November 1940.

Headline Parents' Vain Dash to Coventry Dundee Victim of Raid

A young Dundee soldier Private James Page Black Watch Second son of Mr and Mrs Page 6 Kings Cross Road Beechwood has died in hospital from injuries received in the air raid on Coventry. Last week Mr and Mrs Page received a letter from an officer telling them that their son had been injured but was progressing satisfactorily. On Sunday they received a telegram stating that he was dangerously ill. They set off for Coventry on Monday morning. On arrival they learned that their son had died the previous day. Private Page who was 22 years of age, had been in the Black Watch since February last . He was formerly employed in the Eagle Jute Mills. His elder brother David is in the Navy. Mr . Page served in the last war with the Royal Scots Fusiliers and lost a leg in the Battle of Loos.

An account from Gulson Road comes from Dennis Sadler who was 15 years old.

I left school at 14, and worked on the Co-Op milk round before going on duty at Gulson Road Hospital, this suited me as I could go to bed in the afternoons. I was in the St. Johns Ambulance Brigade as a cadet and volunteered to be a stretcher bearer. When the sirens went I used to go Gulson Road Hospital as I lived close by. The bombs had started falling just after 7pm and we started taking delivery of casualties, they came in, in all sorts of vehicles.

Being a basic first aider, the injuries were beyond our capability and we were trying to comfort people if you had a break in the delivery of casualties. As the night went on it was a matter of trying to find somewhere to put them. A lot of people died from want of attention, there were four doctors and one was a Mr. Beryl. There was not enough staff to deal with all the casualties. Gulson Road Hospital was two stories and the top floor had been cleared in case of an air raid. The hospital was adjacent to Nuffield Mechanisation, this would have been a target if they had known where it was and they made engines there. On the top of the roof they had a Light Anti-Aircraft gun that was barking away all night.

Being on duty in the building you didn't see what was going on all around, only next morning did you see the change. On this ward one of the patients was a woman holding a baby on a stretcher, they were both dead they had been killed by a blast and there was someone my age trying to keep patients comfortable. Being busy with many patients to deal with you weren't really aware of explosions or hearing bombs falling, incendiary bombs had to be dealt with by putting sand on the top.

Gulson Road Hospital was lucky there was not much damage, next morning the matron asked me to go into town and send a telegram to recall the Theatre Sister who was on holiday. A policeman was flabbergasted asking me "what I was doing?", when I told him he replied "Good luck to you, we have no communication with the outside world". No telegram was ever sent.

On the second or third day after the raid, me and my friends were on ambulances taking casualties outside Coventry to Warwick etc. on converted Midland Red Buses and I was asked to go along to escort patients, we ended up in Bromsgrove. I had a bath and got fed. There were 3 or 4 buses each carrying 10 stretcher cases and two sitting cases. My uncle was a casualty at Bromsgrove, and he told me my uncles and aunties 'are here as well'. As I walked down I saw a girl and said "*you live in St. Georges Road as well, I will tell your mum and dad where you are*". A few days after the raid a list was put on the railings at Gulson Road Hospital and my father went over to see my brother in law. Having been on duty for all that time (five days), I collapsed and was treated for pneumonia.

We (cadets) always said there were more casualties from what we saw, one of the days there were removal vans loading the van with plain coffins I don't know where they were going.

James Harold Yarrow has a commemorative plaque in the London Road Cemetery. James was named after his father whom resided at Freeman Street whilst James Harold resided at 675, Stoney Stanton Road with his wife, Julia. He was a native of Cambridge and born there on the 9th August, 1880 and was killed several months after his 60th birthday at Broadgate. James was employed with Coventry Corporation in the Transport Department. His plaque was paid for by J. Yarrow of 69 Dugdale Road on the 8th September 1949 and reads *'Mr James Harold Yarrow Killed in air raid 14th November 1940'*. His burial is listed by the CWGC as within the Borough of Coventry and archive records show that confirmation of his death resulted in a Special Procedure Case.

Broadgate looking towards Owen Owen Store

YARROW Loving memories of dear Harold Always in the thoughts of his loving wife, children and sister Daisy.

Enemy action in the vicinity of 10, St. John Street took the lives of **Joseph Samuel Simpson**, aged 3 and his sister **Muriel Gwendoline Gladys Simpson**, aged 11. Their father served with the Pioneer Corps as Private Walter Francis Simpson. Joseph and Muriel are buried in the London Road Cemetery.

SIMPSON In loving memory of Muriel and baby, Joe. Always in our thoughts, Mum, Dad, David, Billy and sister Eileen, relatives and friends

Along St. John Street at 72, **William Charles Baylis**, was killed aged 36. William was married to Hilda Violet Baylis, whilst his parents, George Henry and E. Baylis (nee Young) also lived in the city at 53, Winchester Street. William was buried in the Communal Grave on the 20th November 1940.

Four members of the Bennett family (father and daughters) died at 52, Trafalgar Street they resided a few doors away at number 46. **Walter Bennett,** was the father and died aged 60. His daughters, **Florence May Bennett** died aged 40, **Eveline Rees** aged 35 and youngest daughter, **Elsie Bennett** died aged 25. Son and brother, Mr. W. J. Bennett resided at 82, Windy Arbour, Kenilworth and identified his father whom was buried on the 23rd November 1940.

BENNETT – Dad and sisters, Flo, Evelyn and Kate – Never forgotten and sadly missed by all, Nell, Frank and David; Bill and Jim; Phyllis, Olive and Fred; Gerald and Tony; Arthur and Eva.

A further five casualties occurred at 77, Trafalgar Street, four of these being members of the Billings family a couple and their two children. **Leonard John Billings** was married to **Eva Billings** and also lost with them was their children, **Aubrey John** and **Marion Grace.** Leonard was aged 29 and his mother Mrs. E. L. Billings resided at Nupend, Horsley, Stroud, Gloucestershire where he was born. Eva aged 26 was born on the 10th May, 1914, at Clutton, nr Briston, Somerset and her parents were Mr. and Mrs. Harris.

Aubrey John Billings was born on the 6th July, 1932 at Nupend, nr Nailworth, Gloucestershire and died aged 9. Marion Grace Billings a younger sister, died aged just 5 months, and was born in Coventry on the 28th March, 1940 at 27, Hope Street. This address was noted as the families residence.

BILLINGS – In loving memory of Eva, Len, John, Marion. Mother, Dad, Albert, Edith, Emily, Beat, Jim and George.

Killed alongside the Billings at 77, Trafalgar Street was **William Henry Harris,** (possibly a relation of Eva Billings nee Harris), William was the stepson of Mrs. U. Harris. He was aged 36 and 77, Trafalgar Street was listed as his residence. William a native of Coventry was born on the 23rd August, 1904 and employed locally with Sir W. G. Armstrong Whitworth Aircraft Ltd.

HARRIS In loving memory of Bill – Dad, Mother, Albert, Edith, Emily, Beat, George and Jim

With a plaque in the War Memorial Park, **Charles Adams** died at his home at 83, Trafalgar Street. He was born 1872 and employed by London Midland Scottish Railway Co. Ltd, Coventry Goods Department, Castle Street. His plaque cost £2-5-0 and was paid for on the 18th February 1949 by Mrs. C. Adams, the application read *'Mr Charles Adams Killed in air raid 14th November 1940'*. The destination for the plaque was originally Stoke Heath and later moved to the War Memorial Park.

```
1939 - 1945

IN MEMORY OF

MR CHARLES ADAMS

KILLED IN ENEMY AIR ATTACK

14TH NOVEMBER 1940
```

Fireman with the Auxiliary Fire Service **Victor Alexander Satchell** died at Messrs. Owen Owen in Broadgate, aged 38. His father, James Satchell of 100, Victoria Road, Bromley, Kent and in Coventry he resided with his wife Leah Satchell, 83, Eastcotes and later 309, Tile Hill Lane. Victor was born on the 6th April, 1902 at Rugby. He was employed by the Coventry Swaging Company Limited and has a commemorative plaque in the London Road Cemetery. His wife Mrs. L. Satchell, of 83 Eastcotes paid for the plaque on the 19th March 1948 that reads *'Mr V. Satchell Killed in air raid 14th/15th November 1940.*

By March 1941 the claim made by Owen Owen in respect of property due to air raid damage was £171, 862. Annual report showed the buildings £143, 937 and contents and fixtures £28,825. Following the raid the firm secured new premises and was out of trading for 28 working days.

Frederick Roberts, was born on the 24th March, 1892 at West Bromwich and died as a result of enemy action at Pitts Head Hotel, Gosford Street aged 50. His parents, Mr. C. Roberts and Mrs. Roberts resided at 83, Colchester Street with Frederick and his wife, Harriet Ellen Roberts living close-by at 55, Colchester Street. Frederick was employed as an Inspector at Rootes Securities Ltd. A casualty from Gosford Street was detained in Warwick Hospital.

ROBERTS Treasured memories of my dear husband Fred Killed by enemy action November 14th 1940 From his loving wife and son Tom

The husband of Dora McInerney, of Nuneaton Private, **John McInerney**, D/14677, 2/ 11th (H.D.) Bn., Royal Warwickshire Regiment died at Parkside, aged 50. John was born on the 21st December, 1889 at Limerick, Ireland and was killed near his home of 58, Parkside. He was employed at Armstrong Siddeley Motors Ltd and enlisted at the outbreak of war. Private McInerney is buried in Grave Reference Square 348. Grave 47. Coventry (London Road) Cemetery. A family member was also treated at hospital.

MCINERNEY (Jack) Treasured memories of a dear husband. From his loving wife and Ronnie

At Armstrong-Siddeley Works, Parkside nearly thirty civilians died and they are listed in alphabetical order.

Norman Allton, an Armstrong-Siddeley employee was the son of George and Maud Allton, of 77, Oldbury Road, Hartshill, Nuneaton. He resided at 34, Ventnor Street, Weddington, Nuneaton and was married to Stella Allton. Norman was born on the 16th June, 1916, at Chapel End and died aged 24. He is buried in Hartshill Cemetery, Nuneaton and a plaque was paid for in his memory at Stoke Heath by Mr. G. Allton, 77 Oldbury Road, Hartshill, Nuneaton on the 16th August 1949; '*Mr Norman Allton Killed in air raid 14th November 1940*'.

Employed as a Coppersmith at Armstrong Siddeley Motors Ltd was **Alfred Barron**. He was born on the 17th August, 1879, at Hebburn, Co. Durham to Thomas and Martha Bulman Barron who later resided at Wallsend-on-Tyne, Northumberland. In Coventry, Alfred resided with his wife, Caroline at 38, Strathmore Avenue. He died aged 61 and has a plaque in the London Road Cemetery that was paid for by his wife, Mrs. C. Barron of 38 Strathmore Avenue.

BARRON Alfred Beloved husband of Kit and dear father of Kathleen and Freda.

John Baxter, aged 44 resided at 3, Market Street, Atherstone with his parents, Mr. Fred J. Baxter and Mrs. S. E. Baxter. His remains were claimed by his mother and John is buried in Atherstone Cemetery.

Sergeant **Alfred John Beck**, 14th Warwickshire (Coventry) Bn., Home Guard was injured as a result of enemy action on the 14th November, 1940, at the works and died of his injuries on the 4th December, 1940 at Rugby Emergency Hospital, aged 42. Alfred was married to Lily Doris Beck, of 12, Barras Lane, Coventry and is buried in Grave Reference. Square 319. Grave 31. Coventry (London Road) Cemetery.

Another victim buried in Atherstone Cemetery, **Arthur William Bown**, aged 23. His parents, Alfred Thomas and Sarah Ann Bown resided at 55, North Street, Atherstone. Arthur was born on the 9th April, 1916 at Atherstone and was employed at Armstrong Siddeley Motors Ltd.

The Collett family, parents (Agnes Elizabeth and Hugh Wilfred) and two sons (Cyril Ernest and Sidney Albert) had a plaque dedicated to them at Stoke Heath and all died at Armstrong-Siddeley Works, Parkside. The family resided nearby at 49 Parkside and the plaque was paid for by F. Collett of 108 Clay Lane on the 12th August 1949 at a cost of £5-5-0 .

Agnes Elizabeth Collett died aged 50 and was born on the 20th April, 1891 at Coventry. Agnes was a housewife whilst husband **Hugh Wilfred Collett** worked at Armstrong Siddeley Motors Limited. He died aged 51 and was also born in Coventry on the 26th May, 1890 at Coventry. **Cyril Ernest** aged 17 was also born in Coventry on the 3rd May, 1923 and was also employed at Armstrong Siddeley Motors. **Sidney Albert** worked at Sir W. G. Armstrong Whitworth Aircraft Ltd and at 19 was two years older than Cyril . Albert was born on the 26th December, 1920.

Armstrong Siddeley employee, **Harry John Collier**, MM died at his workplace and rests in Hartshill Cemetery near Nuneaton. Harry was born on the 13th October, 1897 at Marchington, Uttoxeter, Staffordshire and his parents John and Rebecca Collier, resided in Marchington at Newlands Farm. Harry aged 43 was the husband of Edith Annie Collier, of 15, Green Lane, Nuneaton. Harry's Military Medal would have been awarded during the First World War.

Edith Congrave died at the Armstrong-Siddeley Works, Parkside. Her husband was Lewis Congrave and the couple resided at 59, Whitehouse Road, Dordon, Staffordshire. Edith aged 42 was born on the 3rd May, 1898, at Dordon, Tamworth and employed at the works. Edith is buried in the Communal Grave A Plaque in the War Memorial Park was paid for by L. Congrave, 59 Whitehouse Road, Dordon near Tamworth on the 20th March 1948 reads *'Mrs Edith Congrave Killed in air raid 14th November 1940'*.

Norah Cooper was aged 33 and the wife of Harry Cooper, of 278, Marston Lane, Bedworth. She was buried in the Communal Grave on the 23rd November 1940.

From Belfast, **Robert John Crawford** came to work in the city at Armstrong Siddeley Ltd. His parents, John and Ellen Crawford, resided at 22, Cullingtree Road, Belfast, Northern Ireland where Robert was born on the 14th March, 1893 and died aged 47. In Coventry he resided at 58, Parkside and was buried on the 20th November 1940.

Aged 16, **Edna May Evans** worked at Armstrong Siddeley Motors Ltd. She was born on the 4th June, 1925 and resided in Atherstone with her parents, Herbert and Mary Evans at 154, Long Street, Atherstone. Edna is buried in Atherstone Cemetery.

From 37, Radford Road **Mary Graham** an Occupational Nurse died aged 26. A native of Cookstown, Co. Tyrone, Northern Ireland she was born in 1912. Mary was married to Thomas Graham and buried on the 23rd November 1940.

A commemorative plaque in Longford Recreation Ground was dedicated to the memory of **Constance Mary Jeffery**. She resided with her parents, Mr. C. Jeffery and Mrs. E. Jeffery at 12, Church Street, Atherstone. Constance was born on the 24th January, 1922 at Atherstone and aged 18 was working at Armstrong Siddeley Motor Co. Ltd. She is buried in Atherstone Cemetery. The plaque was paid for by Mr. B. H. Jeffery, 12 Church Street, Atherstone at a cost of £2-5-0 on the 19th July 1951.

Buried in Chilvers Coton Churchyard, Nuneaton is **Clifford David Masser** who died aged 17 and was employed at the Armstrong Siddeley Motor Company Limited. Clifford lived with his mother, Getrude at 96, Coton Road, Nuneaton and was born in Chilvers Coton on the 6th February, 1923.

In Warwick, **Arthur McCormack** is buried in Old Milverton Cemetery and worked at Siddeley. Arthur was born on the 24th June, 1889 at Bramley, Surrey with his parents, William and Charlotte McCormack residing in the county of Surrey at The Common, Shalford, Guildford. In Coventry, Arthur resided with his wife, Alice Maud McCormack, of 33, Watercall Avenue. Aged 51, he was killed at the Parkside works.

In addition to his normal duties at Armstrong-Siddeley, **Horace William Miles** took on the duties of a firewatcher. His parents, William and Lily Miles resided at 80, Far Gosford Street with Horace and his wife May living at 59, Strathmore Avenue. He was born on the 16th October, 1905 at Coventry and died aged 30.

William Mills, aged 38 was employed Armstrong Siddeley Motors Ltd and came to Coventry from Durham, where he was born on the 27th February 1902. His parents, Henry and Harriett Mayor Mills resided in the County of Durham at 53, College View, Esh Winning.

Two days after the raid, **Brenda May Piggon** died of her injuries received at Armstrong-Siddeley Works at Warwick Hospital on the 16th November, 1940. She was 17. Her parents, William and Alice Piggon resided at 36, Hanbury Road, Bedworth. Brenda's grave in listed by the Commonwealth War Grave Commission as Warwick Municipal Borough.

Recorded as dying at Armstrong-Siddeley Works First Aid Post is **Charles Arthur Rooms.** Charles was not employed at Armstrong Siddeley but worked at Moreton and Weaver Ltd. He resided in Coventry at 51, Dulverton Avenue with his parents, Alfred Henry and Ida Rooms, but was born further afield on the 11th February, 1920 at Kirkwall, Orkney Isles.

William Robert Loudon Roper was killed in the raid aged 18. His parents, Frederick and Lena Roper resided across the city in Holbrooks at 110, Nunt's Lane. William was buried in the Communal Grave on the 23rd November 1940.

One of the employees killed was Universal Grinder, **James William Smith,** aged 34. James resided at 211, Hipswell Highway, Wyken, Coventry and was the son of Ada Watson (formerly Smith), of 45, Watersmeet Road, Stoke. He was married to Elizabeth Smith and born on the 29th September, 1906 at Monmouthshire.

Walter Edward Smith aged 30 was also an employee of Armstrong Siddeley. A residence of Coventry he resided at 96, Cranford Road and was born in the city on the 12th March, 1912. Walter was found on the night of the air raid.

SMITH (Walter Edward) Fondest memories of one we shall never forget. Always in the thoughts of his wife, son and relatives of School House, Moseley Avenue.

A victim buried in St. Mary's Churchyard, Cubbington is **Horace Stephens**. At Siddeley he was employed as a rate fixer and carried out additional duties with the Air Raid Patrol as an Ambulance Driver. The connection to Cubbington was from birth as he was born in the village on the 16th April, 1895. His parents, James and Ellen Stephens resided at Penn's Cottages, Cubbington, Leamington Spa and Horace lived with his wife Lucy Stephens at 10, Glebe Terrace, Cubbington.

The last casualty in alphabetical order was fitter **Kenneth John Wood**, aged 23. He worked at Siddeley and was born on the 4th December, 1914 at Carlton-in- Cleveland, Yorkshire. His parents, Edward and Olivia Wood resided at 30, Three Spires Avenue, Coundon. Kenneth also resided in the district with his wife, Edna May Wood at 104, Dallington Road.

Three casualties occurred in the vicinity of Queen Victoria Road. One of those who died in Queen Victoria Road was **Harry Clarke**, aged 39. He resided at the Three Tuns Hotel, Warwick Row and was married to Phyllis Constant Clarke. His parents Robert and Amy Clarke also resided in the city at 23, Lower Ford Street. Refer to Winifred Thorpe.

Injured as a result of enemy action at Queen Victoria Road and dying from his wounds the following day at Gulson Road Hospital was **Roger William Thompsell.** His injuries were possibly incurred at the back of 99, Queen Victoria Road where he resided with his wife, S. E. Thompsell. Roger worked at Bretts Stamping Limited in addition to his role in the Home Guard. A native of Portsmouth, he was born in October, 1900 to Roger T. and Elizabeth M. Thompsell and died aged 39.

At C.W.S. Stores, near Queen Victoria Road **Charles Edward Jackson** died aged 72. He resided at 2, Green's Road, Keresley and was buried in the Communal Grave on the 4th December 1940. His death certificate confirms his death was due to War Operations and he was found on the 15th November 1940 at C.W. S Stores. A certificate to this effect had been received from Frederick Smith, Clerk to Coventry City Council. A resident of No. 32 required treatment, one at 89 treated at First Aid Post and sent home and one person from 103 detained in Evesham Emergency Hospital.

Long Distance Walking Champion C. E. Jackson

JACKSON (C.E). In affectionate remembrance of our dear Superintendent. Sadly missed by teachers and scholars of Keresley Congregational School.

Two men were killed in Chapel Street and both were engaged in fire watching and fire prevention duties. **James Cecil Blagburn**, died as a result of enemy action at Laxons and Co., aged 39. His mother Florence Marian Blagburn resided at 1, Kenpas Highway whilst James lived with his wife, Winifred Blagburn at 167, Whoberley Avenue. James was buried in London Road Cemetery on the 27th November 1940 in a ceremony performed by John Carter in New Grave No. 74 Square 275.

Firewatcher **Harry Gaskine**, died at a location in Chapel Street. He resided at No. 15 and was killed aged 45. Harry was buried in the Communal Grave on the 29th November 1940.

Mary Jane (Polly) Blockley, died at her home address of 6, Court, 6 House, Bishop Street, aged 72. She is buried in the London Road Cemetery and a sister resided in Albion Street.

Husband and wife, **John Thomas Ring** and **Daisy Millicent Ring** were killed at Barracks Square, Hertford Street. The couple resided at 9, Bull Yard. John was aged 64, born on the 14th July, 1875 at Nottingham and employed Daimler Co, Ltd. Daisy was aged 55 and a native of Rugby being born there on the 12th September, 1888. Her occupation was a housewife.

Also killed at Barracks Square was **George Francis Payne.** He was a member of the Home Guard and aged 38. George resided at 120, Poole Road. George was buried in the Communal Grave on the 20th November 1940.

Injured as a result of enemy action, 14th November 1940 at Hertford Street and dying from wounds at Gulson Road Hospital was **Violet Mason**. Aged 16 she was employed as an usherette at the Empire Cinema. Violet was born on the 27th January, 1925 at Coventry and resided at 11, Meadow Street. Her father was a Private G. Mason of the Pioneer Corps. One family member was reported as needing treatment at hospital and a neighbour from No. 13 Meadow Street was detained in Stratford Emergency Hospital.

Died as a result of enemy action on the 14th November, 1940, at Cross Cheaping, whilst on duty was Coventry Fireman **David Ashby.** He was married to Maud Ashby and his parents, Mr. and Mrs. Robert Ashby resided at Thorpe Lane, Wysall, Nottinghamshire. David was born in Banbury on the 8th December, 1912 and died aged 28. In Coventry he resided at Crosbie Road and was employed at Humber Ltd. David has a plaque in the War Memorial Park as part of the Firemans Group and was interred on the 23rd November 1940.

Ashby (David AFS) – He gave his all – Fondly remembered by Amy, Horace, Mal and Ed and fried Billy

Enemy action at the Bull Yard Surface Shelter, took the lives of seventeen civilians. Six of these casualties were amongst the Ball family. **Clara Beatrice Ball** and her five children who resided at 1 Bull Yard took to the shelter when the sirens sounded. Husband and father, Edward Ball returned home and assisted in trying to dig his family out of the remains of the shelter. The children were **Florence May** aged 12, **Thomas Edward** aged 10, **Ada Lillian** aged 9, **William Henry** aged 6 and **Raymond** aged 3. The family are all buried in the Communal Grave.

Age 62, **Thomas Muscott Freeman**, also died in the Bull Yard Shelter. Born in Birmingham on the 19th February, 1879 he was married to Minnie Freeman and resided at 43, Hertford Street. He worked as an Engineer and has a commemorative plaque in the War Memorial Park. The plaque was paid for by M. Freeman of 7 Union Street on the 18th February 1948 and reads *'Mr Thomas Muscott Freeman Killed in air raid 14th November 1940'*. He was named as a victim of the air raid on the 23rd November 1940 and was *'Well known collector of antique cars and bicycles'*.

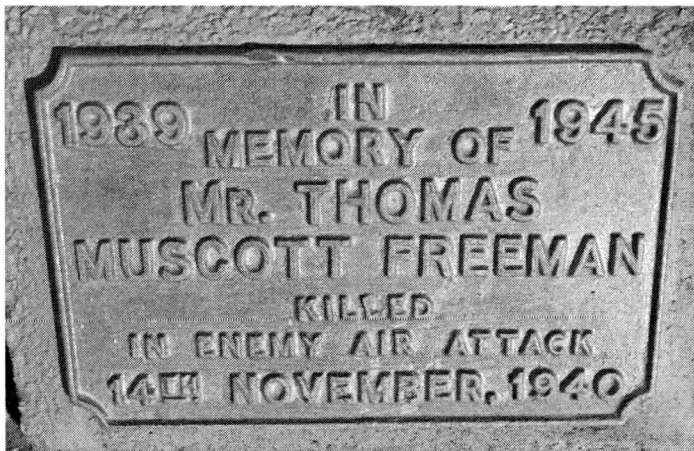

FREEMAN – In memory of Thomas Muscott from his wife and family

Five residents of 11, Union Street died in the Bull Yard Shelter. **Ada Elizabeth Henley**, aged 17, was born on the 30th April, 1894 in Coventry and employed by Humber Ltd. The four remaining victims were members of the Roberts family. **Rose May Roberts** aged 48 was a mother and housewife and born on the 23rd May, 1893 at Birmingham. Her husband, **Ernest David Roberts**, aged 44 was born on the 12th May, 1897 at Coventry to Alfred and Clara Roberts and worked as a labourer at the Standard Motor Company Limited.

Rose and Ernest's children were both pupils of Cheylesmore School. **Ernest Eric** aged 13 was born on the 30th May, 1927 at Coventry and his brother, **Leslie Arthur** was aged 11 and born on the 9th October, 1928 also at Coventry.

HENLEY and ROBERTS Treasured memories of mum. Auntie, Uncle, Ernie and Leslie, Eric and Mabel.
ROBERTS and HENLEY In loving memory of Mum, Dad, Ernie, Leslie and Auntie Ada – Betty (ATS)

Ethel Riley died in the vicinity of Bull Yard, aged 37. She resided at 7, Bull Yard and was married to J. Riley. Ethel was buried in the Communal Grave on the 20th November 1940.

From No. 9 Bull Yard three members of the Tovey family were killed a mother and her two daughters although records indicate the place of death differs across the family and includes Bull Yard Surface Shelter and the Rover Works Shelter. **Daisy Dot Tovey** was aged 33 her eldest daughter, aged 15 was **Doris** who was born on the 4th August, 1924 at Coventry and employed by Thomas Bushill & Sons Ltd. **Daisy Millicent Tovey** was aged 12, born on the 6th December, 1928 at Coventry and attended Cheylesmore School.

Winifred Joan Thorpe, was reported as being killed in the vicinity of Bull Yard, aged 18. She was the daughter of William Arthur and Annie Thorpe, of 102, Bolingbroke Road and born on the 31st May, 1922. Winifred was employed as a Burroughs Operator at Arthur Pattison Ltd.

The headline in *'The Midland Daily Telegraph'* on the 27th November 1940 read *'Coventry Girl Missing Since Raid – Last Seen In Ambulance'*. Mr and Mrs W. A. Thorpe of 102 Bolingbroke Road, Stoke, Coventry are searching the city and neighbourhood for news of their 18 year old daughter, Winifred Joan, who was injured by a bomb in Hertford Street on that terrible night of November 14. Their daughter was seen being lifted into a motor car which was to take her to hospital for treatment and nothing has been seen or heard of her since. Mr. and Mrs. Thorpe have walked or driven miles in their search so far without avail and the absence of news is causing them immense anxiety.

BLOWN OF THEIR FEET

The facts that have been reported to Coventry Police CID which will welcome any information that will help to clear up the mystery as follows:-
Miss Thorpe who was a wages clerk employed at Messrs. Pattison Hobourn Ltd, Foleshill Road went to the Empire Theatre on the evening of the 14 November with a friend George Farndon, 13 Bulkington Road, Bedworth.

Soon after the raid started the couple left the theatre and ran down Hertford Street to take cover in the public shelter in Bull Yard. When a bomb exploded in the vicinity both were flung to the ground and Miss Thorpe was injured. She was assisted into the shelter and later she was carried out again to a waiting ambulance. Her friend remembers seeing her being placed in the ambulance.

POLICE SEARCHING

The Police recovered Miss Thorpe's handbag from the shelter in Bull Yard which was subsequently struck by a bomb, but from the moment she was seen being carried to the ambulance all trace of the young woman has been lost.

Two days later the headline read *' Missing Girl was Killed'*. It has now been established that Miss Winifred Joan Thorpe, the 18-year-old Coventry girl of whom nothing has been heard since she was injured in the mass air raid on November 14, was killed in the car which was taking her to hospital. Yesterday following extensive inquiries by Coventry CID her parents Mr. and Mrs. W, A. Thorpe of 102 Bolingbroke Road, Stoke, Coventry identified at the Casualty Bureau, Council House pieces of clothing belonging to their daughter. She had been buried amongst the unidentified victims of the raid.

Previously the CID had discovered that Miss Thorpe after first being injured near a public shelter had been placed in a car to be taken to hospital. The volunteer driver was a Mr. William Allan, who because he has only one eye had the help of a Mr. Clarke who was a barman at the Three Tuns Public House, to enable him to find his way to the hospital through the debris which was still crashing down under the hail of bombs.

GUIDE ALSO KILLED.

On the way to the hospital Mr. Allan had to stop because the road was blocked and it was whilst he was turning round to seek another way that a high explosive bomb dropped near his car, and both Miss Thorpe and Mr. Clarke were killed. When the bomb exploded Mr. Allan lost the sight of his remaining eye and was eventually rescued by a party of ambulance workers.

Scholar at Junior Technical School, **Dennis Patrick Burns** died aged 14 at 45, Severn Road where he resided with his parents, Thomas and Elsie Burns. He was born on the 24th April, 1926 at Coventry and buried in the Communal Grave on the 23rd November 1940. A family member was detained in the Hospital of St. Cross, Rugby. From No. 21 a person was treated at a First Aid Post and sent home.

Doris May Lenton died at her home, 182, St. George's Road aged 33. She was the daughter of Maggie Sophia Timms, of 16, Bridgman Road, Radford and the wife of Sydney Lenton. Doris was born on the 3rd February, 1907 at Coventry and employed at Lockhurst Lane (Industrial) Co-Operative Society Ltd. She is buried in the Communal Grave.

Also buried in the Communal Grave is neighbour **Brenda Holder** who died at 184, St. George's Road, aged 22.

HOLDER – Loving memory of our dear Brenda died through enemy action. Never forgotten. Grandma, Edna, Reg and Diana.

Two injuries were recorded at No 194 one detained in Evesham Emergency Hospital and the other simply treated. A resident of No 196 was treated at Barnsley Hall Bromsgrove and from No. 202 an injury resulted in treatment at a First Aid Post and sent home. No. 277 had three people treated, two in Barnsley Hall, Bromsgrove.

At Union Chambers, Union Street **Frederick Arthur Cooke** died near his residence of 29A, Union Chambers, Union Street, aged 48. Frederick was the husband of M. S. Cooke and worked as a Building Contractor. Frederick was interred on the 23rd November 1940. From No. 29 a civilian needed treatment at Evesham Emergency Hospital.

Muriel Green was 14 years old and in lived Much Park Street.

In the Autumn we started to get regular air raids and they seemed to have a pattern, we would get home from work, have tea, get washed and changed and the sirens would sound about seven o'clock. We slept down the air raid shelter, we were quite fortunate as we were friendly with the caretaker of Charlesworth Bodies, the factory next door to the court, so we went down the shelter with them and not a public one. The public shelters were very crowded and people had their own little space, they left their bedding in the shelter and just returned every night. When we came out of the shelter there was rubble all around. The court had suffered a direct hit from the bombing.

We only lived about three hundred yards from the lovely old cathedral which was destroyed completely, all the town was flattened, so now we had no home to go to. We managed to salvage two suitcases which my mother had packed with some clothing and the other was packed with sugar, tea and a few items of food that was short, that was all we had. Our friends allowed us to stay with them in the shelter, and eat our meals in their house, fortunately it was still standing. The Army came down our street every night with chocolates, cakes and hot tea, it was all free. The Council erected a stand-pipe in the street and people queued to get water. Dad and I were unable to get to work, the RAF boys picked us up in coaches and took us to the aerodrome. The first day I returned to work, my friends stood with open mouths, they thought our family had been killed as we lived so close to the City Centre, they had been around looking for us. You were with your parents and you felt safe, we lived in the shelter to Christmas as there were no houses to be had.

Aged 46, **William Thomas Keay** died as a result of enemy action at the Greyhound Inn, Much Park Street. He resided at 305, Brearley Street, Hockley, Birmingham and was born there on the 10th September, 1892. In Coventry he was employed at Lea-Francis Limited. William is buried in Handsworth New Cemetery, Birmingham.

At 12 Court, 3 House, Much Park Street **Mary Ann Kendrick** died aged 59 at her residence. Mary is buried in the Communal Grave.
KENDRICK (Mary Ann) Treasured memories of a loving mother. Loved and remembered by her children, Frances, Meg, Betty, Kate and only son, George and wife, Ivy.

From 48, Much Park Street, **Clement Horace Jones**, died at Gulson Road Hospital on the 15th November, 1940, aged 35. He was injured as a result of enemy action on the 14th November, 1940. His father was also called Clement and his mother, Mabel whom also resided in Much Park Street at 118. Clement was born on the 26th June, 1904 at Walsall and employed and resided at Greyhound Hotel, Much Park Street. He is buried in the Communal Grave.

Jane Allitt was killed by enemy action aged 68 on the 14th November 1940 at her home address of 113 Much Park Street. Jane was the daughter of William and Maria Allitt, of 34 Ranelagh Terrace, Leamington Spa and she was born on the 25th May 1871, at Leamington. She is buried in the Communal Grave and the War Memorial Park plaque applied for by W. J. Allitt (Brother) of 22 Irving Road reads *'Miss Jane Allitt Killed in air raid 14th November 1940'*.

He paid for two plaques on the 25th February 1948 one for Jane Allitt the other for Elizabeth Allitt who died from injuries received in air raid on the 13th April 1941. Elizabeth Hannah Allitt, died in hospital after being buried as a result of enemy action in Warwick Row air raid shelter, aged 64. Both sisters are buried in the Communal Grave.

Various injuries were incurred across Much Park Street: No. 5 detained in Shuckburgh Park Convalescent Hospital, Daventry, No. 90 treated at First Aid Post and sent home; No. 101 detained in Evesham Emergency Hospital; Two persons at 105 treated at First Aid Post and sent home; No. 113 treated at First Aid Post and sent home. Three further casualties treated at First Aid Post and sent home, one detained in Warwick Hospital and one detained in Warneford Hospital, Leamington.

Premises along Little Park Street

Further tragedy was to befall the Twamley family on the night of the 14ᵗʰ/15ᵗʰ November with the death of **Oliver**. Like so many families they had lost a relative in the Great War, Private Leonard Twamley who was killed during the Battle of Fromelles on the 19ᵗʰ July 1916. Oliver died at 19, Court, Little Park Street, aged 49. He resided with his wife, Nellie Twamley at 84, Little Park Street and his parents, Herbert and Emma resided at 52, Godiva Street. Oliver was born in 1892 at Coventry and worked in city being employed by Rootes Securities Ltd.

1942 TWAMLEY (Oliver) In loving memory of our dear father also our dear mother (April 1940). Sadly missed by Olly and Barry, also by her Grandma and aunties and uncles.

At No. 103 one occupant was detained in Warwick Hospital, one treated at First Aid Post and sent home and from the Police Station one person treated at Works First Aid Post and sent home.

Plaques in London Road Cemetery were paid for by Mrs. E. G. Leworthy of 29 Lypiatt Tivoli, Cheltenham at a cost of £3-5-0 on the 18th March 1948. They read *'Mr David Geoffrey Leworthy 5 years Killed in air raid 14th November 1940 Mr John Herbert Leworthy Killed in air raid 14th November 1940'*

Father and son, **David Geoffrey Harwood Leworthy** and **John Herbert Leworthy**, died at 12, Minster Road, the family home and are buried in the Communal Grave. David was born on the 23rd April, 1935 at Coventry to Ethel Gladys Leworthy and John Herbert Leworthy. He attended Miss Hoopers Preparatory School, Holyhead Road and is buried in the Communal Grave. His father, John was aged 44 and a Home Guard and employed at Haywards Outfitters. John's parents, Herbert and Hilda Leworthy resided at the Cotswold View, The Reddings, Cheltenham, Gloucestershire, and he was born on the 24th January, 1896 at Cirencester.

LEWORTHY Treasured memories of my dear husband and darling, Geoffrey. His loving wife, mummy and John.

One of those who witnessed the casualties at the West End Club was Harry James who was then 6 years old.

We were living at 26 Albion Street and I was at St. John's School. The ARP Warden, Mr. Hicks who lived across the road came around and told us to get down the shelter as 'it was going to be a bad one, tonight'. My mother was worried as she didn't want to go without her husband so we stayed in the house until my dad came back about 10.00pm. (He was in a reserved occupation at that time). We then went to the shelter in Spon Street. I was grabbed by somebody in the shelter, it was the warden he said 'We've been looking for you in the rubble!" The house had suffered a direct hit and Mr. Hicks had been digging in the rubble until the bombing had got that heavy that he had to leave and come down the shelter.

We came out of the shelter in Spon Street and saw people covered in blankets who had come out of the West End Club. My mum told me they were asleep to protect me, but I knew that they were really dead. When we got home we found a pile of rubble, some friends took us in and then we were helped by the WVS. We had nothing apart

from what we were stood in, after our friends house we stayed at a centre until we were re-housed.

We went back to the house every day to see if there was anything we could salvage and by that time we concluded that 'The cats had it', I was quite upset about this being so young. After three days the cat 'Tim' appeared out of the rubble, he must have managed to claw himself out he was missing half a tail and an ear but he looked happy to see me. The house seemed to implode there were houses within yards that still had their windows. I can remember as well watching a local artist who painted pictures of bombed houses painting our house, I think the picture appeared in the paper.

Mother, son and daughter, **Agnes Maud Chinn, Eric Chinn** and **Vera Maud Chinn** died at West End Club, Spon Street the family resided at 70, Northumberland Road. Their husband and father was Alfred John Chinn. Agnes was aged 43, Eric aged 17 and Vera Maud aged 18 with all being buried in the Communal Grave between the 20th and the 23rd November 1940. Eric was employed with the Auxiliary Fire Service.

Injuries were reported at Northumberland Road, No. 7 detained in Warwick Hospital, No. 9 Treated at First Aid Post and sent home, No. 22 detained in Warwick Hospital and No. 40 detained in Hospital of St. Cross, Rugby.

James and **Sarah Lavinia Cronan** also died at the West End Club although they resided at 11, Swan Street. James, aged 50 was employed Coventry Corporation, Highways Department and Sarah was a housewife. Both are buried in the Communal Grave.

CRONAN (Vin and Jim) In loving memories of mum and dad who were taken from us suddenly. Jim and Rene, Steve and Marg, and baby, Barbara.

One of the youngest victims, **Catherine Elizabeth Haynes** died aged 11. She was the daughter of Mr. A. Haynes and Mrs. E. Haynes (later Kelly) of 18 Norfolk Street. The Haynes family resided at 19 Waveley Road and being of school age she was a pupil of St. Osburg's School. Catherine was born on the 17th August, 1929 at Swansea and died at the West End Club, Spon Street. Catherine is buried in the Communal Grave and her War Memorial Park plaque paid for by Miss M. Haynes of 20 Norfolk Street on the 26th February 1948 reads *'Catherine Elizabeth Haynes 11 years Killed in air raid 11th November 1940'*. At Waveley Road one person from No. 3 was detained in Warwick Hospital and No. 6 one person treated at Warneford Hospital and sent home.

Named on the Corporation Memorial in the Council House is **Arthur Overbury,** City Engineers Department who was in the Civil Division. He died aged 69 at the West End Club, 127 Spon Street. A resident of 42 Croft Road he was born in April 1873 at Birmingham and is buried in the Communal Grave. His plaque was paid for by P. Hinks of Welgarth Avenue on the 13th February 1948 and reads '*Mr Arthur Overbury Civil Defence Killed in enemy air raid 14th November 1940'.*

OVERBURY (Arthur) In loving memory of Dad – Always in the thoughts of Phoebe, Charlie and grandchildren, Derek and Beryl.

Residents of the West End Club, mother **Audrey Annie Roberts** (36) and daughter **Audrey Patricia Roberts** (9) were killed due to enemy action. Audrey Annie was employed as a Stewardess at the Club and the wife of Thomas George Roberts. She was born on the 29th July, 1906 at Pentre, Rhondda. Audrey Patricia was born on the 29th July, 1932 at Coventry and attended St John's School. Both are buried together in Grave Ref. I6. 6/2. at the Communal Grave.

ROBERTS In memory of my wife and child (Audrey and Patricia) – Tom also with treasured and happy memories of a lifetimes friendship Eisle and Will.

Also aged 9 and buried in the Communal Grave is **Margaret Warren.** She resided at 32, Melville Road and was the daughter of Thomas Warren.

WARREN In loving memory of our dear sister, Margaret – Ethel, Ern, Shells, Bet, Harry

Husband and wife, **Alice** and **George Henry Watson** are buried in the Communal Grave, they resided at 30, Waverley Road. Alice was aged 42 and born on the 19th November, 1899 at Bedworth. George was slightly older at 44, born on the 12th September, 1897 at Coventry and employed by Mechanisation and Aero Ltd.

WATSON Treasured memories of my dear son, Harry and wife. Always in his mother's thoughts, remembered always by dad.

Two deaths were recorded in Spon Street. **William Mallard**, aged 67 resided at 7 House, 23 Court, Spon Street and was a native of Northampton. He was employed at Alfred Herbert Limited.

At 51, Spon Street. **Mary Alice Wilson**, died aged 72. She was the daughter of Joseph and Mary Jane Carrington, of Bexhill-on-Sea, Sussex and resided at 201, Attleborough Road, Nuneaton. May was born on the 19th February, 1868 at Rugby and was the widow of Alfred Wilson. A plaque application was received by Mrs. S. C. Green of Victoria Road, Leigh-on-Sea, Essex with an application reading *'Mrs Mary Alice Wilson Died from injuries received in enemy air attack 14th November 1940'*. The plaque application was not pursued, possibly due to location choice.

Resident of No. 21 Spon Street detained in Warwick Hospital, No. 57 received treatment and No. 81 detained in Hollymoor Hospital, Birmingham. With unknown house number, one person required treatment, one detained in Warneford Hospital, Leamington Spa and one person detained in Warwick Hospital.

Charles Southams in Windsor Street is listed as the location of place of death for **John Heath**, who died aged 65. He was an employee of Charles Southams and married to H. Heath, of 69, The Butts. Charles was a native of Hurley, Berkshire and born on the 28th February, 1873. From No. 58 an occupant was detained in Warneford Hospital, Leamington.

Mother and daughter, **Agnes Laing** aged 51 and daughter, **Elizabeth Margaret Laing** aged 31 were killed at Elizabeth's address at 37, Grosvenor Road. Agnes home address was 2, Westfield Crescent, Newport, Monmouthshire and was probably visiting her daughter when the air raid occurred. A further family member was detained in Evesham Emergency Hospital and one in Warwick Hospital. Both Agnes and Elizabeth were interred in the Communal Grave on the 23rd November 1940.

17 Grosvenor Road

Two days after she was injured at her home address of 16 , The Butts **Maria Sarah Kimberley** died at Rugby Emergency Hospital. She was aged 79. Her husband, T. A. Kimberley preceded her in death. Maria's grave details are listed with the Commonwealth War Grave as Rugby Municipal Borough and further investigation revealed Clifton Road Cemetery Grave H208. At the time of her death, Maria's address was listed as 60 Upper York Street, Coventry. On person from 95 Heavy Anti-Aircraft Battery at The Butts received treatment.

Roy Vernon was one of those who lived in this vicinity.

I had just turned seven, I have far memory of that night a lot of what I know now is what I heard from my father. We my friends and I played out in the street (Hope Street) until about five as usual and our family were about to have our tea, faggots and peas, when the air raid warning sounded so we went down the cellar under the house. I played with my toy cowboys and Indian lead soldiers and then went to sleep, but later there were a lot of bangs and the house shook. This and the subsequent happenings I do remember. There was a sound of water and my mum said 'Who's on the lav?" My Dad and Godfather had made a curtained off part of the cellar with a commode in it, the water started to come into the cellar and we had to go to the Anderson Shelter in the garden, it turned out that the water and gas mains had been blown up in the street. As we went out I could see right across the sky it was red in front of us was the YWCA all ablaze. (The Coach House it's ruins were still there in the 1950's).

We stayed out in the shelter until the all clear sounded, but during the night my Dad would keep popping in and out of the shelter once to put out an incendiary bomb at the top of the garden by the chicken pen and as he was a firewatcher he went into the street to see if he could help anyone, he came back once and said Bates (No. 9) and Tidmans (the shop) had gone. When we went out into the street, houses had been destroyed on both sides of The Butts.

Later in life I realized that a stick of High Explosives bombs had been dropped at an angle from about No. 28 across to No. 7 and on to some houses in The Butts. As our house had no electricity in those days and the gas was off mum blew the dust off the faggots and peas and cooked them over the fire for breakfast. We then had to get into the back of Mr. Ceneys coal lorry which took us, dad, mum, my 13 year old sister me some of our friends and neighbours (Mr and Mrs Coppell, Billy my age and Olive about my sisters age) to a Hamlet near Balsall Common called Mear End, we all spent Christmas there getting home in time for the blitz of 1941. Some of my school mates died when there houses were destroyed by fire, they lived in Trafalgar Street.

In Windsor Street there was a brewery called Southams and when my dad went back to the house, next day he found that a large iron girder had been blown from there, after the brewery had been hit be a landmine, through our roof trapping my black cat Joey, he lived on until 1948, the windows in the top shop had been blown out so we stayed at Mear End until March 1941.

David Bee was injured as a result of enemy action at Barracks Market and died at Hospital of St. Cross, Rugby on the 16th November, 1940, aged 37. He was the husband of Annie Maud Bee, of 80, Eden Street, Coventry and rests in Clifton Road Cemetery Grave G427. Indication of being a fireman came from the Rugby Archives that state he was a Member of the AFS, he died at Hospital of St Cross , Rugby and the address at time of death was listed as 111 Hampton Road, Coventry.

One of those seeking shelter was Majorie Viner who was in the Bablake School Shelter.

I had finished at Barr's Hill School and was living with my parents in a large house in Abbot's Lane, opposite the gas works. The house had been damaged by 'bomb blast' in a previous raid, and although my parents were allowed in the house during the day to collect belongings etc we had to find alternative shelters during the night. By the 14th we had been finding alternative shelter at Bablake School for about two weeks, normally occupying a position in the school gym before dark. Prior to this we had sought shelter in a cellar but had been advised to go to Bablake. At Bablake, their were a large number of shelters, and they ran all along the railings nearly to the arches. When we got to the shelter, mother kept walking and walking until she reached the end of the shelter, I would have sat on the first available seat, but her mother kept on walking.

During the night a bomb fell on the front of the shelter. I don't recall getting out of the shelter but remember remarking to mother, that my face was dirty, my mother replied "If you want to wipe your face, you'll have to wipe your face with the water out of the hot water bottle". When the school had been hit, the School Caretaker came out and advised those in the building to take up positions in the school shelter, I crossed to the School shelter with my parents and crossing the school field to the shelters, the ground was rough and uneven as if it had been ploughed and had crops growing on it.

We then went into the City Centre to see what had happened and returned to Bablake the following morning with her parents. A cart that her mother had noticed prior to going into the shelter was now being used to remove the casualties from the shelter into the school building as the school corridor was used as a mortuary, Marjorie's mother informed her that 45 people had been killed.

After the raid my parents went to stay at Warwick and I went to a friend's house in Birmingham. After finding a suitable home, the family returned to Coventry in March, 1941. During the April 1941 raids, the family took shelter in their Anderson Shelter and this house was also damaged by bomb blast.

The bombs that fell on the Bablake School shelters killed a number of people and the School Library was totally burned out. The school corridor was used as a mortuary, Mr. Seaborne the Headmaster had spent the night in Kenilworth and was turned away by the Police when he tried to enter the City.

Three members of the Cooper family whom resided at 9, Mill Street were killed as a result of the air raid. **Florence Lillian Cooper**, aged 50 was married to **Joseph Cooper** aged 54. one of their son **Henry** aged 13, was also killed. An elder son Mr. H. A. Cooper resided at Telfer Road.

The Cuthbertson family also lost three members who resided at 11, Hill Cross. **George** was the father, aged 32 he was born in August, 1911 at Carlisle and employed at the Triumph Cycle Company Limited. His wife, **Mabel** was aged 26 and the daughter of Maria Smith, of 55, Middleborough Road. She was born on the 17th September, 1912 at Nuneaton and a housewife. Their daughter, aged 6, **Joyce** was also killed at the shelter. The family are buried in the Communal Grave.

A native of Bally Connell, Cloghboley, Co. Sligo, Irish Republic was also lost, **Patrick Foley.** Aged 26, he was the son of James and Mary Foley and is buried in the Borough of Coventry. The daughter of R. E. and V. M. Smyth, of 67, Middleborough Road, **Joan Margaret Smyth**, aged 6 also died and she is buried in the Communal Grave. Joan was born on the 2nd December, 1934 at Coventry.

Peter Adams from Briscoe Road was 12 years and attended Bablake School.

In the summer we slept in the Anderson Shelter, my father found bunks and a platform for my sister aged 5, it was like camping out. We were in there for one or two alarms, not serious only when it started to get cold did we come inside. My father brought a bed downstairs and we slept in it. On the night of the November raid we had a bomb land in the back garden and the neighbour lend over the fence to help us put it out.

The raid didn't seem any worse then the rest of the raids. The following morning me and a friend rode to school and got as far as Widdrington Road before we had to walk it. We walked by the rubble of the RAF Depot in Sandy Lane. When we got to Bablake School we received instruction that the school was going to report for evacuation, we had been receiving lessons by a tutorial system and had only used the school shelters for practice not during an actual air raid. To give the information to other pupils we were given a piece of chalk and wrote on any wall we could that the other pupils were to report to school. This was not normal behaviour for Bablake boys and I don't remember getting told off for it. On the 20th we were evacuated from Foleshill Station to Lincoln, to an Old Girls School.

Louis James Daly, died as a result of enemy action, at Highlands Nursing Home, St. Nicholas Street. Aged 72, he formerly resided at 52, Grosvenor Road. Louis was the son of Charles and Maria Lapworth Daly, of 125, Cox Street and the widower of Florence Honora E Reynolds.

Aged 3, **Patricia Ward** died as a result of enemy action at the City Isolation Hospital, Whitley. Patricia was born in 1937 at Coventry to Mrs. D. M. Ward and resided at 25, St. Nicholas Street. A resident of No. 15 Nicholas Street received treatment, No. 40 detained in Hollymoor Hospital, Birmingham and one from The Elms treated at a First Aid Post and sent home.

Michael Joseph Cronin received a Posthumous Commendation by H.M The King for brave conduct in Civil Defence which was citied in *'The London Gazette'* May 1941 as *'those named below have been bought to notice for brave conduct in Civil Defence Michael Joseph Cronin (deceased), Storeman Coventry.'* The story was also covered by *'The Midland Telegraph'* on the 10th May 1941 with the headline - *Gallant Coventry Warden – Honour for Irishman who gave his life in November Raid.* The article continued; *The name of Michael Joseph Cronin of Coventry appears in the latest list of civilian honours. Cronin will never know that his gallant conduct in air raids earned him a National Commendation. An Irishman, living in Middlebrough Road, Coventry. Cronin joined the air raid warden service as a volunteer, and whenever there was enemy action he was in the thick of it. On the night of November 14th he had already accomplished much good work in dealing with incendiaries when he was killed by a high explosive.*

Aged 48, he lived and died at 54 Middleborough Road. Michael was born on the 6th February, 1893 at Charlesville, Co. Cork to John and Josephine Cronin, of Liscullane, Charleville, Co. Cork, Ireland. Locally he was employed as an Assistant Officer-in-charge Regional Store, Home Office Branch, Hinckley and married to Helena Cronin.

He was buried in Astwood Cemetery, Worcester and the connection with Worcester was in line with his plaque application for the War Memorial Park was paid for by Mrs. H. E. Cronin, 4 Park View Terrace, Worcester and reads *Mr. Michael Joseph Cronin Killed in air raid 14th November 1940*. Three occupants of No. 3 Middleborough Road required treatment one was detained in Hollymoor Hospital, Birmingham

Dennis Field resided at Middleborough Road.

I was then at Coventry Technical College and doing my homework when the bombs rained down intermittently and many times we crouched down, expecting the worst or at best hoping not to have a direct hit. Occasionally there were colossal bangs and blasts which blew open the door. I wanted to go out and see what was happening and help if I could but demurred to Mum's pleadings and restricted myself to occasional peers outside. The sky seemed aglow, with the brightest huge conflagration lighting the sky in the direction of the City Centre.

Ten members of the local community were killed taking shelter at the Motor Hotel, Dorset Road and these are mentioned in alphabetical order. A resident of No 11 was treated at First Aid Posts and sent home and No. 30 treated at First Aid Post and sent home. Late in November an 'In Memoriam' notice appeared in the local paper *'Customers and staff of Motor Hotel In memory of our dear friends, from customers and staff'*.

William and Mary Ann Golby, of Lentons Lane, Hawkesbury lost a son (Frederick Golby) and a daughter. Housewife **Eliza Garside** was aged 41 and the wife of Edward Garside. Eliza was born on the 25th December 1899 and resided in Radford at 61 Somerset Road. Buried in the Communal Grave, and to commemorate her loss a plaque was paid for in the War Memorial Park by her husband on the 17th February 1948 from 9 Cheveral Avenue and reads *'Mrs Eliza Garside Killed in air raid 14th/15th November 1940'*. A family member was also injured and treated at a First Aid Post and sent home.

GARSIDE In loving memory of my dear wife, Betty. Sadly missed her husband, Frank and Doris.

Eliza's older brother from 264, Middlemarch Road, **Frederick Golby** died aged 48. He was born on the 16th August, 1890 and employed by Morris Motors Ltd. Frederick was buried on the 23rd November 1940 in the Communal Grave.

John Osborne lost his wife, **Emily Osborne** at the Motor Hotel. She was aged 53, resided with her husband at 212, Widdrington Road and was born in the city in May 1887. Emily was buried in the Communal Grave on the 23rd November 1940. Other injuries from Widdrington road, No. 65 detained in Hollymoor Hospital, Birmingham, No. 110 treated at First Aid Post and sent home, one person treated at Gulson Road Hospital and sent home and a further person received treatment.

The landlady of the Motor Hotel, **Edith Emily Pointon** was lost in the air raid, her husband was Thomas Pointon. Edith was the daughter of Mr. and Mrs. A. Bates, of 79, East Street and born on the 28th February, 1894. She lost her life aged 47.

POINTON (Edith Emily) Ever in our thoughts with loving remembrance Hubby and Eric

Daughter of T. Rowson, of 99, Dorset Road **Emma Amelia Rowson** died aged 31. Emma resided at Hill Crest Cottage, Bentley Road, Short Heath, Wolverhampton, Staffordshire and was employed as a housekeeper. She was born on the 24th January, 1909 at Wolverhampton and is buried in the Borough of Wolverhampton .

From 56, Dorset Road **Elsie Rebecca Spalding** aged 49 died in the air raid. Elsie's parents, Thomas and Sarah Johnson resided at 1, Connaught Terrace, Jarrow-on-Tyne, Co. Durham and she was married to Alexander Spalding. Elsie was buried on the 21st November 1940.

SPALDING (Elsie) In loving memory of my dear wife and Mother – Always remembered by Alec, Allan, Tom and Rene

Lillian Olive Miles, the daughter of George William and Clara Miles, of 40, Godiva Street resided with her parents and died aged 39. The final deaths at the Motor Hotel were three members of the Walters family from 75, Colchester Street. The family members were **Ethel May Walters**, aged 41 and her husband **Richard Walters,** aged 42. Lost with them was their son, **Richard Derrick Walters** aged 12.

MILES and WALTERS Loving memory of our dear sisters, Lily Miles and Ethel, Dick and Derrick Walters – Silently mourned by Nell, Jack, Arthur, George, Bert, Phyllis, Fred, Ernie and Jim.

WALTERS In loving memory of Dick, Ethel and Derek; also Lilly. Sadly missed by mum, dad, sisters and brothers.

Six residents of Springfield Road were killed at No. 13, No. 17 and No. 19. At No. 13, **Bertha Livesey** died aged 30. She resided next door at 11, Springfield Road and was married to A. Livesey. Bertha is buried in the Communal Grave. The residents of No. 13 were **Albert Preston** and **Florence Annie Preston**. Albert was aged 52, born in 1881 at Birmingham and worked locally as a tailor. Florence was slightly older at 55, also born in Birmingham and occupied as a housewife. Both are buried in the Communal Grave.

A further couple were also killed at their home at 17, Springfield Road and buried in the Communal Grave. **Mary Brand Adams** and **William Thomas Adams.** Mary was aged 64 and born on the 5th October, 1879, at Montrose, County Angus. William aged 60 was born on the 3rd January, 1885, at Barrow-in-Furness and employed at Armstrong

Whitworth, Baginton. The couple had a daughter, Mrs Hilda Greaves who lived in Shenton. Mary and Thomas have a joint plaque in Canley Crematorium, that was paid for by Mrs. A. Peel of 128 Beanfield Avenue on the 9th March 1948 at a cost of £2-5-0.

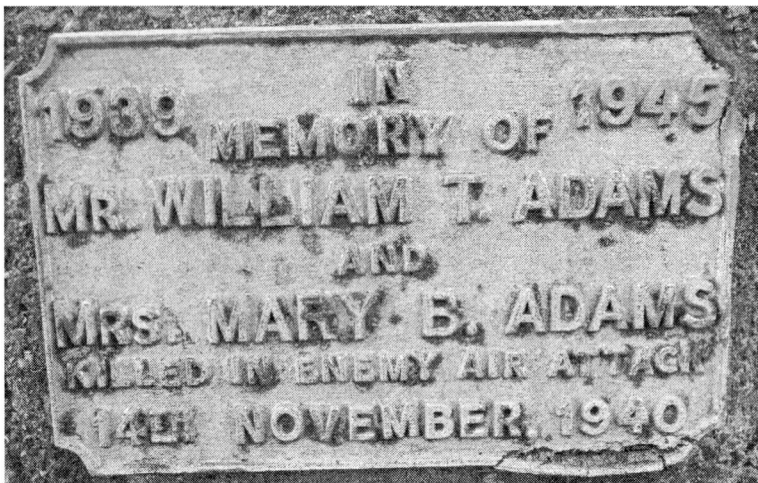

The final death in Springfield Road at No. 19 was **Elizabeth Tanner.** She was aged 85 and one of the eldest victims. She is commemorated on the memorial in the Communal Grave and a plaque was paid for in Hearsall Common. by I. Perkins (Miss) of 13, Bleahley Terrace, Notton, near Wakefield on the 18th July 1952 and reads 'Miss Elizabeth Tanner Killed in air raid 14th/15th November 1940'.

Two residents of No. 5 Springfield Road were injured one detained in Hospital of St. Cross, Rugby and the other in Warneford Hospital, Leamington Spa.

Catherine (Carrie) Barritt, died and resided at 65, George Eliot Road, aged 68. She was the wife of G. S. Barritt and born in 1878, at Coventry and occupied as a housewife. Carrie is buried in the Communal Grave. A resident of No 20 required first aid treatment, one treated at a First Aid Post and sent home from No. 63 and for No. 65 three persons injured one detained in Stratford-on-Avon Emergency Hospital and two detained in Hollymoor Hospital, Birmingham.

Remains of a house on George Eliot Road

Dolly Grinham, aged 53 died at Ford Street Shelter. She resided at 4 Charles Street and was the wife of John Henry Grinham She is buried in I5.3/1. Communal Grave. A resident of 22 Ford Street was treated at a First Aid Posts and sent home.

GRINHAM In loving memory of our dear Mother, sadly missed by all.

A native of Wrexham, **John Cooper Norman**, resided and died at 9, Leopold Road. He was aged 38 and born on the 20th June, 1903. He was employed at Armstrong Siddeley Motors Limited and buried in the Communal Grave.

Buried on the 23rd November 1940 in the Communal Grave was **Martin Florence** and his address was 4c. 5h. Cox Street. A resident was detained in Hospital of St. Cross, Rugby

1939   1945
IN MEMORY OF
FIREMAN
F. KILBUERN
KILLED ON
NOVEMBER 14TH 1940

Leading Fireman **Frederick Kilbuern** died aged 32 on the 14th November 1940. He was the son of Mr. and Mrs. Frederick Kilbuern of 685 Stoney Stanton Road, the couple had three sons and would loose two of then during the war. Frederick was killed whilst on duty at Cope Street, the husband of Lily May Kilbuern they resided at 58 Nuffield Road. His wife applied for a plaque at Sowe Common but this was withdrawn with his allocation at the War Memorial Park. Frederick was born on the 12th September, 1908 at Coventry and employed with Builders E. Harris & Son Ltd., Builders and contractors. He is one of the fireman buried in the Communal Grave. *Kilbuern – Fred (Leading fireman) in loving memory of a dear husband and daddy – Ever in the thoughts of his wife, Lily, John also Mum, Dad and family'.*

Cope Street had one person treated at No. 5, 17 treated at First Aid Post and sent home and along the street one person detained in Barnsley Hall Emergency Hospital, Bromsgrove.

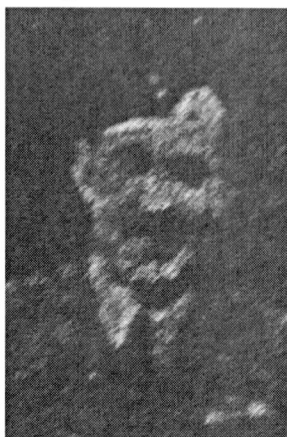

Reported on May 3rd 1941 was *"The death of Sergeant Pilot Ralph Kilbuern of the RAFVR a 23 year old qualified instructor has been reported killed, he was the third son of Mr and Mrs F. Kilbuern of 286 Stoney Stanton road and was married. He was an apprentice of BTH and became a Freeman of the City. On the night of Coventry's big raid Sgt Kilbuern was home on leave and worked hard at a fire station helping to extinguish incendiary bombs. On this night his brother leading fireman Fred Kilbuern was killed in leading at another Coventry Station'.*

Two deaths were recorded in Freehold Street and both are buried in the Communal Grave. At No. 21 **John Ronan**, died as a result of enemy action, 15th November, 1940 at his home of 21, Freehold Street, aged 64. **Barbara Joyce Harrison**, died at 57, Freehold Street, aged 8 although she resided at No. 71. Her parents were Reginald and Mabel Harrison and she was born on the 21st October, 1932 at Coventry. Barbara attended Frederick Bird School.

HARRISON – Cherished memories of our darling Barbara Aunties and Uncles, Granny and Grandpa and cousin Ray.

A resident of No. 21 was detained in Warwick Hospital and one treated at First Aid Post and sent home. From No. 24 one person detained in Warwick Hospital, No. 53 treated and No. 155 treated at a First Aid Post and sent home.

Six citizens lost their lives at the Scala Cinema, Far Gosford Street.

Edna May Doyle, aged 21 was the wife of John Doyle and resided at 446, Stoney Stanton Road. She was born on the 23rd October, 1919 at 3, Vauxhall Street and occupied as a housewife. Also killed with her was her son, **Kevin Anthony Doyle**, aged 18 months. He was born on the 8th May, 1939 at Coventry. Both are recorded as being buried in the London Road Cemetery.

DOYLE – In loving memory of my dear wife and son, Edna and Kevin Doyle. RIP. Sadly missed by husband John.

Injured as a result of enemy action, at the Scala Cinema and dying of wounds at Gulson Road Hospital on the following day was **Ernest Leslie Claypole.** Aged 20, his parents were Arthur and Louisa Claypole and he resided at 3, Harris Road. Ernest was born on the 1st October, 1920 at Coventry and employed at Coventry and District Co-Operative Society Ltd., Binley Branch. He is buried in the Communal Grave.

CLAYPOLE – In loving memory of our dear son, Leslie. Ever remembered by his Father, Mother, brothers (Arthur and Leonard), and Viv.

Also dying of wounds was **Stephanie Kinzett,** she died at Coventry and Warwickshire Hospital on the 15th November, 1940 at the age of 20. She was born in 1922, at Foleshill to Fergus Kinzett and Laura B. Kinzett and resided at 7, Glover Street. Stephanie was employed at the British Thomson-Houston Company Limited and buried in Coventry (London Road) Cemetery on the 4th December 1940 New Grave No. 56. Square 312. The ceremony was performed by L. Bruce.

KINZETT (Stephanie) Treasured memories of a dear daughter and sister. Sadly missed by Dad, Estelle and Brian.

Age 15, **Gwen Ivy Letford**, died at the cinema. She resided at 16, Seagrave Road and was the daughter of Sergeant W. Letford, The Royal Lincolnshire Regiment. Gwen was born 11th August, 1926 at Coventry and worked as a Shop Assistant. She is buried in the Communal Grave. From 31, Heath Crescent and also buried in the Communal Grave is **Gordon John Richardson** aged 23.

An application was made by the wife of Leading Fireman **Frederick Cecil Atkins**, Amy Maud Atkins to have a private plaque in the War Memorial Park but this was superseded by allocation from the Fireman's Group. Frederick was killed age 43 on the 14th /15th November 1940 near Swanswell Pool. The couple resided at 99 Sussex Road. Frederick was born on the 16th July, 1897, at Coventry and was employed locally at Alfred Herbert Ltd. He is buried in the Communal Grave, Coventry Cemetery and was named on the Roll of Honour for Alfred Herbert and listed at the Fitting Department.

Atkins (Fred AFS) In loving memory of our brother who passed to a higher life. Remembered always by Joe, Floss and Nell'.

Also in the vicinity of Swanswell, was Fireman **James Kenny.** He was born on the 5th February 1910 at Newcastle Upon Tyne and in Coventry resided at 16 Sherbourne Crescent. His date of death was listed as the 14th November 1940, he was employed at Riley Motors Ltd and married to Elizabeth Kenney. James is buried in the Communal Grave and has a plaque in the War Memorial Park as part of the Firemans Group.

Eunice Wale (Nee Baxter) was residing at Wright Street, Hillfields.

We were at the full front line as our house backed onto the bus station, we though the Germans this was a factory. The walls were really high and we dreaded moonlight nights, when they build the station before the war the walls were build really high and the properties in Wright Street became really dark. The residents protested so they covered the wall in white tiles, we were sitting targets it used to light up like a mirror. We were moved out of the house three times, the windows were blown in, the roof was blown off and we had to move out due to a gas leak. The warden used to come round and knock on doors and say 'Your alright ?', on one night we were all unconscious. They dragged us out and put us on the pavement and took us to hospital, that was due to a gas leak. The bus station eventually painted the white tiles maroon in a hope that it would deter the bombers from thinking it was a factory but we don't know if it ever did!

Because bombs were dropped in the street, and people were caught in the street mother opened the door after the raid on occasions and found limbs on the doorstep as people had been caught in the blast. We still had to got to school, if we didn't have any water we had to go and find some and then go to school afterwards.

Dad worked nights at the GEC, he was in charge of a shop floor that had disabled workers so he was always the last to leave. On one occasion Dad was buried for two days, he had just bought a new bike and wanted to know where his bike was, he was more concerned about his bike. There weren't many families who stayed in Wright Street at night. Normally there was three off us, mum, my older sister and me and we would sit under the stairs. We had a feather mattress, jigsaws and condensed milk which we used to use with cocoa and a bit of sugar as a treat as we lacked sweetness.

Condensed milk wasn't rationed but it was hard to get hold off. We had lots of gaps in the street and empty land after the war.

Three citizens are recorded as being killed in Berry Street with injuries; two persons at No. 61 detained in Warwick Hospital and one at No. 71 received treatment.

Joseph Palmer Brown died at an unknown location at Berry Street, aged 70. He actually resided at 27, Catherine Street and was born on the 25th January, 1870. He is buried in Grave Ref. O/4 on the 17th December 1940 in the Communal Grave.

BROWN – (of 23, Catherine Street) In loving memory of Dad, Always in the thoughts of Flo, Joe, Vera and Leth.

From No 61, **Pamela Mary Littlehales,** aged 7 died at her home address. Pamela was the daughter of Clarence and Clara Littlehales. She was buried on the 19th December in Grave No. 33. Square 311 at the London Road Cemetery in a ceremony carried out by Paul Stacey. Records show that two family members were detained for treatment in Warwick Hospital.

The eldest victim from Berry Street aged 72 was **Emily Carn.** She resided and died at 67, Berry Street. Her father was Henry Luscombe, of Glenely House, Duncombe Street, Kingsbridge, Devonshire and her husband was John Joseph Carn. Emily's burial took place on the 5th December 1940 in Grave No. 17 Square 191 London Road Cemetery and she came from the Parish of St. Peter. Her remains were found on the 1st December 1940. Her daughter was Mrs. A. Rollason.

CARN- Emily (late of 67, Berry Street). In loving memory of dear, mother. Her loving daughters, Annie, Beatrice, sons-in-law, Reg, Harry, grandchildren, Fred and Pauline

John Jeavons was aged 5.

We lived in an old weaving house in Hood Street. As soon as the sirens went we were down, at that age we didn't remember the danger. I remember coming out of the shelter at British Thompson Houston and Reed Street was covered in litter and glass. Most people had given up with the Air Raid Shelters only when it got serious did they go to the BTH one. I was with my two brothers, William and James and my mother. Father had been called up. In the shelter they had a lot of steel beds and I can remember looking down and seeing water flowing around the shelter floor. Apparently a bomb had hit a static water tank and the water came down the steps into the shelter. Years later I read an account that a lady had been rushing to the shelter and the bomb had blown her into shelter and the water had came in after her.

A number of casualties were recorded in the vicinity of Jordan Well. For hospital treatment a resident of No. 14 was detained in Evesham Emergency Hospital, No. 38 received treatment and two residents detained in Warwick Hospital.

As a result of enemy action, 14th November, 1940 near Gaumont Cinema, Private **Jack Bennett**, 5252648, B Company, 70th Bn., South Staffordshire Regiment died aged 18. His parents were Horace E. Bennett and Nellie Bennett, of Headless Cross, Redditch, Worcestershire and Jack was stationed at Whitley. His was buried on the 23rd November 1940 in the Communal Grave and was identified by Captain Hounslow, 70th South Staffordshire Regiment.

As a result of enemy action at the Gaumont Cinema, **Daisy Violet Duncalf** died at Stratford General Hospital. She was born on the 26th January, 1921 at Shoreham, Kent, resided at 17, Cranford Road and worked at J. Lyons & Co. Ltd. Her father was Ernest William Duncalf. As Daisy died in Stratford she was buried on the 19th November 1940 in grave 4851 at the Evesham Road Cemetery. The ceremony was performed by a Reverend Thomas.

Aged 18, **Wilfred Harold Fern**, was injured outside the Gaumont Cinema and died in hospital. He was employed by Armstrong Siddeley Motors Limited in addition to being a Home Guard. He resided at 18, Severn Road with his parents, Frederick S. and Ellen E. Fern. Wilfred was born on the 7th December, 1921 at Bell Green, Coventry and buried in the Communal Grave.

Also in the Home Guard, aged 18 and buried in the Communal Grave was Volunteer **Sydney Hartopp**, 11th Warwickshire (Coventry) Bn., who died at the Gaumont Cinema. Sydney resided at 2 Court, 2 House, Freeth Street.

Daughter of Oscar and Blanche Miller, of 12, Hugh Road, Stoke, Coventry, **Marjorie Elaine Miller**, was also killed at the Gaumont Cinema, aged 17. She was born on the 19th November, 1923 at Swansea and resided at 12, Hugh Road. Majorie was employed at Walkers, Empress Buildings. Grave Ref. E. 24/4. Communal Grave, Coventry (London Road) Cemetery.

From 5, Huntingdon Road, Earlsdon **George Thomas Parncutt**, died as a result of the enemy action. He was aged 38 and the son of A. and H. Parncutt, of 33, Norfolk House Road, Streatham, Wandsworth, London. George was married to May S. Parncutt and worked for Coventry Corporation in the Electricity Department. He was born in October, 1903 at London and is buried in the Communal Grave.

PARNCUTT – Loving memory of George, loving friend of Mr. and Mrs. North, 359, Grangemouth Road, Radford. Never forgotten.

THIS TREE IS PLANTED
IN MEMORY OF
HARRY BERRY
SP. CONSTABLE
COVENTRY CITY POLICE
KILLED 15.11.40

Harry Berry, aged 34, was a leather merchants buyer and Special Constable with Coventry City Police, he was killed in "Decorwall", Jordan Well Coventry at 1.00am on the 15th November 1940. His widow, May identified him by his glasses, cigarette case, watch and police whistle. The newspaper at the time *'The Midland Daily Telegraph'* stated *'he was killed at the height of the blitz " stripped to the waist, helping to struggle through masses of debris in Jordan Well attempting to extricate thirteen people trapped in a cellar". He was one of many heroes in Coventry that night when, men, women and children died as a result of enemy action'.*

In December his widow May, still hadn't got a death certificate and letters were issued from Detective Inspector Edward W. C. Pendleton setting out the situation as he saw it and the death certificate was issued. In the Council Meeting Minutes 10th December 1940 Chief Constables Report notified that Harry had been killed during a recent air raid attack. A further note on the 24th December 1940 noted that under the Police Pensions Act 1921 and the Special Constables Act 1923 a widows' pension and children's allowances to be granted.

Harry and May resided at 60 George's Road and his parents were Herbert and Rosina Berry of 70, Red Lane where he was born on the 12th January 1906. Harry worked at Messrs. Tooby Adkins and Co. Ltd and is buried in the London Road Cemetery. His plaque in the War Memorial Park was paid for by his wife who was residing at 34 Forfield Road and plaque reads *Special Constable Harry Berry Killed on duty in air raid 14th November 1940'.* As the original was lost a re-dedication was necessary and this was carried out at 11.00am on the 6th December 2002.

'Berry- Tender memories of my beloved husband Harry (Special Constable) who gave his life so bravely. Forever in the thoughts of his sorrowing wife'.

Minnie Stokes, died at her home at 3 Court, 13 Jordan Well she was 71 and buried in the Communal Grave.

E. W. Cooke of 183 Broomfield Road on the 16th July 1951 paid for a plaque in Hearsall Common for the Cooke family, the application read ' *Mr George Edmund Cooke Mrs Louisa Cooke Mr George Frederick Cooke Killed in air raid 14th November 1940'*. The family were killed at home, 13 Court, 5 House, Jordan Well and all are buried in the Communal Grave.

George Edmund Cooke, aged 59 was born on the 9th May, 1881 at Coventry and employed at General Electric Company Ltd. **Louisa Cooke**, aged 57 was born on the 19th July, 1886 at St. Helens, Lancashire and occupied as a housewife. Their son, **George Frederick Cooke**, aged 27 was also killed. He was born on the 15th April, 1913 at Coventry and employed by Daimler Co. Ltd. A further son, Mr. S. Cooke survived the raid.

COOKE – In loving memory of father, mother and brother, George. Always in the thoughts of Edmund, Kate, Norman, Marion and Arthur.

Four members of the Hoare family (two children and parents) died at 13 Court, 3 House, Jordan Well and all are buried in London Road Cemetery. **Margaret Hoare**, was aged three months and her older brother, **John Denham** was aged 7. Their mother was **Hilda May Hoare** who died aged 43 and father was **Walter James Denham Hoare** who died aged 35.

Age 39, **Mary Ann Davis**, resided at the back of 13, Jordan Well. She was the daughter of Mr. and Mrs. Hirons, of Pershore, Worcestershire and married to Wallace Davis. Mary is buried in the Communal Grave.

The Council Meeting Minutes 10th December 1940 and Chief Constables Report noted that the following four policemen and messengers were killed during a recent air raid attack. Two weeks later, on the 24th December 1940 that under the Police Pensions Act 1921 and the Special Constables Act 1923 the following widows' pension and children's allowances to be granted.

Special Constable **William Robert Lambe**, died outside Jordan Well Shelter, aged 26. He resided at 2, Wycliffe Grove, Wyken with his wife, Sarah. His parents were Councillor and Mrs. Robert Lambe, of 3, Somerdale Park, Belfast, Northern Ireland and his names is on the memorial at the Communal Grave. Mrs Lambe £60 13s 6d p.a and children's allowance £12-3-0.

Also lost was at the Jordan Well Shelter was Constable PC 82 **William Alfred Henry Timms**. He was aged 23, and the son of Catherine Josephine Timms, of 48, Millers Road. William was born on the 3rd May, 1917 at Warwick, resided at 52, Quinton Road and buried in Warwick Cemetery. A request to the Town Clerk and City Treasurer was made as to the possibility of a gratuity to the mother of PC 82 W. H. Timms.

Also in the Police was Auxiliary Messenger **Thomas Roland Lowry** who died whilst on duty in Jordan Well aged 16. An employee of British Thomson-Houston Company Limited he resided with his parents, R. H. and Alice C. Lowry at 42 Gordon Street. His name was published locally as a victim on the 23rd November 1940 and it was noted he was a Member of the Police War Reserve. Born in 1924, Thomas is buried in the Communal Grave. His plaque in the War Memorial Park was applied for by his mother on the 1st March 1949 and reads *'Thomas Rowland Lowry Police Messenger 16 years Killed in air raid 14/15th November 1940'*. His death resulted in a Special Procedure Case. From No. 44 a resident was detained in Stratford General Hospital.

PC 25 **Kenneth Charles Rollins**, aged 30 was also lost carrying out his duties. He resided at 111, Sadler Road and was the son of Henry and Rosa Alice Rollins, of 38, Oxford Street. Kenneth was married to Kathleen Annie Rollins and born on the 8th September, 1910 at Coventry. Records indicate he was cremated at Badgeworth nr Cheltenham. Mrs Rollins £76 9s 6d p.a and children's allowance £15-5-0.

A number of casualties were severely injured and taken to Coventry and Warwickshire Hospital where they subsequently died.

Dying at hospital and buried in the Communal Grave was Fireman **Stanley David Endersby** who died aged 30 on the 14th November 1940. Stanley was born on the 6th April 1910, at Fen Ditton, Cambridge and employed with British Pressed Panels Ltd. He resided with his wife, H. A. Endersby and family at 19 Evenlode Crescent.

ENDERSBY – Stanley David AFS beloved husband of Hilda. Always remembered by those who loved him.

Family Photos of Fireman Stanley David Endersby

Scant details exist on **L. Golby** who resided at 118 Stoney Stanton Road. He is buried in the (London Road) Cemetery. An occupant of No. 25 was treated at Warneford Hospital and sent home

Leonard Golby, was injured as a result of enemy action on the 14th November, 1940 at the family home at 115, Bell Green Road, died same day at Coventry and Warwickshire Hospital. He was aged 28. He was born on the 25th February, 1912 at Coventry and employed at the Standard Motor Co. Ltd. Leonard is buried in Bedworth Cemetery.

He has a plaque in St. Pauls Cemetery paid for by Mrs. L. N. Howard 82 Holmsdale Road on the 8th September 1952. His wife, Irene and sons, Neil and Graham were treated at the Hospital of St. Cross, Rugby.

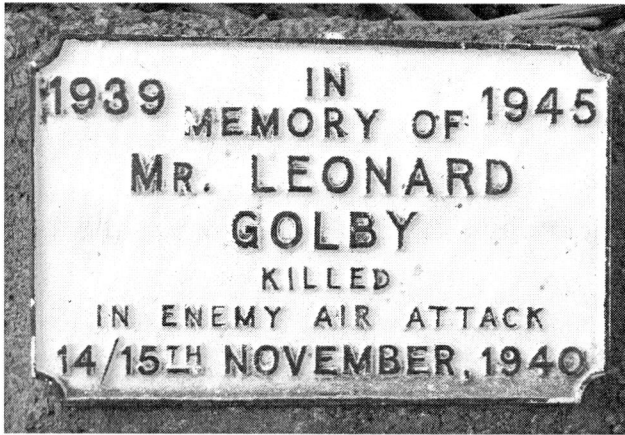

IN
1939 MEMORY OF 1945
MR. LEONARD
GOLBY
KILLED
IN ENEMY AIR ATTACK
14/15TH NOVEMBER, 1940

Neil Golby, Leonard's son provides details of the raid.

We were all in the shelter at Bell Green Road. I was 2, my brother Graham 4, and my Mum and Dad. A land mine one of those ones with a parachute, landed in the back garden and lifted the shelter. We were all injured, mum and the two lads were taken to Rugby and Dad to Coventry and Warwickshire Hospital. It took two days to find my Dad the hospital was so full of injuries that casualties were on the pavement. My Uncle Stan and family friend eventually found my Dad outside the Gas Works, Gas Street on the pavement with other casualties. He had died of his injuries.

We were lucky, he wasn't buried in the mass grave, father's parents knew an undertaker and he arranged for him to be buried in a grave in Bedworth Cemetery. I suppose they were looking for places to bury casualties where they could. A 16 year old girl was also buried in Bedworth at the same time as my dad.

An account in the vicinity comes from May Jenkins (nee Collis) then aged 4.

We lived near the top end of Sewall Highway and Bell Green Road. A bomb splinter came through our house we were underneath the stairs. I was asleep. Sewall Highway was quite intense as it was near Morris Engines and they were trying to get that. No injuries thank goodness, my father made sure we were evacuated and that it would happen again but it didn't.

Fireman, Oldbury, Auxiliary Fire Service, **James Henry Gould**, dies from his injuries at Coventry and Warwickshire Hospital, aged 33. He was the husband of Lily May Gould, of 21, New Street, Oldbury, Worcestershire and has a Grave Reference of Coventry, County Borough.

Also on duty and being mortally wounded was as a member of St. John's Ambulance Brigade, **David Harrison**, aged 57. He resided at 11, St. Christian's Road, Cheylesmore and was the son of John Harrison, of Walsgrave-on-Sowe. David was married to Fanny Harrison and born on the 30th March, 1883 at Walsgrave-on-Sowe. He was employed at Coventry Corporation, Parks Department and is buried in the Communal Grave.

HARRISON (David) In loving memory of a dear husband and father. His loving wife and children and Wallace and Ada.

Birmingham Auxiliary Fire Service lost Fireman, **Arthur Henry Lowe** at 29. His parents were Mr. and Mrs. A. Lowe, of Droitwich House, Henley-in-Arden and he was the husband of Ida Margaret Lowe, of 213, Rocky Lane, Perry Barr, Birmingham. Dying on admission to hospital, he has a Grave Reference of Coventry, County Borough, Warwickshire and is commemorated in the War Memorial Park.

Full time member of ARP attached to First Aid Post, **Alfred Hendry Edward Parsons**, died whilst on duty at Coventry and Warwickshire Hospital, aged 38. A native of Hasting he was born there on the 7th April, 1901, his parents Mr. and Mrs. W. G. Parsons resided at 106, Old London Road, Hastings. In Coventry, Alfred, resided at 74, Morris Avenue, Wyken and is buried in the Communal Grave.

PARSONS (Harry FAP No. 9 late of Hastings) – Although far apart our thoughts are ever with you, George, Budge and sisters, Hastings.

From Erdington, Birmingham Auxiliary Fire Service lost, **Percy William Pyett** aged 31. He died as a result of enemy action, aged 31. In Erdington he resided at 24, Coniston Road, Erdington and was the son of Percy and Kate Eliza Pyett, of 584, Chester Road, Erdington. Percy was married to Hilda Beatrice Pyett and has a Grave Reference of Coventry, County Borough.

On the Communal Grave Memorial is housewife **Bertha Ellen Watkins**, who died of wounds at Coventry and Warwickshire Hospital. She was aged 41 and the wife of Thomas Watkins, of Cash's Lane. Bertha was born on the 4th October, 1900, at Warwick to H. and Bessie Goode, of 2 St Margaret's Road. Thomas paid for her plaque in the War Memorial Park on the 2nd April 1949. At No. 16 a person was detained in Stratford-on-Avon Emergency Hospital, No. 100 received treatment and No. 116 treated at First Aid Post and sent home.

Messenger with Police Auxiliary Messenger Service, **Bertram Whyatt West**, was injured at Holbrooks Lane and died at the hospital on the 15th November, 1940, aged 17. He was the son of Lewis W. and Florence M. West, of 50, Wheelwright Lane and born on the 19th June, 1923 at Eastern, Northamptonshire. In Coventry he resided at 50, Wheelwright Lane and employed at Self Changing Gear Ltd. Betram is buried in the Communal Grave.

WEST Treasured memories of dear Bert. Ever in the thoughts of Mum and Dad.

Corporal, **William French,** 859031, 917 Balloon Squadron, Royal Air Force (Auxiliary Air Force) died of wounds received as a result of enemy action, 11th November, 1940 at Gulson Road. He was born 18th April, 1912 at Northampton and resided at 42, Cowper Street, Northampton. He was employed by Goodall, Lamb & Heighway Ltd., Manchester and enlisted on the 9th May, 1939. His Grave Reference is Screen Wall. Grave 8099. Northampton (Billing Road) Cemetery.

In the 1911 Census there was a French family living at 42 Cowper Street, Northampton, they where James and Annie Jane French, he was a boot finisher, born in Buckingham and Annie was born in Northampton. Other 917 Balloon Squadron members were also killed.

'The Alfred News' covered the formation of the Balloon Squadron, a recruiting office had been set up at 23, Hertford Street and at that time it was planned to have the Town Headquarters in a suitable building in Cow Lane. Three hundred men had enrolled as recruits. The article dismissed the rumour that men were required to ascent with the balloon, this was totally wrong as the barrage was to create a cordon by which the enemy can only pass with great difficulty. The crew of each balloon consisted of ten men and the uniform was that of the RAF, with a minimum of thirty hours training throughout the year for drivers, winch driver, balloon rigger and fabric workers.

City Centre Injuries

From Gulson Road six people required various treatment, two occupants of No. 13 detained in Warneford Hospital, Leamington from No. 27, one detained in Hollymoor Emergency Hospital, Birmingham and one treated at First Aid Post and sent home. Of the two further casualties of unknown address, one treated and one detained in Alcester Emergency Hospital.

From Adelaide Street one person was detained in Hollymoor Hospital, Birmingham and a person from No. 6 was detained in Stratford-on-Avon General Hospital. From No. 60 New Buildings one person was detained in the Hospital of St. Cross, Rugby and from nearby New Street No. 13 one person detained in Stratford-on-Avon General Hospital a further injury from No. 28 was detained in the Hospital of St. Cross Rugby.

Hales Street, No 12 saw one person detained in Shuckburgh Park Convalescent Hospital, Daventry. Five injuries were reported at Chauntry Place; one occupant from No. 7 was detained in Warwick Hospital; one from No. 11 detained in Warwick Hospital and three people from No. 15 received treatment as follows one detained in Hollymoor Hospital, Birmingham, one detained in Warwick Hospital and one treated at a First Aid Post and sent home.

In Warwick Hospital one person was detained from Greyfriars Lane and a further person from No. 11 Strathmore Avenue was also detained in Warwick. Gulson Road Hospital treated and sent home one person from 145 Northfield Road. An injury from No. 4 David Road was treated at a First Aid Post and sent home. Chadshunt Hall Auxiliary Hospital, Kineton detained one person from No. 3 Eaton Road

Four people required treatment from Whitefriars Lane one of these from No. 68 was treated at Barnsley Hall, Bromsgrove. A person from 11a Bramble Street was detained in Warneford Hospital, Leamington and one from No. 65 London Road detained in Stratford-on-Avon Emergency Hospital. No. 2 Friars Road had two people treated at Gulson Road Hospital and sent home with a person from No. 7 requiring treatment. At St. Patricks Road; No. 19 one detained in Stratford-on-Avon General Hospital; from No. 34 treated at First Aid Post and sent home and from No. 38 one detained in Stratford-on Avon Emergency Hospital.

From Paradise Street seven people were treated; No. 12 treated at First Aid Post and sent home; No. 13 two people were treated one detained in Warwick Hospital and one treated at a First Aid Post and sent home; from No. 26 and No. 30 received treatment and a further two people at No. 30 were injured. One detained in Stratford-on-Avon Emergency Hospital and one detained in Warwick Hospital.

At Railway Cottages, Warwick Road one person received treatment from No. 16 and a further detained in Hollymoor Hospital, Birmingham. From No. 3 Brunswick Road two people were treated at Gulson Road Hospital and sent home. A resident of No. 43 was treated at a First Aid Post and sent home as was a resident of No. 65.

No. 8 Hill Street had a person treated at First Aid Post and sent home, two people from 47 Well Street were detained in Alcester Emergency Hospital and further person from a unknown address in Well Street was detained in Warwick Hospital. Nearby in Bond Street, one person detained in Hospital of St. Cross Rugby, a person from No. 50 was detained in Barnsley Hall Emergency Hospital Birmingham whilst persons from No. 50 and No. 56 received treatment.

At No. 19 Upper Well Street a person was detained in Stratford-on-Avon Emergency Hospital. Two neighbouring house in No. 71 and No. 73 Barras Lane had residents that required treatment; one person from No. 71 detained in Stratford-on-Avon General Hospital and four people from No. 73 treated at First Aid Post and sent home. Chadshunt Hall Auxiliary Hospital, Kineton detained a person from 12 Coundon Street and Abbotts Lane had a total of seven injuries; four at No. 9 (one Treated at First Aid Post and sent home, one treated, one person detained in Warneford Hospital, Leamington and one person treated at Warneford Hospital and sent home. From No. 11 two people were treated at a First Aid Post and sent home. The final person of unknown house number was treated at Warneford Hospital Leamington and sent home.
Newfield Road (No. 35) and Aldbourne Road (No. 73) had one casualty each, detained in Hospital of St. Cross, Rugby and detained in Warwick Hospital respectively. Sandy Lane had a total of six casualties as follows:- two detained in Warneford Hospital, Leamington; one detained in Hollymoor Hospital, Birmingham; one treated in Barnsley Hall, Bromsgrove (No. 77) and No. 94 Detained in Warwick Hospital.

No. 55 Harnall Lane West had a resident treated at a First Aid Post and sent home whilst Howard Street had three people treated at First Aid Post and sent home (One from No. 20 and two from No. 45). Hollymoor Hospital Birmingham was the destination for a resident of 30, Church Street and three people from Eagle Street were treated; Treated at First Aid Post and sent home for two persons from 162 and from No. 298 a resident detained in Warwick Hospital.

Corporation Shelter, Leicester Causeway necessitated one person receiving treatment whilst a resident from 117 received treatment at Barnsley Hall, Bromsgrove, No. 166 Leicester Causeway was also treated and a resident of No. 120 was detained in Warwick Hospital.

No. 11 Harnall Lane East one person detained in Evesham Emergency Hospital; No. 212 treated and two people from 236 detained in Stratford-on-Avon General Hospital. No. 6 The Chantries also had one person detained in Stratford-on-Avon Emergency Hospital. A resident of 25 Adderley Street detained in Alcester Emergency Hospital also at 25 was a resident of Alfred Road who was detained in Warwick Hospital.

Oxford Street had three injuries reported; 26 detained in Barnsley Hall Emergency Hospital, Bromsgrove, 27 treated and No. 40 detained in Warwick Hospital. Of a similar number was Cambridge Street; No. 150 Detained in Stratford-on-Avon Emergency Hospital and a resident detained in Hollymoor Emergency Hospital, Birmingham . Detained in Shuckburgh Park Convalescent Hospital, Daventry was a resident of 90 Wright Street.

No. 11 Albert Street a resident was detained in Chadshunt Hall Auxiliary Hospital, Kineton and at No. 59 a person detained in Stratford Emergency Hospital. Not requiring hospital treatment was a resident of 55 Aylesford Street who was treated at a First Aid Post and sent home as was two victims at 7 Yardley Street. Sparkbrook Street (38), Vauxhall Street (14) and Days Lane had one injury each
detained in Warwick Hospital, Barnsley Hall, Bromsgrove and treated at Gulson Road Hospital and sent home respectively

East Street No. 9 had two injuries one was treated at Barnsley Hall, Bromsgrove with a resident of No. 30 and finally in East Street at No.54 required hospital treatment. No. 56 Colchester Street had two people detained in Warneford Hospital, Leamington Spa where as 78 Winchester Street had one person detained in Warwick Hospital. From 70 Vine Street one person was treated at a First Aid Post and sent home and for Lower Ford Street No. 62 two people detained in Evesham Emergency Hospital.

Two injuries at Cow Lane 41, (treated at First Aid Post and sent home) and 42 (detained in Evesham Emergency Hospital). Other injuries in the vicinity were Croft Road 29, (detained in Stratford-on-Avon Emergency Hospital), Freeth Street (treated at First Aid Post and sent home, treated at Gulson Road Hospital and sent home), Godiva Street 88, (detained in Alcester Emergency Hospital), Market Street, 99, Mill Street 23, (detained in Warneford Hospital, Leamington Spa), Park Road 36 (detained in Warwick Hospital), Sherbourne Street 34 (detained in Warneford Hospital, Leamington Spa), St. John Street 11/5 (treated at First Aid Post and sent home), Warwick Road, (Detained in Warwick Hospital) and Augusta Road No. 14.

Coventry North East

Two members of the Lapworth family (father and son) were lost at Coventry Road The family resided locally at 40, Lentons Lane, Hawkesbury. Records indicate **Dennis Lapworth**, was killed outside Wootton House, Longford. He was aged 17 and the son of Joseph Thomas and Annie Lapworth. Dennis was born 16th August, 1923 at Hawkesbury, Coventry and employed at Alfred Herbert Ltd. Dennis was buried at Zion Baptist Church, Hawkesbury. Records indicate his father, **Joseph Thomas Lapworth** is buried in London Road Cemetery. At Lentons Lane one person was treated at Barnsley Hall, Bromsgrove and at No. 126 one person was treated at a First Aid Post and sent home.

LAPWORTH Treasured memories of Dennis killed by enemy action. Always in the thoughts of Kathleen

A plaque in the War Memorial Park paid for on the 16th February 1948 by father and husband, Reginald Walter Hadingham has two names, one his wife the other his son. The plaque reads *"Winifred Blanche Hadingham. Arthur Edward Hadingham 16 months Killed in air raid 14th November 1940'*. The Hadingham family lived at 133 Wyken Avenue, Wyken and this is where **Arthur Edward Hadingham** and **Winifred Blanche Hadingham** died due to enemy action. Arthur was born on the 2nd July 1939, at Coventry and Winifred was also born at Coventry over twenty years earlier on the 30th May, 1919. Both mother and child are buried in the London Road Cemetery.

Electrician **Corbett Egginton**, died at 4, Sommerville Road. He was married to Mrs. A. Egginton and born on the 10th November, 1894 at Wolverhampton. He is buried in Grave Ref. A. 13/2. Communal Grave.

Scott Fensom was seven years old and lived in Wycroft Road, Wyken.

We had an Anderson shelter in the garden, we covered it with two feet of clay. We took to sleeping in it at night. It was OK, we had beds in it and all sorts. We tried to be the first out in the morning so we could collect shrapnel, we were too young to be frightened. My brother Trevor was two years younger then me and my little sister, Mary was in a 'balloon like' carry about thing. The air raids became too much for mum, her sister was in Brownshill in Staffordshire and we had to walk through the city with my sister in this balloon like thing. On the 16th November we were met on the Leamington Road, my uncle ran a mill in Brownshill and they had send the Mill car for us. The city was full of hosepipes is what struck us, we were jumping over the hose pipes going to the Leamington Road and that's how I spent my 8th birthday.

Neighbour Mr M. Rose of 111 Honiton Road paid for a plaque in Stoke Heath to commemorate two members of the Pugh family on the 19th August 1949. **Sarah Pugh** and **William Thomas Pugh** resided at 109, Honiton Road. Sarah was aged 56 and a house wife. She was born on the 26th December, 1884 at Hillmorton, nr Rugby. William was born on the 16th September, 1882 at Coventry and employed at Morris Motors Limited. The couple are buried in graves, I6. 3/2 and I6. 3/3 at the Communal Grave.

At No. 111 three persons required treatment, one being detained in Stratford-on-Avon Emergency Hospital and one detained in Warwick Hospital. A resident of 109 was also detained in Stratford-on-Avon General Hospital.

PUGH (William and Sarah) Always in the thoughts of their daughters Mabel and Kath

Buried on the 23rd November 1940 in the Communal Grave was **Christopher Bennett.** He died at 249, Ansty Road, aged 47. He was the husband of E. M. Bennett, of 163, Stoney Stanton Road and was born on the 14th February, 1893 at Quarry Bank, Staffordshire. He worked as miner.

BENNETT (Christopher) Treasured memories of Dad, Always in the thoughts of his loving daughter, Elsie.

At 276 Ansty Road, married couple, **Maurice William Lovell** and **Ethel Mary Lovell** died as a result of enemy action at their home. Maurice, aged 24 was employed at Daimler Co. Ltd and also in the Home Guard. He was the son of Mr. W. F. Lovell, of 61, Uppingham Road, Leicester and born there on the 20th June, 1916. Ethel Mary Lovell. was the daughter of Mr. and Mrs. Joseph William Spavin, of 52, Messingham Road, Ashby, Scunthorpe, Lincolnshire. Ethel was born on the 14th July, 1914 at Scunthorpe and a housewife. The association with Leicester meant the couple were buried outside the city limits in Gilroes Cemetery, Leicester.

Injuries were recorded along Ansty Road; No. 50 one person detained in Chadshunt Hall Auxiliary Hospital, Kineton, from No. 222 detained Barnsley Hall Bromsgrove; No. 251 detained in Barnsley Hall Emergency Hospital, Bromsgrove; No. 253 treated at First Aid Post and sent home; No. 256 detained in Barnsley Hall Emergency Hospital, Bromsgrove and No. 333 detained at Hospital of St. Cross, Rugby. One person from Caludon Farm detained in Chadshunt Hall Auxiliary Hospital, Kineton.

Two citizens died at 55, North Street and one later died of his injuries. **Arthur William Brown,** died as a result on the 14th November, 1940. He resided at 55, North Street and is buried in the Borough of Coventry. From No. 180 one person treated at Work First Aid Post and sent home.

Ann Marie Ager, also died at North Street, aged 59. Her husband , **John Lovell Ager,** aged 62 died as a result of injuries on the 19th November, 1940 at Gulson Road Hospital. The couple resided at 149, North Street and are buried in the Communal Grave. Ann was born in 1880 at 67, Coventry Street and a housewife whilst John was born in 1877 at 71, Avon Street. A plaque was paid for in Stoke Heath by Mrs. J. E. Watson of 453 Walsgrave Road on the 8th October 1949.

AGER In loving memory of Annie and Jack Ever in thoughts of Alf and Alice

Susannah Nightingale, death was also recorded at 149, North Street. She was 84. Susannah resided at 75, Hugh Road born on the 18th October, 1863 at Coventry and buried in the Communal Grave.

NIGHTINGALE (Susan) Treasured memories of my dear mother. Sadly missed by her daughter, Florrie and Will.

Next door at 151, **Violet May Humphreys**, died at home, aged 16. She was born on the 15th July 1924. and employed at the General Electric Company Limited. Violet resided with her mother, Mrs. Gertrude. Humphreys and records indicate a family member was detained in Warwick Hospital. Violet is buried in the Communal Grave.

HUMPHREYS – In loving memory of Violet who died through enemy action – Silently mourned by her loving mother, sisters and brothers. Safe in Gods Keeping.

Daughter of David Walker and Henrietta Harris, of 175, Cross Road, **Henrietta Masters**, died at 41, Clovelly Road, age 26. She resided at this address with her husband, Reginald Masters. Henrietta was born on the 17th November, 1914. and worked at Morris Motors Ltd. Although she is buried in the Communal Grave she has a plaque in St. Pauls Cemetery. A family member was also injured and detained in Warwick Hospital.

MASTERS (Etta) In loving memory of my dear wife. Treasured memories. Reg

Injuries were also treated from residents at No. 4 treated at First Aid Post and sent home and from No. 174 detained in Hospital of St. Cross, Rugby.

Three members of the Bell family died at 7, Geoffrey Close. **Doreen Betty Bell** (14) and **Raymond Henry Bell** (20) resided at 13, Poole Road. Doreen was born on the 17th August, 1926 at West Bromwich and employed at General Electric Co. Ltd. Raymond was born on the 8th September, 1920 at West Bromwich and worked as a Butcher at Smiths in Far Gosford Street. Both are buried in the Communal Grave, a brother Mr. W. Bell, survived the air raid. From next door, two persons were treated one detained in Hollymoor Hospital, Birmingham the other detained in Stratford Emergency Hospital .

BELL Treasured memories of dear Ray and Betty – Ever in the thoughts of brothers and family

Malvina Bell, daughter of Alfred and Amy Bell, of 98, Bulwar Road, Radford died age 6. She was born on the 20th July, 1934, at Coventry and resided at 7, Geoffrey Close. Malvina attended Stoke Heath School and is buried in the Communal Grave.

BELL – In loving memory of our darling Malvina. Always remembered and sadly missed by Mummy, Daddy, Grandma and family

In Alfall Road, a child and an adult died as a result of enemy action. Aged 4 months, **Anthony Peter Hands**, died at 94, Alfall Road. He was the son of John Herbert and Gladys Mabel Hands and was born in July 1940 at Coventry. Anthony is buried in the Communal Grave.

James Brown, aged 53 died as a result of injuries received at home, 98, Alfall Road. He was born in January, 1887 at Coventry and employed at the Standard Motor Co. Ltd. Records show a J. Brown was treated at Stratford General Hospital and another family member was also treated at hospital. His grave is listed as Stratford upon Avon, Borough.

Fourteen injuries reported along Alfall Road; from No. 11 one detained in Hospital of St. Cross Rugby; No. 39 treated for wounds; No. 62 one person treated and one treated at Gulson Road Hospital and sent home; No. 64 one treated Barnsley Hall, Bromsgrove, one treated at First Aid Post and sent home and a third person detained in Evesham Emergency Hospital; No. 66 one person treated and two treated at Barnsley Hall, Bromsgrove; No. 70 two persons treated at First Aid Post and sent home; No. 80 treated at First Aid Post and sent home; No. 98 one person treated at hospital and a No. 99 one person detained in Warneford Hospital, Leamington.

Thomas John Purchase was injured at 6, Avon Street and died the same day at Ravensdale First Aid Post, Wyken. He was 49 and married to Maud Purchase, of 6, Avon Street. Thomas was born on the 10th November, 1889 at Willenhall, employed by Sir. W. G. Armstrong Whitworth Aircraft Co. Ltd and is buried in the Communal Grave. A resident of No. 12 Avon Street was detained in Warwick Hospital.

PURCHASE (Thomas) In loving memory of a dear husband and father. Always in the thoughts of his wife Maud and daughters. Eva, Norma and Hazel.

Four casualties are recorded in Catherine Street. One at No. 24 and three residents at No. 34. All victims are buried in the Communal Grave. At No. 24, **Elsie Walsh**, died aged 45, her home residence. **Agnes Rollason**, 49, died at No. 34. She was born on the 23rd December, 1890 at Coventry and employed as a Housekeeper. The family that resided in the house were the Storers.

Alice Marjorie Storer, aged 35 was killed along with her father, **Walter Charles Storer,** aged 69. He was born on the 4th November, 1871 at Coventry. Alice was born on the 22nd November, 1906 at Coventry, educated at Barr's Hill School. *'The Barrs Hill School Magazine'* published the following *'Our deepest sympathy goes to the parents and friends of the two pupils and five Old Girls who died as a result of enemy action over Coventry'.*

Joan Alice Tipson, aged 13 years; died November 14th 1940.
Beryl Meek, aged 13 years; died in hospital April 9th 1941.
Joanna Kletzenbauer (1927 – 1932); died September 16th 1940
Doris Scott (1936 – 1939); died November 14th 1940
Mary Baldock (1930 – 1934); died in Birmingham November 25th 1940
Margaret Oswin (1931 1936) died April 7th 1941
Majorie Storer (1916 – 1922); died 14th November 1940

Alice was employed as a Teacher at Coventry Preparatory School, the school employed two Miss Storers, the Girls School, Miss Storer and the Boys School, Miss Storer. They were cousins and Alice was the Girl School teacher.

Mary Maginnis was 10 years old.

November 14th was my last day at Coventry Preparatory Girls School, I never went back it was closed, I was ten at that time. A day or so later we took refugee at the Vicarage in Napton-on-the-Hill as our house in Earlsdon Ave South had no roof and my parents had made contact with a family friend to sort out the accommodation. My mother told me that Miss Storer had been killed, I was very upset. There were two Miss Storer's, the girls Miss Storer and the boys, Miss Storer they were cousins. The girls Miss Storer was lovely, she never had to raise her voice with a class of very well behaved girls!

A plaque to four members of the Elliott family in Stoke Heath was paid for by Mr H. Elliott of 86, Nicholls Street on the 15th August 1949 at a cost of £2-5-0. This was Herbert Nicholls as a tribute to his wife and children whom died at that address and are buried in the Communal Grave.

Housewife, **Annie Elliott**, aged 38 was a native of Bradford and born on the 7th February, 1902. **Ronald Elliott**, 15 was born on the 9th October, 1925 at Hoyland, Bradford. He was employed at Wyleys Limited, Manufacturing Chemists. **Greta Edwina** was the oldest daughter, aged 14. She was born on the 16th October, 1925 at Hoyland, Bradford and employed at Smarts Drapers of Stoney Stanton Road. **Margaret Rose Elliott**, aged 9, was born on the 1st April, 1931 at Thurnscoe, Yorkshire and attended Frederick Bird School.

ELLIOTT In loving memory of Annie, Greta, Margaret, Ron. Dear ones you are always in my thoughts Auntie Clara

Glyn Edwards was 19 years old and in Enfield Road.

Thursday was half day, and I had been to the Gaumont Cinema and chatting to the usherettes, I was only 19 then. I said to one who had just finished her shift that I would walk her home and a load of incendiaries dropped in front of us. We got in a shelter near the Gaumont Cinema and moved to other shelters as we got nearer to her home. We saw the Humber on fire and saw the last planes going over. We never got back home till 7am in the morning. Her father came out of the shelter and told me off for keeping her out all night, I have never seen her from that day to this. That was the worst night of my life for me, and I spent four years in Burma and India.

Remains of a residence in Villiers Street

The names of **Richard Buckley** and **Lizzie Lewis Buckley** appeared in the Births Marriages and deaths in *'The Blackburn Times'* on the 29th November 1940, it simply stated name and Coventry as the place of death. They were buried in Blackburn Cemetery. A letter in the paper on the same day referenced the shelters in Coventry undoubtedly saved lives in Coventry but one citizen was urging the Mayor to stop building surface shelters in Blackburn as they protected against falling tiles and not against a direct hit!

The couple died at their home of 50, Villiers Street. Lizzie, aged 40 was the daughter of John and Anne Bramley, of 16, Dewhurst Street, Blackburn, Lancashire and born on the 16th August, 1900 at Blackburn. Richard was also from Blackburn and the son of Mr. and Mrs. Richard Buckley, of 61, Penny Street, Blackburn. He died aged 41 and was employed in a Local Engineering Factory.

The family grave I 881 contains Richard and Lizzie and also Lizzie parents.

Richard Buckley	Aged 43 years	Buried 25/11/1940
Lizzie Lewis Buckley	Aged 40 years	Buried 25/11/1940
Anne Bramley	Aged 72 years	Buried 18/03/1943
John Bramley	Aged 73 years	Buried 27/11/1944

Kathleen Alice Ager is listed in the Borough of *'Dagenham Book of Remembrance'* as *AGER Kathleen Alice, 885 Green Lane , Civilian*, with no further information. She was aged 21, and had only been married a few months to Frank J. prior to her death. She was the daughter of John and Minnie Helen White, of 885, Green Lane, Dagenham, Essex and born on the 28th September, 1919. In Coventry she resided at 80, Villiers Street where she was killed and in Dagenham her husbands address was 119 Mayfield Road, Dagenham. Becontree Cemetery has now been renamed Eastbrook End Cemetery.

At No. 66 one person detained in Warwick Hospital and at 102 one person treated at First Aid Post and sent home.

At Monks Factory, Richmond Street eight casualties were recorded and all are buried in the Communal Grave. The Barker family resided at 41, Clements Street and were seeking shelter at the factory. They were interred on the 23rd November 1940

Edith Mary Barker, aged 57, was born on the 10th August, 1881 at Wellingborough, Nr Northampton and the wife of **James Barker**. He was aged 58, born on the 2nd May 1882 and worked as a carpenter & joiner at E. K. Youell Limited, Builders. Their daughter aged 16, **Joan Barker** was also killed. She was born on the 31st March, 1923 at Coventry and employed as Shop Assistant at Andertons of London Road.

Husband and wife, **Doris Kate Proctor**, (31) and **Reginald Proctor** (37) of 28, Richmond Street died at the factory. Doris, a housewife, was the daughter of T. P. and L. Mayo, of 83, Binley Road and born in Coventry. Reginald was the son of Mr. T. H. and Mrs. L. G. Proctor, of 15, Bolingbroke Road and employed at Sir W. G. Armstrong Whitworth Aircraft Ltd. Both are buried in the Communal Grave.

PROCTOR Loving memory of Dolly and Reg Always in the thoughts of mum and dad.

Parents and daughter, **Herbert Alec, Olive Annie** and **Christine Mary Whitehouse** are also buried in the Communal Grave and they resided at 32, Clements Street. Herbert was 45, Olive 41 and Christine was aged 13. Olive parents were William Henry and Elizabeth Mary Harrison, of 548, Binley Road. A person was treated at a First Aid Post from No. 4 Clements Street and sent home.

WHITEHOUSE In loving memory of mum, dad, Chris. Ever in the thoughts of their children, Den, Ron, Babs, also mother, dad, brothers and sisters.

Watchman **George Buckenham** was killed whilst at work at Monks Ribbon Factory, 76, Richmond Street, aged 70. He resided at 85 Hastings Road, Stoke and was originally a native of Burgh, Suffolk being born there on the 2nd June, 1870. George was buried in the Communal Grave on the 23rd November 1940. His plaque paid in the War Memorial Park paid for by S. Jeanes, 145 Browns Lane, Allesley reads *'Mr. George Buckenham Killed in air raid 14th November 1940'*.

Buckenham In loving memory of Dad also of mum died October 14th 1918. 'Rest in Peace'. Syd, Ron and little granddaughters June and Pegg'

From No. 70 one person detained in Warwick Hospital and two persons from No. 75 were treated at a First Aid Post and sent home whilst at No.111 a person was treated at a First Aid Post and sent home.

Buried in the Communal Grave is **Frank Clutterbuck,** aged 54. He died and resided at 45, Caludon Road, his parents Thomas and Annie Clutterbuck resided at North Newington, Banbury. Frank was married to Ellen.

CLUTTERBUCK – Treasured memories of my dear husband, Frank (late of 45, Caludon Road). Always in the thoughts of his loving wife.

From No. 4 one person detained in Hollymoor Hospital Birmingham; No. 28 Caludon Road, one person treated and one treated at First Aid Posts and sent home; No. 40 detained in hospital of St. Cross, Rugby; No. 47 treated; No. 53 one person treated at Hospital; No. 55 one person detained in Warwick Hospital and No. 59 detained in Barnsley Hall Emergency Hospital, Bromsgrove.

Warden Records show that Senior Warden **Walter Phillips**, Casualties Post 403B Warden No 617 was fatally killed by blast from a land mine whilst rendering first aid to a casualty. He was killed on duty at Shakespeare Street, aged 43. Walter resided with his wife, Edith Evelyn Phillips at 8, Avon Street. With the couple having two children, Howard and Celia. Walter was born on the 17th November, 1897 at Coventry to Solomon and Mary Phillips, of 192, Farren Road. In addition to his air raid duties, he was employed as a Machine Shop Superintendent at the British Thomson-Houston Company Limited and is buried in the Communal Grave.

PHILLIPS (Wal) In ever loving memory of a dear husband and father. Remembered always by his loving children, wife and mother.

PHILLIPS In memory of our beloved Wal. Every remembered by Mr. and Mrs. Willerton

Father and daughter, **Harold Asa Tarver** and **Doris Tarver**, died at 121, Shakespeare Street. Harold was 57 and married to Mrs. M. A. Tarver. Doris was 29. Both are buried in the Communal Grave. A family member was injured and treated at hospital.

TARVER – Harold and Doris – passed away suddenly – Ever remembered by Mrs. Crutchlow, Phyllis, Mr. and Mrs. Gardner, George, Bill, Edna and Reg.

Along the street at No. 188, **Philip Henry Clarke** died at his home aged 53. His parents were John and Julia Clarke, of 30, King Street and he was married to Lydia Mary Clarke. Philip was born on the 17th April, 1887, at Walsall and worked as a Commercial Clerk, Humber Ltd. On the 23rd November 1940 he was buried in the Communal Grave. A family member was detained in Hospital of St. Cross, Rugby.

CLARKE – Treasured memories of my dear husband Phil. By his loving wife and daughter, Mary.

Frederick Jowett, died and resided at 59, Coventry Street. He was born on the 2nd November , 1866 at Derby and died age 74. He was husband of Margaret Ray Jowett and buried in Coventry (Stoke, St Michael's), Cemetery.

Residents of No. 61 Coventry Street were treated at a First Aid Post and sent home. Two people injured at No. 71; one person detained in hospital of St. Cross, Rugby at No. 77; No. 83 two persons detained in Warwick Hospital and from No.87 one treated at hospital and one person treated at First Aid Post and sent home.

Charles Thomas and Florence Margaret Price, lost their three children in Stratford Street Shelter. The family had taken to the shelter from their home at 72, Stratford Street. **Graham Charles** (6 months) born 2nd May 1940, **June Patricia** (5) born 1st June, 1935 and attended Stoke Council School and **Ruth Ann** (3) born 20th August, 1937. The children are buried in Keresley Churchyard.

PRICE Treasured memories of our dear babies (June, Ruth, Ann and Graham) who have joined the angels. Ever in the thoughts of their mummy, daddy, Auntie Nance, Granddad, Uncle Vic and Joseph.

Edith Annie Parr and **Nancy May Parr** died at home, 67, Stratford Street and are buried in Wolston Cemetery. Edith, aged 54 She was the widow of C. Parr and born on the 3rd February, 1885 at Newbold-on-Stour. Their daughter, Nancy, aged 16 was born on the 13th May, 1924 at Coventry and employed by Woolworth Stores.

Next door, **George Sidney James Evans**, died aged 29. Other family members were injured, one detained in Warneford Hospital, one detained in Barnsley Hall, Bromsgrove and a further resident treated for wounds. George is buried in the Communal Grave.

EVANS (George) In loving memory of a dear son and brother. Always in the thoughts of mother, sister Doris and brother, Bill now a prisoner of war.

The children of Horace and Winifred E. Danes of 73, Stratford Street were lost in the air raid. **Gordon David Danes** was 23 months old and born on the 6th December, 1938 at Coventry his younger brother, **Robert John Danes**, was born on the 18th August, 1940 at Coventry and died aged 2 months. The children are buried in Wolston Cemetery.

At Stratford Street a variety of injuries recorded one person detained in Barnsley Hall Emergency Hospital, Bromsgrove. At No. 64 one resident detained in Warwick Hospital and one in hospital; one person treated from No. 66; No. 69 one person detained in Warneford Hospital, Leamington; No. 79 one person detained in Stratford Emergency Hospital; No. 81 one detained in Barnsley Hall Emergency Hospital, Bromsgrove and from No. 83 one person detained in Stratford-on-Avon Emergency Hospital.

Father and daughter, **Walter Alfred Deacon** and **Ida Henrietta Deacon** died at 35, Burlington Road. Walter was 81 and Ida aged 53. She was born on the 28th June, 1887 at Rochdale, Lancashire and worked as a housekeeper. Wilfred originally came from London where he was born on the 21st April, 1859. Wilfred and Ida are buried in the Communal Grave. Two people from No. 80a treated at Gulson Road Hospital and sent home and one person from No. 95 received treatment.

Bert Rawlins resided at Duke Barn Fields, Barras Heath and was in the Army.

Aged 26, I had only been in the Army a couple of months and at the Barracks. All our leave was cancelled, and we were forbidden to go to Coventry in case it demoralised us although the authorities didn't say what it was. They did a similar thing and kept us away from the Dunkirk veterans at the Barracks. I had been married three years and my wife stayed in Coventry, we had to correspond by letter and all letters were censored by the officers. I came back on leave in April 1941 and helped put out incendiaries as I was on active leave, 'you just had to take conditions as they came along'.

Two families suffered losses at Frederick Bird School, Swan Lane the Olivers and the Suttons. All four victims are buried in the Communal Grave.

The Oliver's resided at 191, Tallants Road, killed were wife and husband, **Edith Evelyn Oliver** and **Jack Oliver.** The both had origins in Lower Heyford, Northampton. Edith was aged 30 and the daughter of Mr. H. Draper and Mrs. E. E. Draper. She was born on the 11th December, 1909. Slightly older, Jack was 32 and the son of Walter Ernest and Ellen Oliver, of 42, Council House, Lower Heyford although Jack was born on the 30th June, 1908 at Brentford. Jack worked at Courtaulds and Edith was a housewife.

Mother and son, **Edith Mary Sutton** and **Kenneth Sutton** of 10, Burlington Road, died at Frederick Bird School. Edith, 35 was born on the 15th March, 1905 at Old Wolverton. Born on the 22nd April, 1930 at Coventry, Kenneth was a scholar at Frederick Bird School and died aged 10. Father and husband was a Mr. Fred. G. Sutton.

SUTTON – Treasured memories of my dear wife, Edith and dear son, Kenneth. Always in the thoughts of Fred and daughter Audrey. Sadly missed by all.

An application for a plaque was received from Mrs. E. Layton, 150 Sewall Highway for George Layton but no reply was received from the Corporation by the 10th August 1949. Indication were the family had moved away. **George Layton**, died at 54, Oldham Avenue, aged 16. His resided with his parents, Raymond and Ethel Layton at 150, Sewall Highway, Wyken. George was a native of Newcastle-on-Tyne being born there on the 10th March, 1924. He worked at the General Electric Co. Ltd and lies in Grave Ref. I.4. 4/5. Communal Grave.

LAYTON Treasured memory of our darling George (Sonnie) Always in the thoughts of Mother, dad, Florence, Iris, friends here and USA

Ernest Harold Beadle and **Irene May Edith Beadle**, would loose their lives as a result of enemy action at 47, Farren Road. Ernest was injured and later died at Gulson Road Hospital the following day. He was aged 35, and the son of William and Constance Mary Beadle, of Radley Cottages, Hooley, Coulsdon, Surrey. Ernest was born on the 27th March, 1905, at New Malden, Surrey and employed at the Standard Motor Co. Ltd.

Aged 33, Irene May Edith Beadle was the daughter of Mr. and Mrs. Fred Ernest Smith, of Church Lane Avenue, Hooley, Coulsdon, Surrey. A housewife, she was born on the 5th June, 1907 at Chingford, Essex. Ernest and Irene were buried in the Communal Grave on the 23rd November 1940.

In memory of **Dorothy Rogers** and **Ernest Rogers** three plaques were paid for. A plaque in Hearsall Common was paid for by Mr. J. T. Rogers of 38 Abercorn Road on the 7th July 1951. Two further plaques in Windmill Road Cemetery were paid for Miss O. Jones of 172 Grange Road, Longford on the 12th July 1951 at a cost of £3-5-0.

The couple resided and died at 184, Hipswell Highway and are buried in the Communal Grave. Dorothy was the daughter of William and Alice Jones, of 172, Grange Road, Longford, and worked at Humber Ltd. She was born on the 23rd January, 1911 at Coventry and died aged 29.

Ernest, aged 31 was the son of Mr. and Mrs. Tom Rogers, of 70, Sir Thomas White's Road, Earlsdon and born on the 11th August, 1909 at Whittlesea near Peterborough. Ernest was employed as a Gardener, W. S. Heatley, St. Paul's Road. From No. 374 one person detained in Stratford-on-Avon Emergency Hospital.

At 37, Hermitage Road and aged 23, **Christina Mary Liggins** died as a result of enemy action. She was the wife of L. Liggins and born locally on the 20th February, 1917 at 1, Courthouse Green, Coventry. Her parents, were William Menzies and Alice Elizabeth nee Lowe. Christina was a housewife and buried in the Communal Grave. From No. 24 two persons treated one in Barnsley Hall Emergency Hospital, Bromsgrove; No. 29 one person detained in Stratford-on-Avon Emergency Hospital and from No. 30 one person detained in hospital of St. Cross, Rugby.

LIGGINS – Ever lasting remembrance of Christina Mary (Menzies) who gave her life – Mother and brothers and sisters, home and abroad. Requiescat in pace

From Newey Road, Vic Terry provides accounts.

I remember hearing the aircraft and seeing the Wyken Green Hill Searchlights and balloons. The usual procedure on hearing the sirens was to dive into our Morrison Shelter which was in the front room and Mum and I waited nervously as Dad went off in his ARP hat and gas mask to meet up with the other wardens at the Wyken Pippen (obviously to protect the contents). There was a big shelter in Newey Road a big thing with a concrete roof. We had a Morrison shelter in the front room, I think dad got in because he was in the ARP as soon as the sirens went we got in it. As a 7 year old we could see barrage balloon from our back window. A bomb dropped on Ansty Road, I heard it but we didn't go but we weren't allowed to go on the Ansty Road. There was a sombre air we could see all the smoke from the centre. As a child I remember there being no traffic I didn't understand or realise why at the time.

Three casualties occurred in a surface shelter at 24, Coleridge Road, their residence and all are buried in the Communal Grave. **Ann Rose** was aged 73. She was born on the 2nd March 1867 at Oakthorpe and married to Percival Rose. The couple had five children Gertrude, Gladys, Ida, Mary and Maud.

Husband and wife, **Christina May Roberts** and **John Roberts** were aged 37 and 38 respectively. John was the son of William Roberts, of 27, Princes Street, Nuneaton and born in the town on the 10th April, 1904. He was employed as a foreman at Smith Stampings Ltd.

At No. 26, four casualties occurred they are buried in the Communal Grave. Two married couples were killed. The first couple were **Arthur Smith** and **Margaret Ettie Smith.** Arthur was aged 36, and the son of Mrs. Smith, of 54, Bridgeman Road. He was born in 1910 and employed as a Transport Driver with Coventry and District Co-Operative Society Ltd. Margaret was aged 30 and the daughter of William Joseph and Gertrude Annie Stephens, of 92, Colchester Street. She was born on the 17th July, 1910 at Coventry and employed as a Shop Assistant, L. H. Fearis & Co. Ltd. At No. 40 one person treated at Gulson Road Hospital and sent home.

SMITH In loving memory of Arthur and Margaret (nee Stephens) late of 26 Coleridge Street. Sadly missed by brother and wife (Stanley and Clarice)

Housewife **Gertrude Annie Stephens** died at 26, Coleridge Road although she resided at 92, Colchester Street with her husband. Getrude was aged 61 and the wife of William Joseph Stephens. She was born on the 11th September, 1879. William was 63, born on the 23rd April, 1877 and from Coventry, he worked in the city as a Storekeeper, Nuffield Mechanisation and Aero Ltd.

STEPHENS In loving memory of William and Getrude late of 92 Colchester Street. Ever in the thoughts of son and wife (Stanley and Clarice)

Coventry North East Injuries

Deedmore Road had a resident treated at a First Aid Post and sent home whilst Henley Road had two people from No. 14 treated at a post and sent home, where No. 22 were detained in Warwick Hospital and No. 228 had a detainee at Warwick Hospital, as did 94 Woodway Lane. Detained in Stratford-on-Avon General Hospital was a resident of 57 Hall Lane.

One injury from each of the following was reported; Wyken Croft (treated at Gulson Road Hospital and sent home), Wycliffe Road (55 detained in Barnsley Hall, Bromsgrove) Wyke Road (26 detained in Alcester Emergency Hospital), Balliol Road (18 detained in Barnsley Hall Emergency Hospital, Bromsgrove), Hartland Avenue (98 Treated at First Aid Post and sent home), Lutterworth Road (42 treated at First Aid Post and sent home), Stubbs Grove (4 treated at Gulson Road Hospital and sent home), Dennis Road (31 Hospital), Wyken Way (103 detained in Warwick Hospital) and Hillside (16 treated at hospital).

From No. 20 Blackberry Lane detained in Stratford-on Avon Emergency Hospital and continuing along the lane, 136 detained in Stratford-on-Avon Emergency Hospital and No. 170 detained in Barnsley Hall Emergency Hospital, Bromsgrove. One injury also reported at 29 Draycott Road who was detained in Stratford-on-Avon General Hospital and 14 Torcross Avenue who was detained in Warwick Hospital. Sewall Highway had four casualties; 17 detained in Hospital of St. Cross, Rugby; 101 treated at First Aid Post and sent home; 103 Hospital and 280 detained in Warwick Hospital.

Across at Heath Road, a resident of No. 49 detained Barnsley Hall, Bromsgrove and a single resident from 2 Druid Road treated at First Aid Post and sent home. Two victims from Burns Road; No. 35 Treated at First Aid Post and sent home and No. 45 detained in hospital of St. Cross, Rugby.

Beaconsfield Road had three casualties; No. 14 detained in Stratford-on-Avon General Hospital and two people from No. 34 Treated at Warneford Hospital Leamington and sent home. Walsgrave Road had various reports of unknown address treated at Barnsley Hall, Bromsgrove and along the road; 209 Detained in Stratford-on-Avon General Hospital; 246 detained Barnsley Hall, Bromsgrove, 325 detained at Hospital of St. Cross, Rugby; 338 detained in Warneford Hospital, Leamington; 352 treated at First Aid Post and sent home and 357 detained in Warwick Hospital.

The 'fields' of Harefield Road and Enfield received injuries, at 133 Harefield a detainee in Alcester Emergency Hospital and from Enfield Road 16 detained in Warwick Hospital and 47 in Barnsley Hall, Bromsgrove. Brays Lane, at No. 25 a resident was detained in Barnsley Hall Emergency Hospital, Bromsgrove and in Central Avenue No.

73 treated at First Aid Post and sent home with No. 4 South Avenue treated at a First Aid Post and sent home.

Shuckburgh Park Convalescent Hospital, Daventry detained a resident of 54 St. Michaels Road whilst a resident of 6 Wren Street was detained Barnsley Hall, Bromsgrove. Treated at Gulson Road Hospital and sent home was a resident of 66 Kingsway. In the vicinity isolated injures were reported ranging from Hamilton Road to Momus Boulevard. No. 50 Hamilton Road, Treated at First Aid Post and sent home and No 56 Detained in Stratford-on-Avon General Hospital; No. 19 Lansdowne Street detained Barnsley Hall Bromsgrove; No. 33 Mowbray Street detained in Stratford-on-Avon Emergency Hospital; No. 30 Lowther Street one detained in Stratford-on-Avon General Hospital and one detained in Hollymoor Hospital, Birmingham; No. 44 Dane Road detained in Stratford-on-Avon Emergency Hospital and No. 79 detained in Nottingham and Midland Eye Hospital.

Nineteen remaining injuries were spread as follows; No. 15 Hastings Road detained Barnsley Hall Bromsgrove, 45 detained in Hospital of St. Cross, Rugby and No. 50 received treatment; Two people at 35 Roman Road treated and No. 40 Roman Road at Hospital; No. 23 Camden Street detained in Barnsley Hall Emergency Hospital, Bromsgrove; No. 73 Belgrave Road detained in Warwick Hospital as 253; Hipswell Highway treated at hospital; Mellowdew Road, two persons at 36 detained in Hollymoor Hospital Birmingham and 98 Treated at Gulson Road Hospital and sent home; 1 Oswin Grove 1 detained in Warwick Hospital; 73 Newey Road treated; No. 46 Longfellow Road detained in Barnsley Hall, Bromsgrove; 20 Bromleigh Drive treated; 30Wyver Crescent Detained in Warwick Hospital; 47 Kempley Avenue detained in Stratford-on Avon Emergency Hospital and 91 Momus Boulevard treated.

Further injuries; Barras Green, Red Horse Inn detained in Warwick Hospital, Bigginhall Crescent 46 detained in Stratford-on-Avon Emergency Hospital, Nicholls Street 77 , treated at First Aid Posts and sent home and Stafford Street, Stoke Barnsley Hall, Bromsgrove

Coventry South East

Three children died at City Isolation Hospital, Whitley. Whoberley School pupil, **Joan Marjorie Eaves**, died as a result of enemy action at City Hospital, Whitley aged 7. Her parents were Edward James and Gertrude Margaret Eaves, of 51, Conway Avenue, Tile Hill and she was born on the 15th January, 1933 in Coventry. Joan is buried in the Communal Grave.

EAVES In loving memory of our dear daughter, Marjorie aged 7 years and 10 months. From mum, dad, sister and brothers

Joan Winterburn, aged 2 was the daughter of Alfred and Elsie Winterburn, of 40, Paynes Lane. She is buried in the London Road Cemetery. Six years older, **Donald Albert Scarrott** was the adopted son of Henry and Lucy Scarrott, of 13, Pine Tree Avenue, Tile Hill. He was born on the 9th July, 1932 and a pupil at Whoberley School. He is buried in Grave Ref. I4. 7/5. Communal Grave.

SCARROT Treasured memories of our little son Donald Ever in the thoughts of his mother, father and auntie

British Thomson-Houston Company Limited employee, **John George Needle**, died in the Humber/Binley Road Shelter, aged 18. He resided with his mother, Margaret Louisa Needle at 182, Gulson Road. John was born on the 15th June, 1922 at Coventry and is buried in the Communal Grave.

Sylvia Mary Bott was injured as a result of enemy action at Binley Road and died at Gulson Road Hospital on the 16th November, 1940. She was the daughter of Leonard William and Evelyn Louisa Bott, of 42, Holmfield Road and died aged 16. Sylvia was born on the 10th November, 1924 at Coventry and worked as a Typist at Maudslay Motor Co. Ltd. Grave Reference in the Communal Grave is E. 22/5.

Aged 56, **Albert Earl Courts**, died and resided at 30, Binley Road. He was born on the 11th May, 1884 at Foleshill and was married. On the 23rd November he was buried in the Communal Grave. Casualties at Binley Road including two at No. 16 one detained in Warwick Hospital the other in Hollymoor Hospital, Birmingham. Residents of 94 and 554 were treated at hospital.

The husband of Ethel Frances Wright, **Francis John Wright** died as a result of enemy action, 14th November, 1940 at 56, The Moorfield. Aged 41. The family resided at 56, The Moorfield. Francis is buried in Grave Ref. I. 4. 8/3. Communal Grave. Injuries were reported at No. 52 and a resident of No. 54 was detained in Stratford-on-Avon General Hospital.

Sheila Thornett one his daughters was eight years old.

There were five houses destroyed. My brother stayed with my father and was in the houses next to ours with my aunties they lived next door. My dad came back from work just after seven he was in the territorial's, I'd don't suppose he'd even had anything to eat by the times the bombs had gone off. My dad popped back in to see they were getting on alright they were passing time by playing film stars and he didn't like to sit in the shelters, he wanted to know what was going on. He said "I'll go and get my overcoat and took the dog and went back in the house, they heard the bomb. Auntie's house got demolished but ours was the main one. They were rescued and went across the road to a neighbour house, my auntie said "my brothers in there", the neighbour said "no he wasn't" and my auntie said "if your not going to dig for him I will".

A man found him the next morning, the house was smoking and was just debris. The dog got out, my dad was buried, they found the dog under the stairs but my uncle had it put down. My other uncle came up and seen the house demolished and didn't know we had evacuated a neighbour told him, his sister and children were alright as they weren't there.

We were evacuated on the Saturday before, Dad heard a rumour at work that there was a Big One coming. Dad rode to Pailton rode on the Sunday across to my aunties and found she already had evacuees staying in her house but he managed to find us a labourers cottage at Pailton pastures. The following Saturday we were evacuated, the coal man took us on his lorry, my dad, sister and me were on the back covered in a tarpaulin as it was cold and my mum with the two babies (two years and thirteen months) was in front. It was like an adventure. The following morning my dad got up and returned to Coventry with the milk lorry, we never saw him again after that. During the week he did write to my mum joking that she had taken all the good knives with her.

On the night we stood in the garden in Pailton just after seven and could see the bombers all going over to Coventry, it was frightening really they were so low, the sky in the direction of Coventry got redder and redder. My mum kept saying over and over "I hope it isn't The Moorfields, I hope it isn't the Moorfields".

I remember seeing my Uncle Bill go past the window and he came into the cottage, he took my mum into the front room and she came out crying she said "It's going to be alright your dad's in the hospital". My sister who was aged 11, realized the truth and screamed asking about my brother as to whether he was alright and he was.

My mum identified my Dad in the Council House , they had his belongings in a little canvas bag and asked if the items belonged to her husband including a grey overcoat, 'yes' they belonged to him she replied. On the way home she was crying and some how managed to get her foot stuck in the bomb damaged pavement, a man saw her and took her into a shoe shop that must of still been in business and bought her a new pair of shoes. People were generous then. My dad was buried next to a 15 year police messenger.

We couldn't go back to Coventry my uncle had his sisters staying with him and an extended family. Mum got us a house in Foleshill and we eventually moved back to the house in Moorfields when it was rebuilt, in fact three of the five neighbours did. My Dad saved our lives really.

A plaque at the London Road Cemetery commemorates **Leonard Lucien Matthews,** and it was paid for by his father, Norman Matthews, of 37 Bollingbroke Road on the 25th February 1948. Leonard resided and died at 68, Hollis Road. Aged 19 he was born on the 3rd December, 1920 at Coventry and employed at the British Thomson-Houston Company Limited. He is buried in the Communal Grave.

Sadie Perry was 21 years old and lived in Hollis Road.

We went underneath the stairs, my sister, Rachel who was two years older and my mum. We used to go to a shelter but it was flooded sometimes we would go to another one otherwise we just stayed in the house. There was no damage to our house. After the raid we went down the town it was terrible, not much left of the town at all! The GEC was bombed so we had no work and went back to Glasgow for four weeks.

13, 15 and 17 Brympton Road incurred casualties. At No. 13, **Ernest William Hydon**, aged 27 was killed. His parents Thomas and Leah Elizabeth Hydon resided at 85, Hugh Road. Ernest was married to Elsie Annie Hydon, and the couple resided at 100, Glencoe Road. He was born on the 28th May, 1914 at Coventry, employed by Rootes Securities Ltd and is buried in the London Road Cemetery.

HYDON Treasured memories of my dearest husband Ernie, sadly missed by his wife Elsie, baby Janet and remembered by his mother and family

At No. 15, **Ethel Moody** and **Percival Clement Moody** died. Ethel was aged 39 and the daughter of Mrs. M. Parkes, of 48, Biggin Hall Crescent. Percival was aged 43. The couple are buried at Wolston Cemetery. On the 15th September 1949 a plaque was paid for by Mr. O. B. Darby 286 Bristnall Hall Road, Birmingham in Stoke Heath.

MOODY (nee Ethel Pakes) Treasured memories of a dear friend. Ever in the thoughts of Nance and Albert.

The last deaths at Brympton Road, No. 17 were residents, mother and son, **Marion Rollins** and **John Donald Rollins**. Marion was 59, the daughter of Benjamin and Elizabeth Darby, of Langley, Oldbury, Worcestershire and the widow of John Rollins. She was a housewife, born on the 13th March, 1882 and is buried in the London Road Cemetery. John, aged 26 was born on the 26th October, 1914 at Coventry. He was employed as a tool maker at Sir W. G. Armstrong Whitworth Aircraft Ltd and is buried in the Communal Grave.

A father and daughter died at Swifts Corner, Whitley. **Alfred Bird** was aged 44 and the husband of Emily Florence Gladys Bird. Aged 16, **Edna Elsie May Bird** was also killed and both her and her father are buried in the Communal Grave. The family resided at 77, Paynes Lane with a further family member treated at a first aid post and sent home.

BIRD (A. T. also Edna) Called away suddenly. Ever in thoughts of his wife, Mary, Bryan and Ed.

Fifty five year old and Swift Corner Cottage resident, **Thomas Richard Elson**, died at Swift Corner Cottages. He was the son of T. and Eliza Elson and born on the 24th September, 1885, at Whitley. Thomas was employed at the City Engineers Department, Coventry Corporation worked at the Pumping Station, Whitley and rests in Grave I. 5. 3/2. at the Communal Grave Cemetery.

ELSON (Tom) Always remembered by his sister, Sara.

From 77, Paynes Lane, **John Henry Hipkiss**, died aged 52 at Swift Corner. He was the son of Stephen Hipkiss and buried in the Communal Grave. Treatment was required for one person from No. 28 and one from No. 40 Detained in Hospital of St. Cross, Rugby.

HIPKISS J.H. Called away suddenly ever in the thoughts of Gladys, Ted, Mary, Bryan.

A plaque in London Road Cemetery applied for by F. Hobday, 134 St. James Lane, Willenhall and paid for on the 3rd March 1948 at a cost of £2-5-0 commemorates four members of the Hobday family (parents and two daughters) who died at Swift Corner Cottages. All are buried in the Communal Grave.

Eliza Hobday and **George William Hobday** were both aged 64. Eliza was born on the 14th January, 1877 at Long Itchington and a housewife. George was born on the 14th December, 1876 at Ryton-on-Dunsmore and employed with the City Engineers, Coventry Corporation, Sewage Pumping Station, Whitley.

Their daughters were **May** aged 32 and **Daisy** aged 21. May was born on the 30th May, 1908 at Pinley, Coventry and employed with Auto Machinery Co. Ltd. Daisy was born on the 27th January, 1919 at Pinley, Coventry and employed at Thos. Bushills & Sons Ltd.

HOBDAY Treasured memories of Dad, Mother, sisters, May and Daisie. Always in the thoughts of family left behind.

Thomas Richard Nelson died as a result of enemy action, 14th November, 1940 at Swift Corner Cottages. He is recorded as being buried in Coventry Borough and found on the 14th November 1940.

Husband and wife, **Ernest Leslie** and **Lillian Hollingsworth**, died as a result of enemy action at 30, St. Christian's Road. Ernest was aged 27 and a member of the British Red Cross Society. He was the son of Mr. W. C. Hollingsworth and Mrs. A. Hollingsworth. Lilian was aged 30 and the daughter of Mr. And Mrs. Davies (formerly Downes), of 31, Pool Street, Macclesfield, Cheshire. Both are buried in the Communal Grave. A neighbour at 32 required treatment.

Three residents of Dillotford Avenue were killed at No. 59. **Florence** and **Walter Thompson** were residents of No. 59 and both are buried in the Communal Grave. Florence was aged 54, born on the 31st October, 1886 at Coventry and a housewife. Walter was also aged 54 and born on the 2nd June, 1886 at Coventry. He was employed as a Works Superintendent at W. W. Curtis Ltd.

THOMPSON Beautiful memories of dearest mum and dad, Sadly missed always by Beryl and Wal.

At 59 Dillotford Avenue, **Edward Jones**, died in his neighbours garage aged 26. Ernest resided at No. 57 with his wife, Getrude May Jones and was born in Coventry on the 20th November, 1912. He was the son of Percy and Agnes Jones of 5 Keresley Road Ernest was employed at Lockheed Hydraulic Brake Co. Ltd commuting to Leamington Spa. He is buried in the Communal Grave. In February 1948 a plaque was paid for in the War Memorial Park by Mrs G. M. Duncan of 57 Dillotford Avenue and reads *'Mr. Edward Jones Killed in Air Raid 14th November 1940'* and she also paid for the plaque of Irene Edith Suddens (killed in the April air raids), with a total cost of £3-5-0. Other neighbours from No. 57 were also injured at 59 Dillotford Avenue and a family member detained in Warwick Hospital.

JONES In loving memory of my dear Ted who passed away suddenly 'Hearts that love never forget'. From his loving wife, May, Father, Len and Bessie

Along the road at No. 80, **Edith Murphy** and **John Irvine Murphy** died as a result of enemy action. They were both aged 42. Edith was the daughter of William and Mary Jane Reynolds, of Habberley View, Lye Head, Bewdley, Worcestershire. John a Home Guard was the son of Mr. and Mrs. James Murphy, of 289, McAslin Street, Townhead, Glasgow, Scotland. Both are buried in the London Road Cemetery.

Chris Hawthorne resided in Woodside Avenue.

We spent the night sheltering with a family in Leek Wootton. There were nine people in the house including a young girl from whom I caught an infection which later turned into a mastoid. A serious condition then, these days rarely heard of and easily treated by antibiotics. However a parachute mine came down the top of Woodside Avenue and Kenpas Highway. The ARP wardens on duty saw it coming and one of them thought it might be a parachutist and ran towards it, the other chap lay down in the gutter. No trace was found of the warden who had run towards it, except I think a shoe. Mr. Randle was not seriously hurt. The mine destroyed nine houses and damaged many more including ours. My mother and I went to stay with friends in Cheddleton near Stoke on Trent, my father remained behind to keep his engineering business going as it was engaged in war work. The view of the City burning is one that I shall never forget.

A friend of Chris, Mike Griffiths was eight years old and at Bathway Road.

We had become accustomed to intermittent air raids since the spring and early summer of 1940, and our reaction had become a routine of taking cover during the daytime and keeping our heads covered at night – wait for the noise to stop and debris to stop falling, then stand up and get on with whatever we were doing. Raids at night rarely started before 9 or 10 o'clock and involved us kids getting out of bed quickly, getting dressed and taking shelter. But on the 14th November I remember we had tea when Dad came home from work, then he went off to check in at the Wardens

116

Post up the road (he was in charge of our local air raid wardens), and we were busying ourselves household jobs, when the sirens sounded the alert at around 7pm. I remember my mum saying ' O Lord they are starting early tonight when almost immediately it seemed we heard the loud roar of German bombers overhead and the thud of bombs exploding.

There were reports of incendiary bombs in numerous locations, but no high explosives in our area. The planes came over in groups of 30 or so, wave after wave and no sooner had one lot passed over to the North the next lot could be heard approaching from the south over the Rugby area. The planes were mainly Heinkel 111 twin engined bombers I believe and the engines were never synchronized which gave them a distinctive throbbing drone which cast a fearful dread in the hearts of those cowering below! It seemed as if there was no end to it all as wave after wave kept coming all night. Occasionally there would be a loud explosion of a bomb close by and all the house and contents would shake. Then on one particular occasion there was an almighty crash as a land mine exploded close by and our windows blew out with a crash (we later heard it was a parachute mine and our two brave church wardens had rushed towards it thinking it was a parachutist landing and no trace of them was ever found again). By about midnight or the early hours the centre of Coventry was well alight and during a brief lull my father came in and gave me a tin hat which was far too big for me and took me to the corner to see the huge fires, one of which was the cathedral fully ablaze. I remember it was very cold (frosty I believe) a brilliant moon but all very exciting for a young lad. Then we heard the familiar drone of more bombers arriving and we scurried back to our safe haven under the stairs!

The raid went on all night. No question of sleep, and our mother kept us amused with various games, No possibility of 'I Spy' of course so being a devoted Coventrian she taught us all about the history of her beloved Coventry. I remember the 'all Clear' sounded at around 6.00am and we all heaved a great sigh of relief. Almost proud that we were OK. I remember Dad coming in soon after looking very tired, and going upstairs to try and grab a couple of hours sleep before going to work again at 8.30am. Then we lads all went to view the bomb sites etc as far as we were allowed, pick up shrapnel and swap stories with other lads. I remember the auxiliary firemen who lived nearby coming home during the morning looking very, very tired and we dared to ask one who lived opposite if all the fires were now out and his shattering reply was unprintable!

Senior Air Warden **Cyril Wyatt Stockton Judd**, died as a result of enemy action age 42 on 14th November 1940, whilst on duty in Green Lane District. He was the son of Harry Stockton Judd and Annie Parkinson Judd of Manor Farm, Ryton-on-Dunsmore and was married to Phyllis Isobel Judd. Cyril was born on the 1st November, 1898 at Leicester and died at the family address of 65 Woodside Avenue, Green Lane. As an employee of Equipment A Department, Alfred Herbert Ltd his name appears in Roll of Honour and he is buried in London Road Cemetery. His wife, Phyllis paid for a War Memorial Park plaque on the 21st February 1949 which reads 'Cyril Wyatt Stockton Judd Mr Senior Warden Civil Defence killed in air raid 14th November 1940'.

Warden Casualty records show he was at Post 606, No. 439 and died on the night of the 14th /15th November 1940 by the fatal explosion of a land mine

'The Alfred Herbert News' reported; "It is with the deepest regret that we have to record the death while on duty as an Air Raid Warden of Mr. C. W. S. Judd. Mr. Judd commenced working with us on February 12th 1923 in the Designs Department under the late Mr. Hawkins and in 1925 was transferred to the Equipment Department where he remained until the time of his death. He will be greatly missed not only by his colleagues but also by the many people whom in the course of his work he had to meet. Everyone pays tribute to his sterling qualities as a worker and he was greatly respected by all who knew him. We extend our deepest sympathy to all his relatives in their very sad loss".

Air Raid Warden **Frederick Thomas Marsden** died at 59, Woodside Avenue. He was aged 50 and the husband of Edith Emily Marsden. He was born at Corley and employed at the Council House. The Warden Records show he was No. 558 at Post 606 and also killed by the fatal explosion of land mine. Frederick is buried in London Road Cemetery. Two people were injured at Woodside Avenue and detained in Warwick Hospital.

Richard Arthur Newall, was killed in Beanfield Avenue and a member of a First Aid Party. He resided at No. 11 with his wife, Sarah Dawson Newall. Richard aged 39 was buried in the Communal Grave.

George Fox Barker (38) and his daughter **Mary Grace Barker** (14 months) were two of the five victims killed by enemy action at 28 Beanfield Avenue. George was the son of Ezekiel Barker and Catherine Mary Barker of 24 Uxbridge Road, Middlesex and born on the 1st November 1902 at Uxbridge. George was employed at the Standard Motor Co. Ltd and married to Nellie Mabel Barker, their daughter, Mary Grace was born on the 31st August 1939 at 28 Beanfield Avenue. George and Mary are buried in the Communal Grave and two plaques in the War Memorial Park were paid for by the wife and mother, Nellie Mabel of 20 Gregory Avenue at a cost of £3-5-0. The plaques read *'Mr. George Fox Barker Killed in air raid 14th November 1940'* and *'Mary Grace Barker 14 months Killed in air raid 14th November 1940'*. A family member was detained at Stratford-on-Avon Emergency Hospital.

Two more deaths were recorded at No. 28., Father and son, **Alfred Ernest Roughton** and **Ernest John Roughton.** They resided at No. 6, wife and mother was Elsie Mary Roughton. Alfred was aged 41 and born on the 12th October, 1899 at Northampton. He was employed at Daimler Co. Ltd. Ernest was 14 and born on the 10th December, 1926 at Bilston, Staffordshire and attended King Henry VIII School, Coventry. Both are buried in the Communal Grave.

A service was held on the 8th December 1946 by the Vicar, The Reverend Canon A. M. Startin at St. Barbara's Church. The service was attended by about three hundred friends and relatives. The lesson was read by Mr. Dennis Whitehouse with Mr. E. R. Shaw one of the School Music Staff at the Organ. After the sounding of the Last Post the names of the fallen were read by the Headmaster, and this reading was undoubtedly the most impressive part of a memorable and solemn ceremony. The names of those who died from King Henry VIII School.

The Names

DERRICK BOUCHIER BAILEY	JOHN HOLROYD
BERNARD RICHARD BOOTH	ROBIN SCOTT JACK
THOMAS HENRY BROWN	JOHN BERNARD JOHNSON
PATRICK TAWSE CATTO	RONALD WILFRED LANGSHAW
BERNARD LAWRENCE CRAWFORTH	JOHN LOWE
ALBERT ALAN CROSS	RONALD DAVY MALLET
JOHN DALY	KENNETH GORDON MITCHELL
ARTHUR GEOFFREY HOWARD DAVIES	STANLEY NEVILLE PICKERING
LEONARD ROY EGGINTON	RONALD ERIC PLANT
HAROLD SANDERS FROST	JACK REYNOLDS
FRANK WILLIAM GILBERT	ROYSTON THOMAS RICHARDSON
JOHN DOUGLAS GORDON	JOHN ERNEST ROUGHTON
HERBERT BARRINGER GOULD	VICTOR HARRY TAYTON
ANTHONY EDWARD GRUBB	RONALD HENRY THOMAS
KENNETH WILLIAM HEARD	JOHN GRANT TURNBULL
	JOHN HENRY WARREN

A. R. R. BOWER

E. A. WEBB

David Arthur McMurdie was injured as a result of enemy action at 28, Beanfield Avenue and died at Hospital of St. Cross, Rugby on the 27th December, 1940. He was aged 4 and resided at 6, Beanfield Avenue,. His Grave Ref. is given as Rugby Municipal Borough and his parents were Arthur Oswald and Ivy McMurdie. Warwickshire A family member was detained in Stratford Emergency Hospital and one treated at hospital.

Various injuries were recorded across Beanfield Avenue; 4 (detained in Stratford-on-Avon Emergency Hospital), No. 5 (detained in Hollymoor Hospital, Birmingham) No. 6 (one treated and one detained in Stratford Emergency Hospital), 20 (treated at First Aid Post and sent home), 27 (treated at First Aid Post and sent home), 28 (detained in Stratford-on-Avon Emergency Hospital), 29 (one detained in Hospital of St. Cross, Rugby and one treated at Gulson Road Hospital and then sent home and No. 32 detained in Rugby Emergency Hospital.

Coventry South East Injuries

Six people treated from Bolingbroke Road, No. 13 detained in Alcester Emergency Hospital; No. 22 detained Barnsley Hall, Bromsgrove; No. 34 treated at First Aid Post and sent home; three people from 179 (two detained in Warneford Hospital, Leamington and one treated at Warneford Hospital and sent home). Humber Road saw injuries at No. 27 detained in Alcester Emergency Hospital, 210 treated at hospital and 242 detained in Warwick Hospital. No, 15 Greenfields had one person detained in Alcester Emergency Hospital as did 29 Bulls Head Lane one person detained in Stratford-on-Avon Emergency Hospital and 14 Coombe Street treated at First Aid Post and sent home.

One person at Glencoe Road detained in Warwick Hospital and one from 75 Treated at First Aid Post and sent home. Emscote Road had three injuries; No. 1 treated at First Aid Post and sent home, No. 11 Treated at First Aid Post and sent home and No. 30 detained in Warwick Hospital. Wycliffe Road had four reports : 42 detained in Warwick Hospital; Two people at 53 treated at First Aid Post and sent home and No. 81 detained in Chadshunt Hall Auxiliary Hospital, Kineton. The number injured at Binley Road (490 treated at First Aid Post and sent home), Whitley Village (14 treated at First Aid Post and sent home); Shortley Road (3 treated at First Aid Post, 7 detained in Evesham Emergency Hospital and sent home and No. 31 Barnsley Hall Bromsgrove) and Tonbridge Road (9 detained in Evesham Emergency hospital).

London Road five injuries occurred at the Plough Hotel treated at First Aid Post and sent home; No. 39 detained in Barnsley Hall Emergency Hospital, Bromsgrove; 119 Detained Barnsley Hall, Bromsgrove and two victims at 173 received treatment at First Aid Post and sent home. Isolated incidents were reported at 96 Millers Road (Detained in Alcester Emergency Hospital);27 Woodcote Avenue ; 84 Rutherglen Avenue (detained in Hollymoor Hospital Birmingham); 6 Ridgeway Road (detained in Stratford-on-Avon General Hospital); 51 Knoll Drive 51 (treated at First Aid Post and sent home); 91 Ulverscroft Road ; 33 Joan Ward Street (treated at First Aid Post and sent home); 19 Mile Lane 19 (treated at Gulson Road Hospital and sent home); 15 John Grace Street (Barnsley Hall, Bromsgrove); 14 Seedfield Croft 14 (detained in Warwick Hospital); 23 Montalt Road 23 (Detained in Warwick Hospital); 64 Erithway Road 64 (treated at First Aid Post and sent home); 1 Kingscote Grove 1 treated at First Aid Post and sent home); 48 Benedictine Road (Detained in Barnsley Hall Emergency Hospital, Bromsgrove); 1 Asthill Grove 1 (detained in Stratford-on-Avon General Hospital) ; King Johns Road and 73 Wainbody Avenue (detained in hospital of St. Cross, Rugby).

At Crecy Road, six injuries were reported; One at No. 12, four residents at No. 20 Treated at First Aid Post and sent home and a resident of No. 22 detained in Warwick Hospital. At Cecily Road, five injuries were reported; No. 33 Treated at First Aid Post and sent home, 38 Treated at First Aid Post and sent home, 46 detained in Nuneaton

Emergency Hospital and treated at First Aid Post and sent home and at 64 a person treated at First Aid Post and sent home.

Five injuries also reported at Kenpas Highway; No. 5 treated at First Aid Post and sent home, No. 25 One treated and one detained in Warwick Hospital, 54 detained in Stratford-on-Avon Emergency Hospital and 66 treated at First Aid Post and sent home. Three injuries occurred at Daventry Road, one person from 62 Detained in Warwick Hospital and two people from No. 120 were detained in Warneford Hospital, Leamington. Three people also injured at Purefoy Road and Green Lane. Purefoy Road one injured at unknown address, two at No. 18 one of which was detained in Hospital of St. Cross, Rugby. No. 15 (treated at First Aid Post and sent home), No. 16 and No. 17 (detained in Stratford-on-Avon Emergency Hospital) all had one casualty at Green Lane.

Two people were injured in each of the following streets; Martyrs Close (3 detained in Warwick Hospital and 17 detained in Warwick Hospital); Wrigsham Street (4 detained in Warneford Hospital, Leamington and 22 detained in Warneford Hospital, Leamington), Quinton Road (9 detained in Evesham Emergency Hospital and 105 treated at First Aid Post and sent home), Kenpas Highway (9 detained in hospital of St. Cross, Rugby and 25 detained in Warwick Hospital), Leamington Road (144 detained in Hospital of St. Cross, Rugby and detained Rugby PA Hospital) and finally Anchorway Road (28 detained in Stratford-on-Avon Emergency Hospital and detained in Stratford General Hospital).

Further injuries at two at Swift Corner Cottages 23 one person at Barnsley Hall, Bromsgrove, Thomas Lansdail Street 19 Detained in Evesham Emergency Hospital, Blondville Street 26 Detained in Warwick Hospital and Thomas Lansdail 19 treated at hospital.

Coventry South West

Beryl Worswick was eighteen years old.

We lived on the corner of Fir Tree Avenue and Jobs Lane. It was an ordinary Thursday until the night time. I think I slept through the raid. I never went in the shelter I used to stay in bed, mum and dad used to try and rake us out, but I would never go to the shelter. Tile Hill was worse off in the later raids we had lots of damage but not so much at that point. On Friday morning I was having a conversation with my mum about going dancing and my brother who was 21 had been into town as he had a little car and said "Going out! Can you hear our Beryl, Mum she thinks she's going out!". My brother was in the Oxford and Bucks and had been evacuated from Dunkirk.

The shelter my dad used to sit in just fell down, that's how well it was built. I eventually got into town on the Saturday and it really struck me then, there were so many people lost. We did the best we could, and that was my youth!

Mainly isolated incidents were recorded along the following addresses with most casualties recorded at Tile Hill Lane; Gerard Avenue (17 detained in Shuckburgh Park Convalescent Hospital, Daventry), Torrington Avenue (140 detained in Stratford-on-Avon General Hospital), Middlecotes (106 treated at First Aid Post and sent home), Eastcotes 164 (detained in Isolation Hospital, Coventry), Eastcotes 26 (Detained in Stratford-on-Avon Emergency Hospital), Westcotes 22 (detained in Warwick Hospital), Standard Avenue (122 detained in Warneford Hospital, Leamington Spa), Tile Hill Lane (102 and 114 detained in Warwick Hospital and 281), Elm Tree Avenue (76 detained in Alcester Emergency Hospital), Ash Tree Avenue 26 (detained in Barnsley Hall Emergency Hospital, Bromsgrove), Lime Grove (12 Barnsley Hall, Bromsgrove) and Pine Tree Avenue (8 detained in Warwick Hospital).

Coventry North West

Age 72, **Walter Gough** died at Prince of Wales Road. He resided at 11, Canterbury Street and was the husband of Mary Jane Gough. Walter lies in the Communal Grave. A family member was detained in Warwick Hospital and an occupant from No 77 detained in Warneford Hospital, Leamington.

GOUGH (Walter) Treasured memories of dear husband and father who passed away. Memories are treasured no-one can steal. From his loving wife, son and daughter.

Injuries were recorded from No. 96 to No. 117 as follows; 96 (detained in Stratford-on-Avon Emergency Hospital, one treated at First Aid Post and sent home and one treated), 98 (one treated, two treated at First Aid Posts and sent home and two detained in Warwick Hospital, 100 (hospital) and 117 (two treated at First Aid Post and sent home).

Three deaths were recorded at the Alvis Works. Home Guard **Thomas Digby Jones**, 7th Warwickshire (Coventry) Bn., was aged 45. He was married to Ethel Jones, of Queensferry, Cheshire and born on the 26th June, 1895 at Abertillery. He was an Alvis employee, resided at Grosvenor Road and is buried in the Communal Grave.

Buried at Chyll Churchyard **is Edgar Inman** who was injured as a result of enemy action, at Alvis Works and died at Coventry and Warwickshire Hospital on the 15th November, 1940 aged 33. He was a Works Fireman with the Alvis Ltd. Fire Brigade and resided at 9, Melville Road. Edgar was the son of John Blades Inman, and Clara Inman, of 72, Colne Lane, Colne, Lancashire and married to Hilda Inman.

Garnet Shore, died at the Alvis Works, Holyhead Road, aged 32. He resided at 144, Fir Tree Avenue and buried outside the city at Risca Cemetery. From No. 59 one person was treated at a First Aid Post and sent home.

Four casualties occurred at Gorseway. At 28, Gorseway, **John Matthew Davis**, died aged 27. His parents were Mr. and Mrs. James Davis, of 74, Earls Road, Nuneaton and he was born close by on the 27th December, 1913 at Gun Hill, Arley. John resided at 203, Allesley Old Road and employed by Sir W. G. Armstrong Whitworth Aircraft Ltd. He is buried in the Communal Grave.

1942 DAVIS (John) In remembrance of John, Marjorie.

At 35, Gorseway **Harry Taylor d**ied at his home, aged 30. He was married to D. Taylor and born on the 5th November, 1910. Harry was employed as a Fitter, Standard Motor Co. Ltd and is buried in Grave Ref. A. 21/4. of the Communal Grave.

TAYLOR Treasured memories of my dear husband Harry. Always in the thoughts of his wife, Doris, Father and Mother (Mr. and Mrs Hutt).

Also employed at the Standard Motor Co. Ltd was **Alfred Eli Britt**, MM. He died at 37, Gorseway, aged 46. His mother was Lucy M. Mercer (formerly Britt), of 111, Liverpool Road, Reading, Berkshire. Alfred was married to Gertie and buried in the Communal Grave. From No. 20 a person was detained in Warwick Hospital

Frederick Solomon Strong was injured on the 14th November at the rear of 37, Gorseway whilst on duty as a Constable in the Police War Reserve and died aged 34 on the 17th November 1940. He was the husband of Elsie Strong, and fatally injured a short distance from his home at 43, Gorseway, Coventry. As Coventry Hospital had reached capacity, those injured were taken to surrounding hospitals. Frederick was taken to Warwick Hospital but died as a result of his injuries. Frederick was the son of Soloman and Emma C. Strong of Stepping Stones Road, Coventry and had attended Bablake from 1917 to 1922.

The Council Meeting Minutes 10th December 1940 Chief Constables Report killed during a recent air raid attack, Police War Reservist 20. On the 24th December 1940 that under the Police Pensions Act 1921 and the Special Constables Act 1923 the following widows' pension and children's allowances to be granted. Mrs Strong's pension and allowance will be a matter for the Ministry of Pensions.

Freeman of the City, **Frederick Samuel Yeomans**, died at 8, Palmerston Road aged 70. His father was Samuel Yeomans and he was born on the 7th May, 1870 at Coventry. Frederick was a Manufacturer at 48, Spon Street and buried in the Communal Grave. His death was covered locally; *"Former member of the City Council. Retired from the council some years ago after having served as a representative of Bablake Ward for six years. He was a well known watch manufacturer in Coventry, members of his family have been associated with the watch making trade almost from it's inception in the city".* One person at 45 was treated at a First Aid Post and sent home.

Ann Yardley is buried in the Communal Grave, She died at her home address of 25, Bristol Road, aged 56. Three family members were treated at a First Aid Post and sent home.

YARDLEY Ann, the beloved wife of Joseph T. and mother of Frank, Mary and Vera. Treasured memories of a gracious companion. Sadly missed.

Bristol Road had casualties at 25 to 74: No. 25 (three persons treated at First Aid Post and sent home), 27, (two persons treated at First Aid Post and sent home) and one person at 40, 53 and 63. A resident of No. 74 was detained in Warneford Hospital, Leamington Spa.

Sarah Ann Toney aged 75 died at her home, 26 Kensington Road. She was born in 1872 at Coventry and was buried in the Communal Grave. A plaque in the War Memorial Park paid for by Miss M. J. Toney, 40 Queen Victoria Road reads *'Miss Sarah Ann Toney Killed in air raid 14th November 1940'*. From 25 two people were treated at First Aid Posts and sent home.

John Roberts resided in Winifred Avenue

One of my starkest memories of the November 1940 blitz was being briefly allowed by his Father to leave our bolthole under the stairs to see the huge red burning centre of the city from our front window vantage point near the top of Winifred Avenue in Earlsdon.

Officially named as an Air Raid victim on the 23rd November 1940 was Senior Air Raid Warden, **Harold Frederick Harrison**, the local paper stated *'He conducted a manufacturers agent in Queens Road and lived at Kenilworth Road. He achieved prominence on the amateur stage having many roles and several official positions during his long association with Coventry Dramatic Society and Coventry Amateur Operatic Society'*.

Harold died as a result of enemy action age 56 at "Sunridge" 8, Kenilworth Road, his residence on the 14th November 1940 and was a Member of both the Civil Defence Wardens Service and Royal Observer Corps. Originally from London he was born on the 18th September, 1883. He is buried in the Communal Grave and his plaque in the War Memorial Park was paid for by Mrs A. D. Harrison of 227, Leamington Road. Warden Records show he was at Post 604, service No. 772 and was killed on the night of the 14th/15th November 1940 by a HE bomb. One person from No. 8 was treated at a First Aid Post and sent home at No. 65 (one person treated and one treated at Gulson Road Hospital and sent home).

HARRISON (Fred) In memory of one who put service before himself.

Husband and wife, **Albert Victor** and **Ada Lockett** died as a result of enemy action at 224, Earlsdon Avenue. Albert was aged 57, born on the 2nd February, 1883 at Leeds, worked at Alvis and is buried in the Communal Grave. Ada, aged 53, was injured and died at Emergency Hospital, Old Stratford on the 23rd November, 1940. She was born on the 4th March, 1887 at Coventry and a housewife. Records indicate she is buried in Leamington Cemetery. A further family member was treated at hospital. From Earlsdon Avenue a resident of 54 was detained in hospital of St. Cross, Rugby, No. 71 detained in Stratford-on-Avon Emergency Hospital and No. 137 detained in Stratford-on-Avon Emergency Hospital.

LOCKETT (Albert) Dear Dad loving remembered by sons, daughters-in-law and grandchildren

Richard Aldridge was nine years old living in Coniston Road.

The road backed on to Hearsall Common which was very different to the expanse of grass and fairground park that it is today. For some reason my mother had decided instead of going to the shelter we would go under the stairs that evening, a popular measure in those days. Our cubbyhole was fitted with a mattress on the floor, with extra blankets to supplement our 'siren suits' in keeping us warm. Lighting was one of those stubby candles called nightlights that you put in a saucer of water; we also had a torch for emergencies. That night I had one of my favourite possessions with me a toy searchlight, that really worked it proved rather useful!

It was soon apparent that this wasn't a routine raid, unlike the usual routine of the sound of a few bombers accompanied by some loud bangs from guns and bombs, shortly to be followed by the ALL CLEAR, the noises went on and on. To this day my blood still runs cold whenever I hear a recording of that engine noise, whilst I cannot

help but cringe when I hear the air raid sirens in a film or on the radio sounding the rising and falling wail of the AIR RAID WARNING, RED.

Wearing my 'siren suit' a hooded overall made from an old blanket by my mother, I was wedged into the narrow space where the stairs come down to the hall, next to one of those ventilator bricks through which the sounds came with great clarity. It was a tight squeeze, because two of our friends, Desmond and Gerald Carman, who lived a few hundred yards away in Earlsdon Avenue, had been visiting us when the raid started and obviously they had to come in with us.

After a while during a lull in the bombing, they set off for home, only to return some time later. They were distraught, having found their home empty and the street shelter that was just around the corner in Highland Road badly damaged with no signs of either their parents or younger brother, George. A little later they set off again, and although we didn't realize it at the time we were not to see them again for a full year. Meanwhile it seemed as if the raid would go on and on forever. The noise of the bombs and anti-aircraft guns mingled with the tinkling of the glass from our windows as they succumbed one by one to the blast from the Bofor guns at the end of the garden.

Then, at last came "our" bomb. It takes very little stretch of the imagination for me to recall that whistle of its descent, the previous raid had made me an expert by this time and I knew that this one was going to be very close indeed. For the second time in the war I thought I was about to die, and that is a very frightening thing when you are nine years old. I huddled up even tighter into the corner and waited to see what it would be like.

I don't remember the sound if the explosion at all, it was so close that I probably never even heard it, bomb blast could behave like that, but to this day the memory of the screams I heard coming from the street shelter can still bring tears to my eyes, so perhaps I was more affected by it than was believed at the time.

As we were to find the next morning, the house had received little real damage, some plaster came down from the ceiling, one or two off the doors were off the hinges and some tiles came off the roof, but nothing to render the house uninhabitable by wartime standards. However, it was quite enough to make my mother decide to get out while the going was good, and we clambered, scrambled over the mess, aided by the light from my toy searchlight, and made a run for it to seek shelter from a neighbour.

Also in Coniston Road was Tony Duffy, eight years old.

This was much the same as other nights really. I was washing in the kitchen prior to going to bed, I could hear the drone so you knew it wasn't one of ours I looked out of window and was whipped under the stairs. There was me, my mum, dad and Sister, Winifred Joyce. My brother was out as he was older and on Home Guard duty, my dad was a Home Guard as well. A shelter within about a quarter of mile took a direct hit, so that was pretty close, this blew the windows out and my dad was holding on to the under stairs door and the handle was pulled out of hand and he was blown against the wall. So it must have been a far old size. We could hear the Bofor Guns going but they stopped after a while, people said they ran out of ammunition but I think now they overheated.

I collected shrapnel like other boys but I don't remember being allowed out after that. The road had had a sprinkle of incendiaries as they were going for nearby factories. My parents got me to an old friends house in Northampton after that, my sister and mother spent a week with me in Northampton and I went to school there, it was relatively safe. I came back just before the April raids.

From 111, Broomfield Road, three members of the Marley family were killed and are buried in the Communal Grave. **Herbert** aged 56, and his two daughters, **Iris** aged 15 and **Olive Lily** aged 13. A family member was treated at a First Aid Post and sent home. At No. 6 one person treated at First Aid Post and sent home, 113 treated at First Aid Post and sent home, 141 detained in Warwick Hospital and 155, treated at First Aid Post and sent home.

The Council Meeting of the 9th November 1940 stated *'Committee membership – Non-Council Members. In pursuance of the Standing Orders the Council received nominations of the following persons (not being members of the Council) for appointment to membership of the Committees stated in accordance with the scheme governing these Committees ; and appointed the persons named below to hold office until the date when the Council appoint non-Council members to serve for 1940-1941:- Horticultural Committee Mr A. Jones, Mr. W. P. Perkins, Mr. W. T. Newlove, Mr. F. G. Randle and Mr. J. G. Witcomb'.*

The Council Meeting of the 24th December 1940 recorded for; *'Appointment of Non-Council Members of the Committee. To make appointments to fill vacancies on the following committees. Horticultural Committee M. J. G. Witcomb has died'.*

Five members of the Witcomb family were killed at 111, Beechwood Avenue, they are buried in the Communal Grave. Father and mother were **John Gregory** (47) and **Ethel** (38). The children were **Sylvia** (17), **Joan** (11) and **Christine** (7). Local reports state; *'A bomb demolished their house. Mr. Witcomb was a prominent horticulturist and seedsmen. He was regular prize-winner at big shows in various parts of the country. Ground secretary of Earlsdon LTC he was also known as a tennis player'.*

WITCOMB Loving memory of John, Ethel, Sylvia, Joan, Christine, taken away but never forgotten by dear mother, father, sister and brothers.

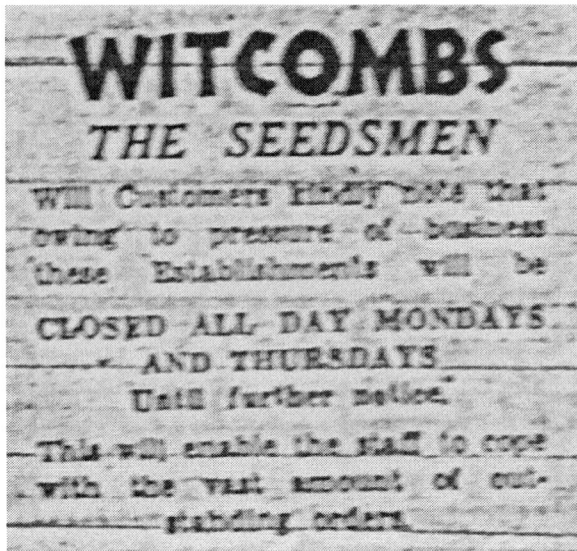

Aged 3, **Simon William Heynes**, died at 167, Beechwood Avenue. His parents were William Munger Heynes and Evelyn Heynes. Simon was buried in Milverton Cemetery. A family member was detained in Warwick Hospital and one treated at Gulson Road Hospital and sent home. From 169 one person detained in Evesham Emergency Hospital and one treated at First Aid Post and sent home.

Sergeant **Lionel Scott**, 11th Warwickshire (Coventry) Bn., Home Guard was injured as a result of enemy action on the 14th November, 1940 at Albany Road whilst on duty. He later died at Gulson Road Hospital on the 16th November, 1940. He was born on the 10th August, 1916 at Coventry to William and Ruth Scott, of 23, Vincent Street. Lionel was married to Eileen Mary Scott and resided at 191B, Albany Road. He was employed as a Fitter at Singer Motor Company and is buried in the Communal Grave.

At No. 147, **Anne Elizabeth (Dorothy) Wright**, was injured and died the following day at Coventry and Warwickshire Hospital, aged 69. She was the wife of Thomas H. E. Wright and born in August, 1871 at Melton Mowbray. Anne was a housewife and buried in Exhall (St. Gile's) Churchyard.

Beatrice Ada Mansfield and **John Osborne Jones** died as a result of enemy action at their home of 158, Albany Road, they were both in their fifties and are buried in the Communal Grave. Beatrice's parents were Rachel Jackson, of 15 , Ton Mawr Road, Blaenavon, Monmouthshire and she was a native of Abergavenny, Monmouthshire born there on the 23rd July, 1885. Her occupation was a housewife. John was the son

Thomas and Elizabeth Jones, of Dany-y-Parc, Stanhope Street, Abergavenny, Monmouthshire. He was born on the 18th October, 1883 at Talywain, Monmouthshire.

At 161a (treated at Warneford Hospital and sent home), 181a (detained in Warwick Hospital), 191a (treated), and two persons at 193c treated at First Aid Post and sent home.

Also buried in the Communal Grave are **Frances Nelly** and **Peter Robinson**. They died at 53, Mickleton Road. Frances, aged 63, was the daughter of Mr. and Mrs. Moreton and born on the 31st December, 1878 at Coventry. Peter was the Son of Daniel and Esther Robinson and was born on the 17th August, 1880 at Prescot, Lancashire. He worked at Armstrong Siddeley Motor Co. Ltd., whilst Frances was a housewife.

ROBINSON In loving memory of Nellie and Peter Ever in the thoughts of Horace, Gordon Ellen, and John, also Gertie, Will and Mary and our families

No. 60 Sir Thomas White Road

Two casualties recorded at 76, Sir Thomas White's Road was Retired Coach Builder **Arthur Edward Smith** and daughter **Phyllis Cicily Smith**. Albert was 58 and Phyllis aged 30. She was born on the 18th September, 1910 at Coventry. Father and daughter are buried in the Communal Grave.

At Sir Thomas White's Road, eleven casualties were recorded as follows: No. 35 (detained in Warwick Hospital), 54 (three detained in Warwick Hospital and one treated at First Aid Post and sent home), 76 (hospital and one treated at First Aid Posts and sent home), 78 (treated at First Aid Post and sent home) and at 160 (two persons detained at Warneford Hospital, Leamington Spa).

A plaque in Hearsall Common was paid for by Mrs. G. Elliott formerly 12 Heathfield Road then 22 East Road, Brinsford Covey, near Wolverhampton on the 11th July 1951. The plaque commemorates **David Wilson Burrows** who was injured as a result of enemy action, at 12, Heathfield Road and died at Warwick Hospital on the 17th November, 1940. He was 33. David's parents were W. D. and A. E. Burrows, of 53, Walsgrave Road, Coventry and he was married to G. Burrows. David was born on the 19th September, 1907 at Coventry and employed at Three Spires Electric Co. Records indicate he is buried in Warwick Municipal Borough.

BURROWS – In loving memory of Wilson – Marie and Frank

Next door at No. 14, **Wilfred Henry Tong**, died as a result of enemy action. His parents were William Henry and Edith Mary Tong, of Gravel, Llanbister Road, Radnorshire, Wales and Wilfred was born on the 7th December, 1911 at Llandrindod Wells. His wife was Marjorie Olive Tong and Wilfred was employed as a Aircraft Worker. Aged 29, he was buried in Wales at Gravell, Llanbister Road, Llandrindod Wells, Radnor, Wales.

Nine casualties occurred in Mount Street and all are buried in the Communal Grave. **John Alfred James**, was killed in Mount Street Shelter, aged 27. He resided at 15, Mount Street with his wife, Barbara Olive James. He was a native of Nottingham and born their on the 9th May, 1913. His parents, John Alfred and Sarah James, resided in the city at 20, Taylors Cottages, Nelton Street, London Road. John was employed locally at the Standard Motor Co. Ltd.

Seven members of the Bass family were killed at 14, Mount Street along with Air Raid Patrol, Messenger **Colin Arthur Dingley.** Warden Record show he was at Post 613, service No. 4298/M and was killed by a HE Bomb aged 18. His parents were Arthur Henry and Winifred Jane Dingley, of 62 , Queen Margaret's Road, Canley.

Sixty five year old, **Thomas William Bass** was married to **Annie Elizabeth Bass** ,aged 53 and they died along with four children and a daughter in law. She was **Doris Hilda Bass**, aged 21, the daughter of Arthur and Annie Nash who was married to Walter Thomas Bass. The couple resided at 43, Mount Street, Chapel Fields.
BASS (Doris) – Memories are treasures no one else can steal. Mum, Dad, Sisters and brothers

Thomas and Annie's children were **Joan Mary** (18), **Leonard James** (16), **George Arthur** (14) and **Clement Alfred Gordon** (12). Joan Mary was born on the 21st June, 1922 and employed at Renold & Coventry Chain Ltd. Leonard James was an Air Raid Patrol Messenger and records show his Post was 600, his number 438M and he was fatally injured by a HE bomb. Injury at No. 13 result in a detainee in Alcester Emergency Hospital and two injuries at 43, one detained in Stratford-on-Avon Emergency Hospital and one in Warwick Hospital.

BASS In loving memory of messenger J. Bass – Remembered by wardens and messengers of Posts 600 and 601

Alan Hartley was sixteen years old with Warden Post 607.

The sirens went around 6.30pm. We reported to the ARP post, and when we got down there the warden said, 'Look, it's only a purple warning, rather than a red warning.' That meant aircraft in the vicinity, rather than overhead. So he said, 'For the moment lose yourselves, but don't go far.' There were four to five ARP Messengers at Grayswood avenue, a photographer had started up in the area and we were posting leaflets through peoples doors for 6 pence a hundred. On the evenings before this we played Monopoly. Over Coundon I saw a parachute drop and I said to the guys we better get back.

All of a sudden over the north side of Coventry I saw a parachute flare, then another one to the left, then another and another, until soon the whole city was ringed by flares. Watching these flares come down filled me with dread. I knew we were being targeted. Within 10 minutes, bombs started falling in the east of the city. They were coming straight for us; it's the most terrifying experience to stand there, hearing these bombs from a distance and them getting louder and louder and louder, wondering how many have they got left and are you going to be the next one.

The Germans bombed Coventry very systematically. They bombed in straight lines from east to west, and then they started from south to north. It was like darning a sock. Just occasionally you would catch sight of a German plane, like a little moth caught in the searchlight beam. Then all of a sudden, it would fly out of the beam and the searchlights would go frantically round the sky, trying to pick it up again.

About one o'clock in the morning, one of the wardens at his post suffered a serious injury, when an incendiary exploded in his face. The man needed medical treatment and, with the telephone wires down, Alan cycled the two and a half miles into the city centre to get an ambulance. Shrapnel was falling – big, red-hot shards of shrapnel hitting the road; the searchlights were swinging; and I could see the glow in the sky as Coventry burned. Marks & Spencer was burning on one side, Woolworths on the other, the cathedral was in flames, and the air was full of brick dust, smoke and sparks. I had to carry my bike through one huge crater, but got to the town hall, from which rescue operations were being conducted. The warden, though severely burned, survived. Mrs. Whitmore the deputy warden didn't want me to go but I wanted to.

Alan was still in the centre of town when the all-clear sounded in the early hours. It was a terrible scene, the shops were burning, all the windows had gone, lamp-posts were leaning down, cars were burned out, it was chaos. To my great surprise, at six in the morning, a tea wagon arrived within minutes of the all-clear sounding and the rescue squads were queuing up and having tea.

Nearby Gladys Codling twelve years old and Joan Ince, eleven years old lived in Sherbourne Crescent.

My father in law worked at the Gas Works in Gas Street and a hole was blown in the gas tower and him and a team of men filled the hole with clay. A HE bomb dropped in the yard and caused a blast and killed some men, my father in law was badly burnt and his coat was burnt he was awarded the MBE. (Refer to Codling).

I went into town the following day with my mother and father, I don't know how we got in the bridges over the Holyhead Road was down and two houses were on fire. I will always remember the acrid smell of smoke. I was under the stairs, there wasn't much room under there so mum and dad stayed in the room in the house. My father wanted to go back for a pork pie, you can see how much we valued food, my mother said to him your not getting yourself killed for a pork pie. By the time we got back to the house after the bomb had been defused, the pork pie had gone off.

Accounts from Joan Ince (nee English).

We were evacuated on the night to Southbank Road, to Coundon School due to Unexploded Bomb they called a landmine. It landed exactly in the crescent but didn't go off, so we were evacuated for three days whilst they defused it. I was with my parents and younger brother (aged 7) when the ARP warden called out, with the whole off the crescent we had to walk to the school with just an eider down, the bombs were still raining down then. The water main had burst and was flowing down the hill, so me and my brother had to be carried over the water. On the way to the school there was a very high wall at one point we had to lay flat on the ground as a policemen yelled out 'everyone down'. The bomb landed about 50 yards away and destroyed a house in Southbank Road. In the three days in the school all I can remember eating was bit of fruit cake and some cocoa that we had been given by the WVS, we hadn't brought anything with us. It was scary I suppose, at that age you don't realize what could happen.

Father worked at the water department and went back to work in Spon End, he wanted to get his bike, officially he wasn't allowed to go but with his position he was allowed. In the end up he carried it most of the way past the rubble along the Holyhead Road and the Alvis. He went back in to supervise getting the water sorted out.

At 63 Brown's Lane, **Agnes Harriett Ince**, (Nee Steel) died as a result of enemy action, aged 46. She was the daughter of Mr. and Mrs. Steel, of Highlands, Channel View Road, Brighton, Sussex and the wife of Arthur Ince. Agnes was born on the 24th May, 1894, a housewife and buried outside the city limits at Brighton Cemetery.

The House destroyed

Arthur Ince son of Agnes.

I went to Bablake School until the 14th November 1940 and never went back. Our house was probably targeted as an Electricity Sub-Station was close to our home in Browns Lane, we think that six to seven land mines had landed in the vicinity. During the raid we took shelter underneath a table, a land mine landed nearby which completely destroyed the house which Father had built prior to the war. The explosion killed my mother, caused injury to my father and severe injuries to myself. My father was taken to Warwick Hospital and I was taken to Hollymoor Hospital in Birmingham. I suffered a fracture to the base of my skull and severed an optic nerve which caused blindness in one eye, I spent four months in Hollymoor Hospital.

I came out of hospital in February 1941 and cared for by my Aunt who lived in Wellesbourne going to Stratford Grammar School, I became an apprentice with the Standard as a metallurgical chemist. A note was made in the Bablake School Magazine that Agnes Harriet Ince also died on the 14th November at 63 Browns Lane and she was the mother of Arthur Ince. Arthur pictured with his mother, father and grandparents.

Three people at No. 69 Browns Lane were treated at a First Aid Post and sent home.

Gordon Moyes then fourteen was a close friend of Arthur Ince, Butt Lane.

We were at home with my parents and went down the shelter (parents and brother , Ken aged 19) and stopped there the whole night long, like everyone else. My father had dug a trench in the garden and covered it over with corrugated iron, we didn't have an official shelter! There were four of us in the shelter at 61, Butt Lane. It was brilliant moonlit night ideal for bombers, we stayed in the shelter till 6 o'clock the following morning.

On coming out we found the windows had been blown in and the ceiling was down. A land mine affected all the houses in Butt Lane, that was the land mine that killed Arthur Ince's mother. The all clear did not sound, people were traumatised and come out of the shelter and moved about, it was a right mess.

My father had a friend, and he took his wife and his baby son on a tandem with a sidecar attachment into the city, they were horrified. It was then arranged for all of us to be evacuated to a farm house in Meriden. They had a big room with an open fire, all seven of us stayed there. (Father, Mother, brother, fathers friend, wife and baby). The Corporation eventually replaced the windows with a canvas type material dipped in resin, it was meant to stop the wind but it didn't.

We were close friends of the Ince family, several weeks after the raid, Mr. Ince still in a state of shock with his arm in a sling came to our house asking for the whereabouts of his wife and son. Mother offered sympathy but could do no more and Mr. Ince, disconsolate, walked away, at this point. my 'Mother, burst into tears'.

Walter Cooper was aged 23 and evacuated from Dunkirk.

We were stationed in a commandeered workshops it was the 'Model Garage'. I had come back from France out of Dunkirk, that was a horrible experience on it's own for a young person. In Coventry we had the ex-naval three guns, the .37 Ack Ack guns, In Coventry there was 23 of them the same age as me see. I was a Staff Sergeant at the time, an Armament Staff officer in charge of maintenance of the guns. I was off duty but we knew from information we had that it would be Coventry that would be bombed, but not until 3.00pm that day until the Germans switched on their ray machine, Churchill didn't know until that time. I was out my wife's house in Millicent Wood at about 7.30pm when the sirens went, they came over Meriden and the Cotswolds. The first bombs they dropped were on Millicent Wood, I was upstairs in the house, I hated the shelters my wife was down the shelter with her family.

We saw the flares over Coventry, that the Germans were dropping with Heinkel 111, they were used for distance and so they could get back for the next load and then come back. A Hillman utility vehicle came to pick me up and take me back to the camp and we got a team together and went into town. The Hillman had a soft roof and was useless even against our own shrapnel, so we commandeered two Daimler buses and used those to bring people out of the shelters and away from the centre of Coventry, we only used the bottom deck as shrapnel was piercing the tops of the buses. We made six trips in and out of Coventry bring people back to the camp. The last one was at 3.30am and aircraft were still coming over. We got out of the bus at the top of Hertford Street and could see the cathedral burning, we spoke to the Provost but he wanted to stay with the Cathedral that was well alight. On the third trip we were just under the Alvis bridge, there was a Shell tanker place that stored fuel that received a direct hit and went straight up in flames, I can still see it now.

On the last trip in, the Holyhead Road was blocked with fire engines that couldn't get in and off course there was now water by this time. We had to go down the by-pass and into town on the Warwick Road. Going up Hertford Street their were bomb holes all the way and had to drive the bus around to get up to the top before coming back to camp. The following morning we put the double deckers on Windmill Hill just by the bus stop and contacted the bus company to collect the buses. The amount of ammunition fired that night was 1200 – 1500 rounds per site and that wasn't counting Bofors that was just on the 37mm. The Bofors were 30mm quick firing guns, and stationed at Packington Park and came into Coventry going around the factories whose ever turn it was, the depot that supplied ammunition to the guns was the other side of Meriden.

The following day, there were two guns based at Stoneleigh and a shell had burst in the barrel peeling it back like a banana, we had to burn the end of the barrel of with an oxy-acetylene torch to get them out.

Sheila Duffy from Oldfield Road was aged four.

I can remember being bustled under the stairs, we had a concrete shelter but mother wouldn't go in it. There was me, my brother Derek aged 13, mum and dad. Derek had a rug under the bottom step and I was on my mums lap next to the gas meter. I was young but I can remember my brother going out to look for shrapnel.

Coventry North West Injuries

At No. 89 Berkeley Road and No.10 Stoneleigh Avenue one person from each was detained in Warwick Hospital. From No. 10 Stoneleigh Avenue a further person was treated at a First Aid Post and sent home as was No. 4 Osborne Road. In Earlsdon Street three reports; No. 30 (treated at First Aid Post and sent home), No. 65 (detained in Stratford-on-Avon General Hospital) and No. 80. Providence Street didn't fair any better with two people injured at No. 18 and No. 42 Detained in Stratford-on Avon Emergency Hospital. Stanley Road incurred eight casualties; 51 (detained in Hollymoor Emergency Hospital, Birmingham), 57 (Treated at First Aid Post and sent home), 61 (one treated and one detained in Hollymoor Hospital, Birmingham), 63 (One treated and one at Hollymoor Hospital Birmingham and 67 (Two people treated at First Aid Post and sent home). Three people were treated at First Aid Post and sent home from at No. 174 Earlsdon Avenue and three from 115 Highland Road . Injuries also recorded at No. 9 Treated at Gulson Road Hospital and sent home, No. 111 treated at First Aid Post and sent home and No. 117 detained in Stratford-on-Avon General Hospital.

Three injuries at Hearsall Lane; two at 163 who were Treated at First Aid Post and sent home and on at 184 Treated at First Aid Post and sent home. One person from various addresses was reported; No.11 Collingwood Road (treated at First Aid Post and sent home), 44 Shakleton Road, 50 Kirby Road (detained in Alcester Emergency Hospital), 8 Farmen Road (treated at First Aid Post and sent home), 30 Latham Road (detained in Warwick Hospital), 9 Ludlow Road (treated at First Aid Post and sent home), 51 Melbourne Road (treated at First Aid Post and sent home), 47 Kingston Road (detained in Alcester Emergency Hospital), 20 Broadway, 53 Stanway Road (Treated at First Aid Post and sent home), 181 Broad Lane (detained in Stratford-on-Avon Emergency), 61 Harewood Road (treated at First Aid Post and sent home), 15 Billing Road (detained in Warneford Hospital, Leamington Spa), 34 Maudslay Road (detained in Hollymoor Hospital, Birmingham), 42 Turner Road (treated at First Aid Post and sent home), 24 Cranford Road (treated at First Aid Post and sent home), 12 Leyland Road (treated at First Aid Post and sent home), 4 Lake View Road, 25 Malvern Road (treated at Warneford Hospital and sent home), Fire Station, Butt Lane (Detained in Warwick Hospital), Harvest Hill Allesley (Detained in Shuckburgh Park Convalescent Hospital, Daventry), Dockers Farm, Washbrook Lane (detained in Stratford-on-Avon General Hospital) and 10 Washbrook Lane (treated at First Aid Post and sent home).

In Centaur Road 41 two people were Treated at First Aid Post and sent home one at No. 41 the other No. 51. Two people were also injured in Sovereign Road one at 175 Treated at First Aid Post and sent home the other at 218 was detained in Warwick Hospital. Four people from Newcombe Road were treated No. 2 Treated at First Aid Post and sent home and at No. 8 three people were Detained in Warneford Hospital, Leamington Spa. Close by in Spencer Avenue injuries were reported at 17 Spencer Avenue, No. 26 Spencer Avenue and at No. 77 one Detained in Stratford-on-Avon Emergency Hospital.

At Huntingdon Road No. 16 one person Treated at First Aid Post and sent home and at No. 38. Three injuries at Allesley Old Road at 148, 410 (Treated at First Aid Post and sent home), and 448 Treated at First Aid Post and sent home. From Whoberley Avenue No. 121 detained in Warwick Hospital and at 155a Detained in Warneford Hospital, Leamington. In Kingsland Avenue at No. 100 one person Treated at First Aid Post and sent home and another person from the street Detained in hospital of St. Cross, Rugby. Craven Street had three casualties, No. 74 Treated at First Aid Post and sent home No. 121 Treated at First Aid Post and sent home and No. 131 Treated at First Aid Post and sent home

In Abercorn Road one person from No. 19 was detained in Warwick Hospital and one from No. 27. In Sherlock Road one person from No. 1 Detained in Hollymoor Hospital, Birmingham, one person Treated at First Aid Post and sent home and at No. 11 one person Detained in Warwick Hospital. At No. 3 Fife Road one person Treated at First Aid Post and sent home, whilst in Oldfield Road No. 61 Detained in Alcester Emergency Hospital, No. 152 Treated at First Aid Post and sent home and at No. 155 Detained in Warwick Hospital. Sussex Road one person from No. 64 Barnsley Hall, Bromsgrove, No. 76 received treatment and one person Detained in Warwick Hospital.

Coventry North

Dennis Howard Holland, died on the 15th November, 1940 at Radford Road, aged 29. He resided at 5, Meriden Street and was born on the 24th February, 1912 at Newbury where his parents resided at George Henry and Elizabeth Holland, of 14, St. George's Avenue, Newbury. Dennis was employed at Coventry Engineering Co. Ltd and buried in the Communal Grave. Two injuries reported at No. 1, one at 193 treated Barnsley Hall, Bromsgrove, one at 248 treated at First Aid Post and sent home and one at 266 detained in Barnsley Hall Emergency Hospital, Bromsgrove.

Named locally as a victim of the air raid on the 23rd November 1940 was Station Officer **William Henry Kimberley**, aged 41 who died on the 14th November 1940 in the vicinity of Stoney Stanton Road. William was married to Ada Winifred residing at 17 Chauntry Place, Hales Street. He was born to James and Alice Kimberley, of 8. Godiva Street on the 14th October 1899 at Coventry and his obituary noted; *'He was one of the best liked officers at the Central Fire Station'*. William was buried in London Road Cemetery and has a plaque in the War Memorial Park. Appeared on the list of Retired Fire Members as dying in 1940.

Resident of 5, Stoney Stanton Road. **Reschotti Podesta**, died aged 60. She was born in 1877 at Gloucester to Lazarus and Catherine Podesta and employed in the Equipment Department of the Royal Air Force. She is buried in the Communal Grave.

PODESTA Ever in the thoughts of Ada, Victor, nieces and nephews.

From 28 Station Street a person detained in Alcester Emergency Hospital, 64 detained Barnsley Hall, Bromsgrove, 104 detained in Stratford-on-Avon General Hospital, 382 Detained in Hollymoor Emergency Hospital, Birmingham, 419 detained in Stratford-on-Avon Emergency Hospital and at 1 Wood Buildings, Stoney Stanton Road detained in Hollymoor Emergency Hospital, Birmingham .

Husband of Fanny Hobbs, **Albert Hobbs**, died at Old Church Road, aged 70. He resided at 34, Old Church Road, Bell Green and was a native of Neithrop, Banbury being born there on the 16th June, 1869. In Coventry he was employed at Charlesworth Bodies Ltd and is buried in the Communal Grave.

Warden Records show that **Charles Archer,** worked at Post 307E, service No. 2781 and was found killed on the night of the 14th/15th November 1940 at Lythalls Lane whilst on duty, aged 42. He was the son of James Archer, of 247, Kingfield Road, Foleshill and married to Lily Archer. The couple resided at 11, Bartlett Close, Lythalls Lane. Charles was born on the 11th September, 1898 at Coventry and employed locally at Courtaulds Ltd. He was buried in the Communal Grave on the 23rd November 1940.

Two people at No. 4 required treatment one at Barnsley Hall, Bromsgrove and one treated at First Aid Post and sent home. At 333 one person detained in Chadshunt Hall Auxiliary Hospital, Kineton and at 343 one person treated at First Aid Posts and sent home.

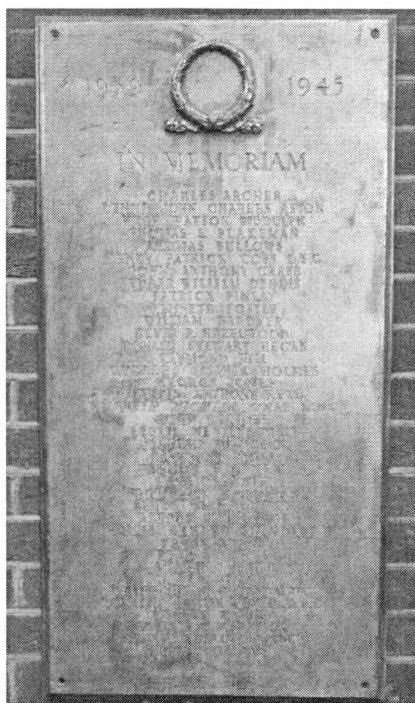

St. Pauls Memorial, Foleshill Road

ARCHER. C. – In affectionate memory of Warden Charles Archer. Loved and remembered by Peggy and little son Tony

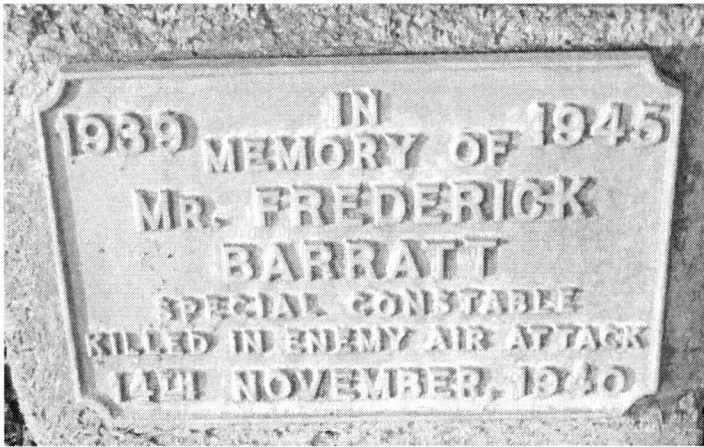

Special Constable **Frederick Barratt** died aged 50. He was the husband of Florence Barratt of 135 Poole Road. Frederick was injured at Lythalls Lane and died the same day at Coventry and Warwickshire Hospital. He was born on the 14th March, 1890, at 25 Drapers Field and worked for the Corporation as a Park Keeper. As such he is named on the Corporation Memorial in the Council House. Fredericks cremated remains were placed in a Family plot in Square No 164 Grave No.6 in the London Road Cemetery on the 29th November 1940. Ceremony performed by Edward J. Bostin from the parish of St. George in the opening of Grave No. 6. Square 164. His wife Florence remains were placed with her husband on the 5th June 1971 having lived a further 31 years with her loss.

George Barratt had purchased the plot and also interred in the plot are Sarah Jane Barratt (53) died 1918, George Barratt (68) died June 1st 1940, Ethel King died 1963 and Harry King (81) died 1971.

His plaque in the War Memorial Park paid for by his wife on the 16th February 1948 reads; *'Mr Frederick Barratt (Special Constable) Killed in air raid 14th November 1940'*. In Memoriam in 1942 Council Meeting Minutes 10th December 1940 Chief Constables Report killed during a recent air raid attack. 24th December 1940 that under the Police Pensions Act 1921 and the Special Constables Act 1923 the following widows' pension and children's allowances to be granted. Mrs Barratt £65 0s 0d p.a and children's allowance £26-0-0.

BARRATT (Frederick Special Constable) In proud and ever loving memory of a dear husband and father sailed to a higher service. Remembered always by his loving wife and children

Father and son, **Walter Henry Edwin** and **John Edwin Brown** died at their home address of 177 , Lythalls Lane. William, the husband of Kate Brown was aged 58 and their son was aged 34. William was born on the 22nd June, 1882 at Coventry and employed at Alfred Herbert Ltd. John born on the 10th May, 1906 at Coventry was employed at Rootes Securities Ltd. He was also a stretcher bearer with the ARP. Father and son were cremated at Perry Barr Crematorium and sister and aunt was a Miss G. Brown of Radford.

St. Pauls Cemetery contains a plaque for **Robert Kemble**, he died at 181, Lythalls Lane aged 78. His mother, Mrs. Kemble, resided at 3, Hinckley Road, Nuneaton although Robert was born on the 3rd February, 1862 at Devonshire. He was married to Ada Frances Kemble and his plaque was paid for by R. T. Kemble 45 Lutterworth Road, Nuneaton on the 16th September 1952. Robert is buried in the Communal Grave.

A SYMBOL OF FAITH

St. Nicholas Church, Coventry, lies in ruins but the living faith is symbolised by the wooden cross denoting where the altar stood.

Alan Hiscocks died aged 19 on the 14th November 1940 in defence of the sister church of Holy Trinity, St. Nicholas Church. Alan was the son of Francis Edward and Lillian Hiscocks of 60 Dugdale Road, Radford and born on the 29th January 1921. He attended Bablake from 1932 to 1937 and was employed by E. T. Peirson & Son accountants. The Vicar of Holy Trinity church, G. W. Clitheroe dedicated his book *'Coventry Under Fire'* to Alan (a Server of the altar) and his companions Alec McArthur (Server of the altar, aged 22), Bernard Harbourne (Server of the Altar, aged 15) and Douglas Hill (Scout aged 16) who were all killed on fire guard duty at St. Nicholas Church when it was completely obliterated by a high explosive bomb. In addition to the fatalities, the curate in charge of the fire guard, the Reverend John Lister was blinded. Alan is interred with his father, Francis Edward in Radford Cemetery, in the grounds of St. Nicholas Church not far from where he was killed and his headstone reads "*We shall remember*". He has a plaque in the War Memorial Park, paid for by his mother which reads "*Mr Alan Hiscocks Killed in air raid 14th November 1940*".

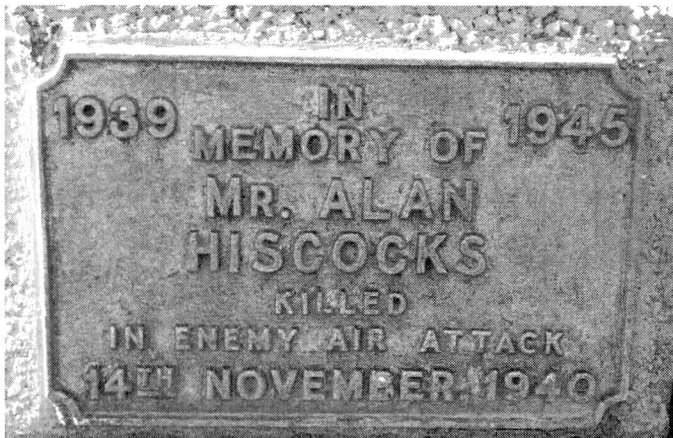

HISCOCKS – Loving memory of Allan died Radford Church. We shall remember, Frederick, Edward and mother.

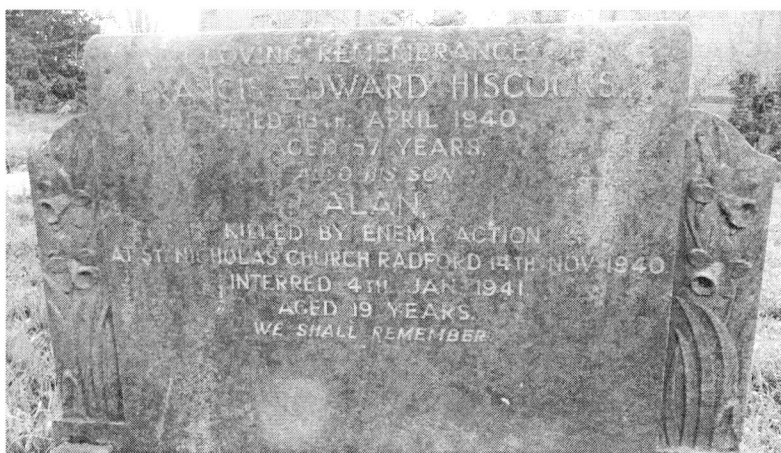

The Headstone of Alan Hiscocks

St. Nicholas Church with the passage of the Nave cleared of debris.

Bernard Harbourne and Douglas Hill are buried in the Communal Grave. **Bernard Harbourne,** was the son of Mr. and Mrs. Charles Harbourne, of 124, Moseley Avenue, Radford and born in Coventry on the 15th November, 1924 and never reached his 16th birthday. He was employed at Coventry & District Co-operative Society. **Douglas Hill,** of 70 Telfer Road was the son of James William and May Hill and born on the 4th May

1924 at Marrangaroo, New South Wales, Australia. He attended Barker Butts School and the Technical College. His mother was also killed at Telfer Road.

More tragedy came to the McArthur family with the death of **Alexander Thomas**. His father, Corporal A. McArthur was killed in action on the 20th October, 1918 during the Great War. Age 22, Alexander was a member of St. John's Ambulance Brigade and resided at 25, Lanchester Road. His mother was Florence McArthur and he was born on the 28th July, 1918 at Coventry being employed by Alfred Herbert Limited. Alexander is buried in Bedworth Church Yard.

Born on the 25th April, 1917 was **Phyllis Thomas** and she died aged 23 at 9, The Jetty, Broad Street. She was the daughter of A. and Mrs. White, of 705, Stoney Stanton Road and the wife of A. F. Thomas. Her death was a Special Procedure Case and she is interned in London Road Cemetery.

THOMAS (Phyllis) In loving memory of Phyl, taken away suddenly. Always in our thoughts Flo and Fred.

Firewatcher **Reginald Felgate**, aged 49 died and resided at 61, Broad Street. An employee of Sir W. G. Armstrong Whitworth Aircraft Limited, he was married to Florence G. M. Felgate. A native of London he was born on the 2nd February, 1891 and now rests in the Communal Grave. No. 45 Broad Street one person detained in Stratford-on-Avon Emergency Hospital, one injured at No. 120 and one detained in Stratford-on-Avon Emergency Hospital from The Jetty.

FELGATE (Reg) in loving memory of a dear husband and father. Never forgotten and sadly missed by his wife, Mavis and Leslie.

Eighteen casualties occurred at the Foleshill Union Shelter. **William Frederick Edmunds** was aged 60 and resided at 957, Foleshill Road. He was born on the 6th March, 1880 at Blaenavon and employed at Sterling Metals Ltd. He is buried in the Communal Grave and subject of a Special Procedure Case.

Plaques in St. Pauls Cemetery were paid for by Mrs W. E. Daines of 10 Goring Road and dedicated to **Ada** and **Walter Daines**. Father and daughter are buried in the Communal Grave, were on duty at the Lythalls Lane First Aid Post and resided at 89, King George's Avenue.

Ada, aged 41 was a member of the Civil Defence Warden Service. Warden records show she was at Post 307E and had Service No. 2353. Ada was born on the 7th December, 1898 at Manchester and employed at Dunlop Rim and Wheel Co. Ltd. Walter, aged 68 was born on the 28th January, 1872, at Leicester and worked as a tailor.

Aged 44, Sergeant in the Home Guard **William James Albert Dennis** died in the shelter. He was married to Hilda May Dennis, of 12, Chapel Square, Foleshill Road and born on the 20th October, 1896, working locally at Rootes Securities Ltd. William is buried in the Communal Grave. Three family member were injured, one detained in Stratford-on-Avon General Hospital, one treated in hospital and one treated at a First Aid Post and sent home.

No. 1 Chapel Square

From 870, Foleshill Road, **Mary Hannah Isitt**, died as a result of enemy action aged 27. She was born on the 14th September, 1910 at Tonypandy, South Wales. A housewife Mary was married to W. Isitt. A family member was detained in hospital of St. Cross, Rugby. Mary is buried in the Communal Grave.

Four members of the Orton family from 3, Lythalls Lane were killed and all are buried in the Communal Grave. The parents were **Olive Ida,** aged 36 and **Percy Lionel** aged 38. Housewife, Olive was born on the 26th December, 1903 at Nuneaton. Percy Lionel worked at Albion Drop Forgings Limited, his parents were Isaac and Leah Orton and he was born on the 1st June, 1901 at Bedworth. Olive and Percy's children were **Colin** aged 8 months and **Thelma** aged 10.

Elsie Marjorie Randall, died aged 23. She resided at 13, Curzon Avenue and was the daughter of Mr. and Mrs. A. J. Dwyer, of 156, Frankland Road, Croxley Green, Hertfordshire. Elsie was married to Cyril John Randall, born on the 28th November, 1917 at Willesden and a housewife. She is buried in Grave Ref. A. 19/3. Communal Grave.

Mother and daughter, **Harriet** and **Hilda May Redgate** died in Foleshill Union Shelter. Harriet was aged 68 and Hilda aged 29, they resided at 36, Victory Road, Foleshill and are buried in the Communal Grave. Father and husband was John Redgate. Harriet was born on the 1st April, 1872 at Walsall and her daughter, Hilda was born on the 13th November, 1911 at Walsall.

REDGATE Treasured memories of our dear Mother and sister Hilda – Always remembered by all.

G. E. Ruddick lost his wife, **Florence Lavinia** aged 37 and son, **Malcolm George** aged 4. The family resided 19, Beresford Avenue. Florence and Malcolm are interred in Grave Ref. I4. 4/3. Communal Grave.

Three resided of 43, King George's Avenue were killed and are buried in the Communal Grave. Employee of Websters Brick Works, **Edward Tallis** died aged 64. He was born on the 24th October, 1876. Mother and daughter, **Clara** and **Phyllis Marguerite Allport** lost their lives aged 60 and 22 respectively. Clara was the widow of Alfred Allport and born on the 16th September, 1880. Phyllis was born on the 3rd August, 1918 and employed as Clerk Typist with Alfred Herbert Ltd.

ALLPORT and TALLIS – Treasured memories of sister Clara, niece Phyllis and brother Edward Tallis – Not forgotten by Kate and family

Buried in Treorchy Cemetery, South Wales is **Harriet Mary Shillcock.** She was 36 and the daughter of William H. and Mary Floyd, of 5, Stuart Street, Treorchy, Rhondda, South Wales. She was married to Fred Shillcock, resided at 74, King George's Avenue, and born on the 22nd April, 1904 at Treorchy, South Wales. Locally she was employed as a Miller for Morris Motors Limited.

SHILLCOCK (Mary) In loving memory of my dearest wife. Sadly missed by husband Fred

Kenneth Gamble Fourteen years old Foleshill King Georges Avenue

We lived not far from the Foleshill Tram Depot at 54, King Georges Avenue. My mother and father and two sisters, Phyllis (19) and Doris (23) where under the stairs. It's strange really it started quiet early and went on all night. There was no damage to our house. My dad said to me to go and see if my older was alright in Green Lane as she had just got married and moved over there. I headed off on my bike but couldn't get down Foleshill Road, Eagle Street and Springfield Street were heavily bombed. I had to push my bike over bomb craters and God knows what! I had to push my bike all the way until I got the other side of town. It took a couple of hours to get there. They were alright, we had a couple of bombs up this end but they were OK. On the way back home, I went back up Foleshill Road, the trams used to go up there, where the bombs had hit the tram lines they were standing in the air. It was quite something really, the tram lines were about 6" to 8" thick, they were like girders just sticking out of the road.

On a prior riad, my brother, garaged his car at Masons Coalyard, Foleshill Road and a blast knocked him off his feet and killed his girlfriend Violet Howard. She was buried in Bedworth. He was blown clear and suffered a bang on his head and Violet was buried under rubble.

Being one of the main arterial roads in Coventry, casualties were recorded at business and private premises along Foleshill Road, many of the victims are buried in the Communal Grave. No Chapel Square, (treated at First Aid Post and sent home and one detained in Stratford-on-Avon General Hospital), 107 (detained in Warwick Hospital), 157, 405 (Barnsley Hall Emergency Hospital, Bromsgrove and treated at posts and sent home) 557 (treated at First Aid Post and sent home), 619, Bk 640 (detained in Warneford Hospital, Leamington), 693, 701 (detained in Hospital of St. Cross Rugby), 743 (treated at First Aid Posts and sent home), 870 (detained in Hospital of St. Cross, Rugby), 949 (treated at First Aid Post and sent home), 957 (detained in Evesham Emergency Hospital) and 1127 (detained at Hospital of St. Cross, Rugby).

Bomb damaged properties along Foleshill Road

Air Raid Warden **Raymond Moss**, died at Courtaulds, Foleshill Road, aged 41. He was a native of Handsworth, Birmingham, born on the 28th April, 1899 and married to S. B. Moss, of 138, Heath Road, Bedworth. He worked at Courtaulds Ltd.

Five deaths were recorded at Air Raid Patrol, HQ, Foleshill Road whilst they were on duty. Aged 16, **Gordon Edwards** was a Civil Defence Messenger and the son of Albert and Lillian Edwards, of 12, Proffitt Avenue, Bell Green. He was born on the 28th January, 1923, at Coventry and employed at Rover Co. Ltd. Warden Records show he was at Post 308E and No. 4663/M. Gordon was cremated at Perry Barr Crematorium and his ashes buried at St. Lawrence's Church, Foleshill.

EDWARDS – Treasured memories of our beloved son, Gordon. Loving remembered by Mum and Dad.

William Edward Hartell on the 1911 census lived with his parents, William and Ellen. He was born on the 5th September, 1905 at Northampton. The father was born in Worcester and a boot finisher, the mother born in Leicester. They where living at 133, St. Edmunds Road, Northampton and the time of his death his parents resided at 50, Cloutsham Street, Northampton.

William Edward was aged 35 and Divisional Secretary with the A.R.P he resided close-by at 2, Lythalls Lane, Foleshill with his wife, Margaret E. Hartell. On his death he was buried in Billing Road Cemetery, Northampton and Warden Records show his number was 3294 and he died due to a 'HE bomb on HQ'.

Member of the Civil Defence Messenger Service, 4226/M, **John Harry Wood Leedham** died aged just 15 on the 14th November 1940, whilst on duty at Foleshill Divisional ARP Headquarters. He resided with his parents, John Henry and May Leedham at 24 Beresford Avenue, Foleshill. John was born on the 3rd June, 1925 at Coventry and attended Junior Commercial School, Technical College. He is buried in the Communal Grave and his father paid for his plaque in the War Memorial Park that was originally destined for Foleshill Cemetery.

LEEDHAM (Harry) J. H. W. Warden Messenger Foleshill DHQ age 15 dear beloved only child of J. H. and M. Leedham, 24, Beresford Avenue- Always in the thoughts of loving mummy and daddy

Dental Surgeon **Charles William Randall**, L.D.S., R.C.S died age 60 on the 14th November 1940 as a result of enemy action. He joined the Civil Defence Wardens Service in 1939 and had achieved the level of Deputy Divisional Warden at the time of his death. He lived with his wife Hannah Kennaway Randall at 643 Foleshill Road. Charles's parents were William Langley and Annie Randall, of Spencer House, Hertford where he was born on the 11th February, 1880. Deputy Divisional Warden Randall, No. 120 is buried in the Communal Grave. A plaque application by Mr. Paul Randall, Foleshill Road was originally planned for Longford Recreational Ground and later moved to the War Memorial Park. He was named locally as a victim on the 23rd November 1940.

Air Raid Patrol, Messenger, **Dennis John Smith**, died at A.R.P. Post, Foleshill Road. His parents were Frederick John and Dorothy Alice Smith, of 39 , Benthall Road, Little Heath. He was born on the 14th July, 1926 at Coventry and resided with his parents. Dennis was employed as an Electrician, Messrs., G. Laird and is buried in the Communal Grave. A plaque was paid for by D. A. Smith, School House, Ulverscroft Road on the 16th July 1951.

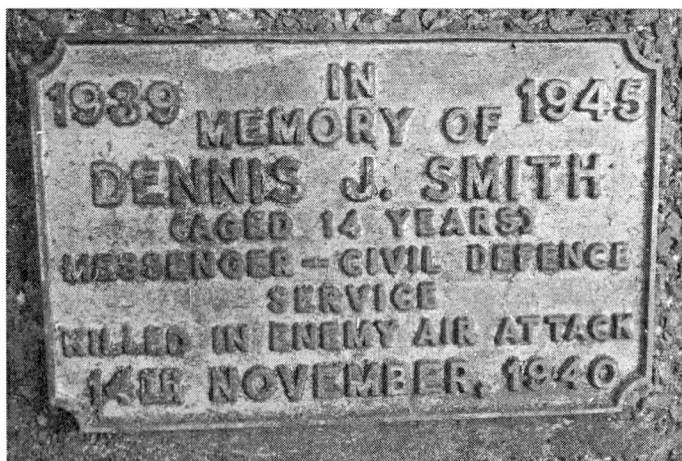

Two deaths were recorded at the Parkstone Club, 846, Foleshill Road and both are buried in the Communal Grave. They were **Bertram Barrell** and **Arthur Print.** Betram aged 47 resided at the Parkstone Club with his wife, Amy. His father, John Barrell lived at 689, Foleshill Road.

BARRELL – In affectionate remembrance of our dear brother Bert. Ever in the thoughts of his two sisters, Muriel and Gert.

Arthur Print was killed at the club but resided at 17 King George's Avenue with his wife, He was born on the 15th March, 1885 at Brinklow and worked at Courtaulds Limited.

PRINT Treasured memories of a dear husband and father who died suddenly. Always in the thoughts of his wife and family

Also buried in the Communal Grave is two members of the Price family, a family member was detained in Evesham Emergency Hospital and they were killed or injured in the shelter at the Old Foleshill R.D.C. Offices.

Delise Price, aged 39 was married to **Harold Ewart Jayne.** Price, aged 41 and they resided at 957, Foleshill Road. Housewife, Delise was the daughter of Joseph and Charlotte Elliott, of Osbourne Cottage, Keepers Road, Blaenavon, Monmouthshire and born on the 5th January, 1900. Harold was the son of William and Margaret Price, of Cwmavon Road, Blaenavon, Monmouthshire. He was born there on the 15th August, 1898 and employed Lockhurst Lane (Industrial) Co-Operative Society Ltd.

Lavinia Norman's death was recorded at the Foleshill Air Raid Shelter, aged 65. She was married to E. A. Norman and born in 1876 at Hemel Hempstead. In Coventry she resided at 38, Dunster Place and was a housewife. She is buried in Grave Ref. I5. 2/3. Communal Grave.

NORMAN (Lavinia) Treasured memory of my dear wife, killed by enemy action. Ever in the thoughts of Ethel, George, Len, Mabel and Norman

Warden Records show that **Eveline Sharrocks** from Post 307E No. 3037 was killed as a result of enemy action also at Foleshill Road Shelter, aged 29. She resided at 77, King George's Avenue, Foleshill and her father, Mr. H. Sharrocks was of 7, Fairfield Road, Southall, Middlesex. She was also buried in the Communal Grave.

SHARROCKS In loving memory of my dear sister Evelyn. Ever in the thoughts of Edith, Alice, Mabel, Marion and Jim.

SHARROCKS and ALLPORT In loving memory of Evelyn and Phyllis who entered into eternal light. Greatly missed by St. Lawrence's Bible Class.

Demolition Workers in 1942 bringing down the remains of O'Brien's

At O'Brien's Shelter, Foleshill Road, **Rosina Carvell**, died aged 68. She resided at 15, Jesmond Road and the widow of George Carvell. A housewife she was born in 1872. Her son, Mr. H. Carvell resided at Leicester Causeway. Rosina is buried in the Communal Grave.

Buried in Exhall, St. Gile's Cemetery is **Violet Grensill**, who died at Foleshill Road. Her father was John Howard, of 294, Goodyers End, Exhall and aged 22 she was married to. J. Grensill. Violet was born on the 2nd November, 1918 at Exhall and employed by Armstrong Siddeley Motors Limited.

Grave Ref. O/4. Communal Grave that was used for burials after the main internments contains **Alice Elizabeth Rooke** who died at her residence of 148, Foleshill Road, aged 77. Her parents were Francis and Sarah Garrett, of Lamb Street and she was the widow of George Rooke. Alice was born on the 30th March, 1863 at Warwick. A casualty from No. 8 Lamb Street was detained in Barnsley Hall Emergency Hospital, Bromsgrove.

Eight casualties occurred at 152, Foleshill Road, this included residents and neighbours. The main contingency were the Stubbs family. To commemorate them, two plaques were paid for in Hearsall Common by F. H. Stubbs, 9 Linden Road, Northampton at cost of £3-5-0 on the 9th February 1949.

Arthur John and **Marjorie Stubbs** are buried in Grave B. 4/2 of the Communal Grave and **Dorothy** and **Irene** in D. 4/1. Arthur, aged 63 was born on 12th February, 1877 at Northampton and employed as an Engineer, Humber Ltd. The remaining three members of the Stubbs family were daughters of Frederick Henry and Rose Stubbs. Marjorie, aged 24 was a member of the British Red Cross Society and born on the 23rd June, 1916 at Northampton. She was employed as a Clerk, Courtaulds Ltd. Dorothy, aged 23 was born on the 19th July, 1917 at Northampton and employed by General Electric Co. Ltd. The youngest daughter, aged 19, Irene was born on the 13th June, 1921 at Northampton. She was an employee of Messrs. Rotheram & Sons Ltd.

71 year old, Housewife **Elizabeth White** died as a result of enemy action. She was the wife of Thomas White and born on the 4th December, 1869 at Northampton. Buried in the Communal Grave she is also commemorated in Hearsall Common.

Thomas, her husband plaque is missing from Hearsall Common. He was aged 67, retired and born in 1874 at Sysesham. Thomas is buried in the Communal Grave.

Neighbours from 154, and 155 were lost at 152 Foleshill Road both lie in the Communal Grave. **William James Hughes**, died aged 47. She was the husband of Annie Jane Hughes and born on the 1st July, 1893 at Trelewis and found on the 19h November 1940.

Born on the 23rd January, 1885 at Orleans, America as **Frederick Robinson** and he died aged 55. He resided at 155, Foleshill Road and the son of James Norfolk Robinson, and Harriet Robinson, of 24, Regent Street, Shipley, Yorkshire. In Coventry he was employed as a Time Clerk at Courtaulds Ltd.

At 154, **Clara Ward** died alongside **Harold Benjamin Hughes.** Clara, aged 66 was born on the 30th January, 1873 and buried in Grave Ref. I6. 4/1. Communal Grave. Harold was born on 1st September, 1887 and is buried in Grave Ref. I.6. 2/2. Communal Grave.

WARD (Clara) In loving memory of a devoted wife and mother, died November 14th 1940. Ever in the thoughts of Dad and Family. (Jim, Amy, Cis, Handel, Pop, Bill, Ben and Braith).

Although a resident of 156, **John Tansey** died at 154, Foleshill Road. He was aged 39 and the son of Mr. and Mrs. A. P. Tansey. John was married to Mary Tansey and buried in the Communal Grave. At 155, **William Henry Guest** lost his life aged 80 and lies in the Communal Grave,. He was born on the 13th December, 1860 at Northampton.

The plaque for members of the Beasley family was originally in Longford Recreational Ground but over time was moved to the War Memorial Park. It was paid for by Mrs. E. Beasley, 15 Mellowdew Road, Wyken. With three names it reads *'Mrs Dorothy Beasley Barbara Beasley 4 Arthur Leonard Beasley 3 Killed in air raid 14th/15th November 1940'.* The family died as a result of enemy action at 156 Foleshill Road. Their father and husband was Mr. L. S. Beasley. All members of the family were born at Coventry. **Arthur Leonard Beasley** was born on the 28th November,1937, his older sister **Barbara Beasley** was born on the 11th October 1936 and their mother **Dorothy Beasley** was born on the 9th August, 1914. The family are buried in the Communal Grave.

Stephen and **Isabella Steele**, also died at 156, Foleshill Road they were both aged 52. Isabelle was a housewife and Stephen employed at Rootes Securities Ltd. They are buried in Grave Ref. . I6. 3/1. and D. 4/1. Communal Grave.

The Butterfields and Lewin were lost at No. 158. Salesman **Alfred,** aged 55, was married to Housewife Dorothy Elizabeth aged 59 and they are both buried in the Communal Grave. **Alec Edward Lewin**, age 42 was married to **Gertrude Emily Lewin** aged 44. He was the Son of William and Annie Selena Lewin, of 9, Carmelite Road and employed at Morris Motors Ltd. Getrude was the daughter of Frederick Cross Cumberlidge and Gertrude Cooper Cumberlidge and employed by Alfred Herbert Ltd. They are buried in the London Road Cemetery.

LEWIN –In loving memory of Alec and Getrude. Ever in the thoughts of Dad, Mum, Arthur, Eunice and Doris

Young married couple, **Ada** and **William Malcolm George Sinclair**, died at 405, Foleshill Road. Ada was 20 and William aged 21, they are buried in Bubbenhall Cemetery.

SINCLAIR (nee Ingram) In loving remembrance of dear Ada and her darling husband Malcolm – Ever in the thoughts of her Dad, sisters and brothers.

Next door at 407, **Annie Wiseman**, died aged 25. Annie was the daughter of John and S. Carlin, of 127, Middlecotes, Tile Hill and the wife of Richard Wiseman. She was born on the 12th November, 1914 at Londonderry and a housewife. Annie is buried in the Communal Grave.

The remains of 409 Foleshill Road

159

Dying of his injuries at the Hospital of St. Cross, Rugby was 54 years old, **Alfred Eaton**. He was married to Elizabeth Eaton and resided at the back of 640, Foleshill Road. Alfred was born on the 3rd December, 1885 at Weston-under-Weatherley, Leamington Spa and employed with Coventry Corporation, Gas Works. He has a grave reference of Lockhurst Lane Cemetery.

EATON (Alfred) In loving memory of my dear husband, Alf. From his loving wife, Lizzie.

15 year **Wesley Allen Edmunds,** died at 949, Foleshill Road. He was born in 1925 at Birmingham to Mr. & Mrs. M. B. Edmunds. The connection with Birmingham, saw him buried in Yardley Cemetery.

EDMUNDS In treasured memory of our beloved son, Wesley. Ever in the thoughts of loving mother and dad.

Foleshill Road

Born on the 11th September, 1876 at Leamington Spa was **Elizabeth Collingridge** and she died as a result of enemy action age 64 on the 14tH November 1940 at 36 Lawrence Saunders Road. This address was also where she resided with her husband, Bernard Collingridge. Elizabeth is buried in the Communal Grave. A plaque in the War Memorial Park was paid for by G.M Taylor of 57 Lavender Avenue and reads *'Mrs Elizabeth Collingridge Killed in air raid 14th November 1940'*. One person from No. 10 detained in Warwick Hospital.

COLLINGRIDGE (Elizabeth) Treasured memories of a dear wife and mother, who was killed by enemy action. Remembered always by her loving husband, also daughters, Rosie, Gladys and Hilda and sons-in-law Bert, Jack and Bill, also grandchildren Tony, Julie, Terry and David.

Nellie Cramp, died at Freehold Street she resided at No. 72 and her mother was W. L. Cramp. Born on the 19th March, 1926 at Coventry she was just 14 years old and employed at Goodwin Foster Brown Ltd. Nellie is buried in the Communal Grave.

Buried in Baginton Churchyard is **Walter William Watson** killed by enemy action age 72 on the 15th November 1940 at 40 Moseley Avenue where he also resided. He was born on the 17th April, 1868, at Helidon, near Daventry and his plaque paid for by D.E Watson of 40 Moseley Avenue; . Walter was named as a victim on the 23rd November 1940 and his obituary noted *'Secretary to Coventry Diocesan Conference. Prominent workers of St. Johns Church, Coventry and a tribute to his services paid by the Bishop of Coventry (Dr. Mervyn Haigh) yesterday at a conference of Coventry Clergy'.*

S. F. Haines of 56 Rutland Street, Leicester paid for a plaque on the 5th June 1951 to commemorate **Albert Thomas Woodfield** and **Frances Zena Woodfield** who died and resided at 133, Moseley Avenue. Albert aged 33 was born on the 15th January, 1908 at Coventry and employed as a Wages Clerk, Standard Motor Co. Ltd. Housewife Frances Zena, aged 35 was born on the 16th August, 1905 at Leicester. They are buried in Welford Road Cemetery, Leicester. Four residents treated at hospital, two detained in Warneford Hospital, Leamington Spa and one in Warwick.

Gerald Patterson 39 Cedars Avenue thirteen years old.

My Dad had come over to Coventry from Northern Ireland to get work and we followed him over later. I went to Christ the King School. We were in an Anderson Shelter at the back of the house. There was me, my brother (Joe), two sisters (Mary and Lily) and my mother. My dad was working in the Part Store at Siddeley and he hadn't come home by the time the raid started. The door of the shelter was blown in on top of us, and I can remember my mother roaring and shouting to make sure we were alright. The next door neighbour, Mr. Thompson from Northern Ireland came over to check we were alright, (his children had already gone back to Northern Ireland), Ma shouted to him, 'What about the houses, Mr. Thompson ?', he replied "You won't have to worry about cleaning your windows, Mary?".

Father came back from Siddeley and was delighted to see his family. Bombs had come down, the parachute aerial mines and had blown the windows in, plaster of the ceiling and tiles of the roof. When you stood in the house you could look up through the roof. I can still hear the sound of the tiles falling of the roof when we were in the shelter. In the house the window frames as well as the windows were blown in and bits of glass were stuck all over the wall, the porcelain white sink also had glass stuck in and the lead water pipe were full of glass. The back door had been blown in to the front door and the lino had been torn up off the floor.

We were send back to Limerick about a week after that. I never came back to Coventry until almost seventy years later.

Warden Records show at Post 200 Warden Number 1761, Doris Lampitt of 12 Crampers Field death was caused by explosion of land mine outside Crampers Field Shelter whilst on duty, aged 45. In addition to a warden she was the Proprieties of The Wool Shop, Crampers Field. Her parents were Henry and Mary Lampitt, of Station House, Fladbury, Pershore, Worcestershire. Where she was born on the 24th September, 1896. The association with Fladbury continued in her death as she is buried at the local cemetery.

LAMPITT In loving memory of warden Doris Lampitt who died in the service of others. Always remembered by Mr. and Mrs. Knight and family

Father and daughter, **William** and **Mavis Evelyn Newson**, died at 16, Crampers Fields. Their wife and mother was Hannah Newson. Air Raid Warden, William was aged 62 and born in August, 1880 at London, he worked as a Chimney Sweep. Mavis, aged 25 was born in June, 1913 at Sheffield and employed General Electric Co. Ltd. They are both buried in the Communal Grave. At No. 20 Crampers Field one person was detained in Warwick Hospital.

NEWSON (Cramper's Field) Mavis and her father - Fondly remembered by the Millward family also Sec .2 3 GEC late of Whitefriars

Four members of the Briers family were killed at No. 18, a mother and three children , they rest in Gilroes Cemetery, Leicester. **Jessie Briers**, aged 39 was the daughter of Frederick William and Lillian Appleby, of 27, Abingdon Road, Leicester and the wife of Lewis Harold Briers. She was born on the 8th March, 1901 at Leeds and a housewife.
Alan aged 6. was born on the 4th November, 1934, at Coventry and attended Radford School. **Doris Jean** aged 10 was born on the 6th November, 1930 and attended Barker Butts School. **Sheila Lillian** aged 12 was born on the 11th November, 1928, at Coventry attended Wheatley Street School and died just after her twelfth birthday.

Joan Willoughby resided in Poole Road.

On the night of the 14ᵗʰ November 1940 I got home from work about 5.30pm from the Humber Works using the inner circle from Gosford Street it used to stop near the house. I remember thinking it was a beautiful bright night. I had my tea and went to the Radford School Shelter about 6.30pm as we felt something big was going to happen. It was me, my mum, the next door neighbour, the neighbours baby and their dog. My dad and the next door neighbour were on air raid duty. The shelter had bench seats against the walls and was divided into various parts, they were 30 – 40 people in our area squashed up and probably about the same in the other part.

When we came up the street, what a mess! All the windows were blown out and the curtains were pitted. Two houses at the junction of Lawrence Saunders Road and Poole Road had been hit by a land mine and our house and other houses had got the blast from it. The house were up but badly damaged, the houses at the end of the street weren't damaged so much. In the shelter we never thought it was as terrible as it was and then you started thinking who was alive and who wasn't.

After that we went to Leamington for a while, but mum used to go back and check how the house was coming along. One day mum went back and found the Corporation men having sandwiches in the living room, she was bit upset by that. We got back in just before the April Raid, we had our lives and that was OK, people were very kind in those days.

Standard Motor Co. Ltd employee and Home Guard **Harold Bullock** was killed age 40 at Three Spires Avenue near his home at No. 52. He was married to Ada and originally came from Manchester being born on the 5ᵗʰ July, 1900. He was buried in London Road Cemetery. He wife paid for his War Memorial Park plaque. He was subject of a Special Procedure Case and a family member was treated at a first aid post and sent home.

From 66, Three Spires Avenue, **William Arthur Jones**, died at Three Spires Avenue, aged 26. He was the son of Evan John and Harriet Jones, of 44, Napier Road, Cowley, Oxfordshire. A Special Procedure Case he is buried in London Road Cemetery.

A Plaque in Hearsall Common was paid for by a Miss E. S. Roberts, 10 Lloyd Street, Caerau, Bridgend, Glamorgan on the 17th July 1951.Also at Three Spires Avenue was **Herbert William Roberts**, aged 27. He resided at 19, Three Spires Avenue and his parents were Hugh and Ann Roberts, of 10, Lloyd Street, Caerau, Bridgend, Glamorgan, Wales where he was born on the 11th September, 1913. A bricklayer, he was also a Special Procedure Case and has a Grave Reference of Coventry, County Borough.

ROBERTS In loving memory of Herbert also Herbert Bausor who passed away, always in our thoughts of Bunny and Bert

The son of Mr. and Mrs. Edward Sear of 38 Cedars Avenue, Member of Civil Defence **Stanley Arthur Sear,** was killed by enemy action age 25 on the 14th November 1940 and subject to Special Procedure Case. He resided with his wife, Kathlyn E. Sear at 40, Middleborough Road. Stanley was born in Coventry on the 1st September 1915 and employed as a gas fitter with Coventry Corporation Gas Department. He died at Three Spires Avenue and is buried in London Road Cemetery. The plaque was paid for by Mrs E. F. Sear on the 18th February 1949 and reads *'Mr Stanley Arthur Sear Civil Defence Service Killed in air raid 14th November 1940'.*

Resident of 19, Three Spires Avenue, **Herbert Bausor,** died aged 39 with the Auxiliary Fire Service and a Special Procedure Case. He was the son of Harry and Eliza Bausor, of Spon End and the husband of Gladys May Bausor. He has a plaque in Hearsall Common and a Grave Reference of Coventry, County Borough. Plaque was paid for on the 21st July 1951 by his wife.

BAUSOR (Bert) – In loving memory of my dear husband who passed away in tragic circumstances also Rob, ever remembered by wife and children, Derek and John.

ROBERTS In loving memory of Herbert also Herbert Bausor who passed away, always in our thoughts of Bunny and Bert

Three members of the Williams family died and resided at 23 , Three Spires Avenue they are buried in the Communal Grave. **Mary Ann Williams,** was the eldest at 58. She was the widow of Llewellyn Williams. And born on the 12th February, 1882 at Coventry. Housewife **Catherine Nora** her daughter was aged 31, the wife of **John Emlyn Williams** and born on the 14th August, 1908 at South Wales. John was also killed, the son of Mr. and Mrs. Williams, of Cadoxton, Neath, South Wales.

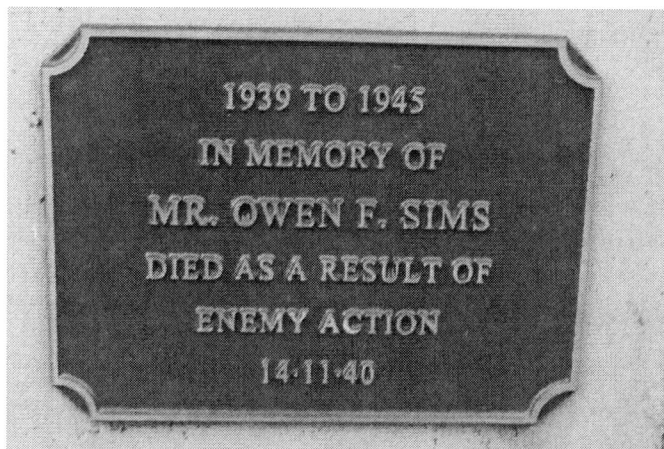

Also killed at Three Spires Avenue, was **Owen Francis Sims**, age 71 who resided at No. 25 where he was killed. Owen was born on the 12th March, 1869 at Highgate, London and was retired. He is buried in the Communal Grave, and his wife, Mrs. Alice Maria Sims paid for his War Memorial Park plaque on the 18th March 1949 *'Mr. Owen F. Sims Died as a result of enemy action 14th November 1940'*. At this point she was residing at Engleton Road.

A plaque in Hearsall Common, was applied for by Mr. H. Holland, Jesmond, Needlers End Lane, Balsall Common on the 5th June 1951. Almina and Raymond resided at 27, Three Spires Avenue, Almina was 15 and Raymond aged 23. They were the children of Harold and Grace Holland. Almina was born on the 19th April, 1925 at Coventry and employed by Alvis Ltd. Raymond was born on the 30th April, 1917 at Coventry and employed by the General Electric Co. The siblings are buried in the Communal Grave.

HOLLAND Treasured memories of Almina and Raymond who passed to a better world. Ever in the thoughts of mum, dad and Desmond.

Robert Wilton Wood, at 56 was killed aged 30. His parents were Mr. and Mrs. Reuben Wood, of 66, Newhey Road, Milnrow, Rochdale, Lancashire and he was taken to Milnrow Cemetery for burial. A family member was detained in Warwick Hospital, one treated in Warneford Hospital and sent home and one treated at First Aid Post and sent home.

Seven year old**, Maureen Patricia Morrell**, died at 58, Three Spires Avenue. Her parents were Mr. and Mrs. Patrick Joseph Morrell and Mary E. Morrell and she was born on the 9th August, 1933 at Kenilworth. Maureen attended Barker Butts School and is buried in Kenilworth Cemetery. Five family members were treated at First Aid Posts and sent home. The family also lost Gunner, Robert Henry Morrell who died on active service, 19th General Hospital, Middle East Force, on the 22nd December, 1941.

MORRELL In loving memory of our Maureen The hearts that loved you never forget – Mam, Dad, Sisters, brothers,. Also never forgotten by Mary

.

Injuries were obtained at 31, 52, 56, 58, 62, 68 and 152 most which were treated at First Aid Post and sent home.

'Barrs Hill School Magazine' read *'Our deepest sympathy goes out to the parents and friends of the pupils and five Old girls who died as a result of enemy action over Coventry Doris Scott (1936 – 1939) died November 14th 1940'.*

Father and daughter were killed at 12, Addison Road. **Doris** (17) was born in 1922 at Wolverhampton, educated at Barr's Hill School and employed by Rotherham & Company Limited. Father **Frank** was married to Laura Scott, and injured he later died at Warwick Hospital on the 17th November, 1940. He was born in 1898 at Birmingham and employed at Armstrong Siddeley Motors Limited. Father and daughter are buried in St. Phillips Church Yard, Wolverhampton. From No. 12 a person was detained in Warwick Hospital and one person from 14 received treatment.

SCOTT Treasured memories of my dear Husband and daughter, Frank and Doris who died by enemy action. Missed and longed for by a sorrowing wife and mother

Next door at No. 14 a mother and daughter were killed **Rose** and **Josephine Ann. Smith.** Rose was injured and died the same day at Coventry and Warwickshire Hospital aged 26. Josephine aged 3 was killed. They were the daughter and wife of T. N. Smith and both are buried in the Communal Grave.

SMITH In loving memory of my dear wife, Rose and daughter Ann. Ever inn the thoughts of husband and family.

Ron Suddens 17 years Old, Lock Close, Keresley

I was at home when it happened it was bright moonlit night a bit on the frosty side. One bomb dropped in the street, a small one mind, that just blew the windows out. A large one killed some people in a house nearby, one of the indiscriminate ones landed where Addison Road joined Scotchill. I knew the girl that was killed, she was in her teens. I had father who was a fatalist, if it's got your name on it your get it that's how he got through World War 1. He was at the Somme so you can imagine.

We were on the outskirts so we didn't get it as bad. I went into town the following morning, we didn't stay off course it was absolute wreck. Round about the Rialto cinema had it bad too and it was in that area when I saw the King when he came to inspect the damage. I joined the RAF less then a year later in September 1941.

William Thomas Clarke died and resided at 6, The Scotchill, Keresley. His parents were William Henry and Annie Clarke, of the Elms Farm, Appleby Magna, Burton Upon Trent, Staffordshire and he was married to Mary Clarke. William is buried in the Communal Grave. His War Memorial Park plaque was paid for by Mrs M. Nutt 6 The Scotchill Keresley and reads *'Mr. William Thomas Clarke Killed in air raid 14th November 1940'*. A supplementary added to the application noted *'Not red cherry tree preferred'*.

Eileen Mary Clarke, died at Warwick Hospital on the 16th November, 1940, aged 25. She died at 6, The Scotchill and resided at 4, The Scotchill, Keresley, Coventry. She was the daughter of Mrs. E. Cotton, of 107, Kingston Road, Earlsdon and the wife of Kenneth Stockley Clarke. Her grave reference is given as Warwick Municipal Borough.

Housewife **Hilda May Partington** was interned in the Communal Grave she died at 8, The Scotchill, aged 27. She was the daughter of Oliver and Sarah Pickard, of 106 , Station Street East and the wife of Norman Partington. Hilda was born on the 4th August, 1914 in Coventry and the brother of Syd Pickard. One person at No. 6 detained in hospital.

PARTINGTON (nee Pickard) In loving memory of Hilda. Ever in the thoughts of Norman, Mam and Dad, and Syd, Wife and family

Mother and son, **Kate** and **Christopher Patrick Dawson**, died as a result of enemy action at 58, Telfer Road. The father and husband was Harry Dawson. Kate, a housewife, aged 40 was the daughter of Richard and Hanna Stephenson, of Hutton Buscel, West Tyton, Scarborough, Yorkshire and born their on the 22nd January, 1901.
Age 11, Christopher was also born at Hutton Buscel, Nr Scarborough on the 8th March, 1927. A schoolboy he attended Barker Butts School. Mother and son are buried in the Communal Grave.

At No. 70, Telfer Road, further tragedy came to James William Hill with the death of his wife, **May.** Their son, Douglas was killed at St. Nicholas Church. May died at 62, Telfer Road, aged 49. She was born on the 31st May, 1892, at Heywood, Lancashire and buried in the Communal Grave.

From Houldsworth Avenue, 18, 21, 25, 26, 32, 33, 34 and 39 were either treated at First Aid Post and sent home, detained in Stratford-on-Avon Emergency Hospital, detained in Hospital of St. Cross Rugby, detained in Evesham Emergency Hospital and detained in Warneford Hospital, Leamington.

Four civilians were killed in an Anderson Shelter at 26, Houldsworth Avenue, Exhall and all are buried in Bedworth. **Frederick Holt** was aged 35. One family member was detained in Stratford-on-Avon Emergency Hospital and one in Evesham Emergency Hospital. G. W. Howells lost his wife, **Winifred May Howells**, aged 37 and his children, **Keith** aged 2 and **Royston Charles** aged 9.

A plaque in London Road Cemetery was paid for by Mrs J. H. McGarrity, 22 Canning Place Glasgow on the 13th March 1948 for her husband, **Michael McGarrity**. He died and resided at 49, Dunster Place He was aged 40. His parents were James P. and Janet McGarrity, of 22, Canning Place, Townhead, Glasgow, Scotland where he was born on the 25th March, 1900. Buried in the Communal Grave, he worked at the Humber Ltd.

Injuries recorded at 53 detained in Nuneaton Hospital, 74 detained in Warwick Hospital, 76 treated at First Aid Posts and sent home, 84 treated and one person detained in hospital of St. Cross Rugby.

Mary Porter, died aged 76 at 2, Edgwick Road this was also her residence. She is buried in Grave Ref. A. 20/4. Communal Grave.

Two fireman were killed at the Rover Company Ltd, Helen Street and both are buried in the Communal Grave and have plaques in the War Memorial Park. Station Officer **William Alfred Edward Jackson**, aged 57 was married to E. Jackson residing at 125 Oliver Street and has a plaque in the. Fireman **Frederick Neville** died age 45 and was born in 1895 at Bond Street. He was also a resident of Oliver Street.

JACKSON Station Officer Bill Killed by enemy action Ever remembered by his Fire Brigade Colleagues.

NEVILLE (Fireman Fred) Killed by enemy action. Ever remembered by Fire Brigade colleagues

At 81, Smith Street, **William Henry Jones**, died aged 38. He resided at 81, Smith Street and was the son of Mrs. E. Vickers (formerly Jones). Found on the 14th November 1940, he is buried in the Communal Grave. No. 16 treated, 24 detained Barnsley Hall Emergency Hall Bromsgrove, 67 detained in Barnsley Hall Emergency Hospital, Bromsgrove and 79 detained in hospital of St. Cross Rugby.

JONES (William Henry) In memory of my dear friend Bill Remembered by Mr. and Mrs. Vickers and family. In silence we remember.

Mother and daughter, **Florence Yates** and **Elizabeth Yates**, died at 64, Cromwell Street and both are buried in the Communal Grave. Florence aged 59 was born in June, 1883 at West Bromwich and a housewife. Elizabeth was born on the 31st December, 1922 at Coventry and employed by General Electric Co. Ltd, aged 18. Arthur Yates was the husband and father.

Charles John Lewin, was injured at No. 66 and died at Emergency Hospital, Old Stratford within Stratford Upon Avon on the 17th November, 1940, aged 70. He was the Husband of Louisa Lewin and is buried in the Communal Grave. A family member was treated at a First Aid post and sent home.

Civilian **Charles Jennings** died as a result of enemy action age 71 on the 27th January 1941. He was the husband of M. J. Jennings of 72A Cromwell Street, Coventry where he was fatally injured on the 14th November 1940 at his home address. Charles died at Hollymoor Emergency Hospital, Northfield, Birmingham and it is known that a number of casualties from Coventry were treated here for wounds. Charles was born on the 25th April 1869 at Court House Green Coventry and employed by Maudslay Motors Ltd. He is buried in St. Paul's Cemetery, Foleshill, Coventry. A family member was treated at a First Aid Post and sent home.

His plaque in the War Memorial Park was paid for by his wife who had by 1948 moved to 1 Norman Place Road, the plaque reads *'Charles Jennings Mr Died from injuries received in air raid 27th January 1941'*. An additional note added *'Request copper birch tree if not silver birch tree'*. Form No. 66 one person treated at First Aid Post and sent home and one person detained in Stratford-on-Avon General Hospital.

Amongst the names on the Civil Defence Roll of Honour for Alfred Herbert is **Dennis** and **Edward George Brown**. The Roll notes Brown, *'D. Not an employee but assisting his brother, E. G. Brown'*. They both died at Alfred Herbert's Fire Station, Cross Road, lived at 54, Beacon Road and were the sons of Albert Brown. Dennis, aged 19 was born on the 14th February, 1919 at Wheelwright Lane, Exhall and employed by the Standard Motor Company Ltd. Edward George a 16 year old Messenger with the Works Fire Service was born on the 19th December, 1922 at 102, Whitmore Park Cottages. Both brothers are buried in the Communal Grave. The Alfred Herbert Roll reads *'Brown, Edward George Age 17 Service Works Messenger Department Foundry'*.

Works Fireman **Frank Richardson** was killed in the Fire Station at Alfred Herbert Ltd, whilst on duty age 19 on the 14th November 1940 and was listed in the firm's Roll of Honour as Civil Defence Works Messenger Fire, Foundry Department where he worked as a wood pattern maker,. He was the son of Samuel and Lucinda Richardson of 22 Keresley Green Road, Keresley although he was born at Accrington, Lancashire on the 5th July 1921. Frank is buried in the Communal Grave and has a plaque in the War Memorial Park.

RICHARDSON To the memory of Frank our dear son who gave his life (on duty). From mother, father and Leslie (on service)

Also killed at Alfred Herbert's Fire Station whilst on duty was **Frederick Arthur Morris**, Works Auxiliary Fireman was employed in the Grinding Department. His parents were T. S. and S. A. Morris of 5 Poddycroft Terrace, Rudge Road where Frederick also resided. Frederick had just turned 20, he was born on the 3rd September 1920 at Coventry and is buried in the Communal Grave.

MORRIS (Fred) In ever loving memory of Fred – Never forgotten by Mother, Dad, brother and sisters, also Jim, Frances, Edna and nephew, Brian.

The third death was that of **Richard John Richardson** aged 40 who died at Alfred Herbert's Works, Cross Road. Richard was the husband of Violet Jane Richardson, of 662 Sewall Highway, Bell Green and was employed as an inspector in Detail Inspection Department and joined the Works Fire Brigade on the 31st July 1940. A native of Birmingham he was born on the 9th November 1900 and was buried in the city at Handsworth Cemetery.

RICHARDSON (Fireman) In loving memory of my dear husband Richard John Ever in the thoughts of his wife and children.

The Civil Defence Roll of Honour for Alfred Herbert reads *'Robbins, Peter Edgar Age 16 Service Works Spotter Department Fitting'* he died whilst on duty. Peter resided at 42, Moat Avenue, Green Lane and was the son of Squadron Leader A. S. Robbins, R.A.F. He was born on the 22nd March, 1923 at Leamington Spa and cremated at Perry Bar Crematorium.

ROBBINS – With many very treasured memories of our dear beloved and loving son, Peter (aged 16 years and 8 months). Love and remembrance from Daddy, Mummie and Thelma at Marji House, Alness, Ross Shire, Scotland

Mother and son, **Ethel Frost** and **Leonard Frost** died as a result of enemy action on the 15th November 1940 at the family's home at 62 Cross Road and both are buried in the Communal Grave. Ethel aged 48 was the wife of S. P. Frost, and their son Leonard was born on the 28th August, 1928, at Coventry and attended Broad Street Boys School. The plaque in the War Memorial Park was paid for by J.C. Frost of 576 Allesley Old Road and reads *'Mrs Ethel Frost killed in air raid 14th November 1940 Leonard Frost 13 years killed in air raid 14th November 1940'.* Mother and son had stayed at home as Leonard was not feeling well and sheltered under the stairs.

Ellen Whitwood daughter stated "*I had just got married so we didn't know what was going on the other side of town. The following day I rescued a photograph that was burned around the edges of Leonard Morris who was killed in The Great War*".

FROST – In loving memory of our dearest mother, Ethel and little brother, Leonard. Sadly missed by Dad, Jack, Ellen, Sue, George and Harry.

Resident of 243, Cross Road, housewife **Elizabeth Faulkner** died aged 65 and her husband, **William Joseph** aged 67. They are both buried in the Communal Grave.

In Cross Road at 66 one person detained in Warwick Hospital, 121 treated at Works First Aid Post and sent home, 147 detained in Evesham Emergency Hospital and 181 detained in Nuneaton Hospital, Chilvers Coton.

Council Meeting Minutes 10th December 1940 Chief Constables Report stated that **Albert Ernest Bawden** was killed during a recent air raid attack. 24th December 1940 that under the Police Pensions Act 1921 and the Special Constables Act 1923 the following widows' pension and children's allowances to be granted. Mrs Bawden £60 13s 0d p.a and children's allowance £12-3-0.

Special Constable **Albert Ernest Bawden**, was injured as result of enemy action, at Red Lane died same day at Coventry and Warwickshire Hospital on the , 14th November, 1940. He was aged 38, a bricklayer and the son of Ernest John and Elizabeth Bawden, of 138, Stoney Stanton Road. Albert was the husband of Florence Bawden, of 13, Newdigate Road and born on the 8th October, 1902 at Coventry. He received a Posthumous Commendation by HM the King for brave conduct in Civil Defence. A plaque in Stoke Heath was paid for by H. J. Bawden 92 Blackberry Lane on the 27th August 1949 and he is buried in the Communal Grave.

Reported locally *'Bawden, Albert Ernest. (deceased), Special Constable, Coventry Special Constabulary. 25th February 1941. National Commendation for work prior to this death in an air raid. Married man, member of the mobile section, B Division, Special Constabulary. He went out time after time, returning from incidents under the most hazardous conditions of danger. He was a gallant man and set a high example to others by complete disregard for himself. A partner in a firm of decorators, Special Constable Bawden is believed to have met with his death when the car he was driving crashed in a bomb crater and another bomb fell alongside'.*

BAWDEN (Albert, Special Constable) In ever loving memory of my dear Dad, 'Memories ever green are always with us ' His only son John and all his family.

Housewife, **Agnes Baseley** was born on the 8th September, 1868 at Bubbenhall and resided at 134, Crabmill Lane where she was killed aged 73. She is buried in the Communal Grave. One person treated 126 and from 134 one person detained in Rugby Emergency Hospital.

BASELEY (Agnes) Tender memories of our dear mother – Remembered always by her children and grandchildren

The son of Joseph and Rosina Banyard, **William Joseph Banyard**, died and lived at 196, Queen Mary's Road aged 33. He was born on the 11th March, 1907 at Coventry and employed by Coventry Gauge & Tool Company Limited where he worked as an Engineer Miller. A plaque in St. Pauls Cemetery, was paid for by Mr. J. Banyard on the 8th September 1952. He is buried in the Communal Grave. A family member was treated at First Aid Post and sent home. People also injured from 138 and 158.

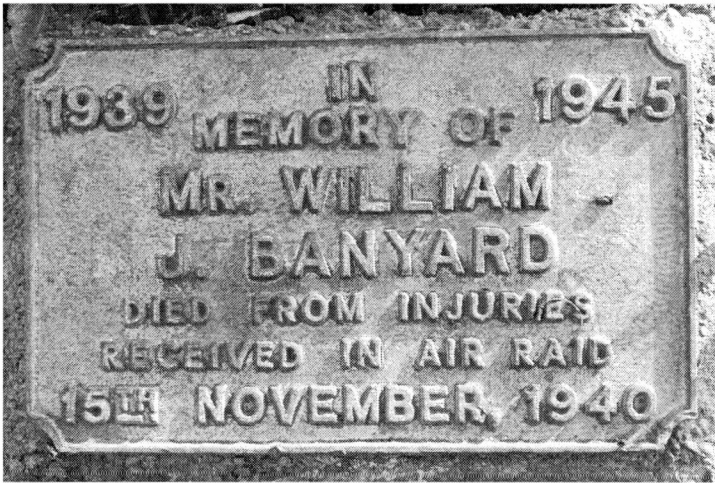

Banyard – In ever affectionate remembrance of Bill – Always remembered by Mum and Dad, Win, Cliff and Doreen (of Dundee), John and Freda.

Albert Lindon aged 5

We were bombed out of 170, Queen Mary's Road and moved to Black Heath Road, Coundon. That house wasn't much better then the one we'd just left. In Queen Mary's Road we had a night under the stairs a bomb blast had pinned us under the stairs. The ARP got us out we had no roof or windows. A bomb had dropped in the bay window of next door blew a door between our under stairs door and the hallway jamming us in. We went under the stairs at 7.00pm and never came out till the next morning. There was me, my mum and my sister. Dad worked at Webster and Bennett Machine Tools and didn't get out off there until the following morning but we were out by then.

The house up the road was also a sweet shop and the blast blew out the windows. It was a normal house front with a little garden and there were adverts and smashed jars lying in the road. On of the mornings in Black Heath I used to go out too look for souvenirs, bullets etc. On one occasion I dragged a big green parachute home, it was gigantic to me then. The rope was about half an inch thick and made up of strands and we split it down into separate pieces for shoe laces, string etc. The centre core was a lighter green colour. I used to trade it for other bits and bobs.

'The Barrs Hill School Magazine' published the following *'Our deepest sympathy goes to the parents and friends of the two pupils and five Old Girls who died as a result of enemy action over Coventry'.* **Joan Alice Tipson,** aged 13 years; died November 14th 1940.

Joan was killed alongside her mother, brother and sisters. They resided at 30, Astley Avenue and the family are buried in the Communal Grave. Joan was born on the 24th January, 1926 at Pinner, Middlesex. **Alan Roy** her 3 year old brother (born on the 24th July, 1936), **Pamela Elizabeth** her 6 year old sister (born 3rd November, 1932 at Pinner, Middlesex) both siblings attended Windmill Road School. A further sibling, **Patricia Ann** was just 8 months and born on the 3rd April, 1940 at Coventry. Husband and father was S. W. Tipson.

Selina Miles nine years old. 31 Woodshires Road, Rowleys Green

The RAF had taken over the nearby field for barrage balloons. The Germans dropped a big bomb at the back of Salem Chapel, we had all the windows blown out in the house and quite a lot of structural damage. We ended up having a metal thing put through the structure. We must have been very brave as we didn't have any counselling, like they have today. My dad was in the AFS in Radford and he came back the next morning covered in dust, he didn't want to talk about it. It was a bit shocking to see your dad like that.

We had quite a big house with stairs in the middle of it, we used to go in the air raid shelter but mum was worried about going to the shelter in case of germs as people use to spit in there. Dad did up under the stairs and we used to go to sleep there. I always thought'd we were safe, you don't realise at the time do you ? There was three children aged 9,7 and 4 and my Great Uncle Jack. He wouldn't come under the stairs and took shelter under the table. He wasn't injured, when the windows were blown in, his name wasn't on that bomb!

Ron Miles 14 years Old Sydnall Road above the pie shop.

We were surprised it lasted so long. We were under the table (children being Ron, Allan, Norman and Cyril) in the front room, mum and dad were in their chairs hoping for the best. When there was lull in the bombing we went to the outside toilet, we had a toilet upstairs but nobody would go to it. We could hear all the noises but we didn't really know which ones were bombs or our guns. We were worried about my older sister Ruth.

She had gone to the cinema with her boyfriend who was on leave with the RAF. We later learned that she was on Eagle Street when the bombing stared and took shelter in the Five Ways pub. Eventually you got used to it. We were waiting for the all clear and were glad to get to bed and get some sleep. We did look towards Coventry and see the sky red, but we didn't see any immediate damage so we went to bed, not back to bed as we hadn't even got in it.

Five members of the Walford family and two of the Villiers family died at Miles Meadow. They all died at 12, Miles Meadow, the Walford residence and are buried in the London Road Cemetery. **Esther Villiers**, aged 67 was the wife of A. W. Villiers, of 37, Hartlepool Road. Her son, **Harry** aged 39 also died. He was born in Coventry and employed at Humber Ltd.

VILLIERS and WALFORD In loving memories of mother, brother, sister, brother in law, also their dear children (Norman, Edwin and Esther). Always remembered by Lil, Elsie, Edith and Louie.

Parents **Edwin** and **Esther Walford** died with their three children, **Norman, Edwin** and **Esther.** Edwin aged 32 was the son of Edward and Annie Elizabeth Walford, of 33, Princess Street and born on the 12th February, 1908 at Coventry. Wife, Esther was 32 the daughter of A. W. Villiers, of 22, Hartlepool Road. She was born in 1909. Both parents were employed at the British Thomson-Houston Company Limited. The three children were Norman (12) who was born on the 25th April, 1928, school boy Edwin (10) who was born on the 8th April, 1930 and Esther (4) who was born on the 7th April, 1937.

WALFORD and VILLIERS – Treasured memories of our dear mummy, daddy, brother, sister, also grandma and Uncle Harry. Always remembered by Joyce and Harry

Husband and wife, **Raymond** and **Jane Leeson** died and resided at 45, Pearson Avenue, they were aged 24 and 25 respectively. Jane a housewife was born on the 15th January, 1916 in Belfast . Her husband, Raymond was the son of John and Lillian Leeson, of 34, Rogerson Terrace, Croxdale, Co. Durham and born on the 15th May, 1915 at Stockton-on-Tees. Raymond was employed at Rootes Securities Limited. **Timothy Nolan**, also died and resided at No. 45, aged 39. He was married to Mary Nolan. All three residents are buried in the Communal Grave.

LEESON In loving memory of Mr. and Mrs. Leeson, also Ted of Pearson Avenue – Always in the thoughts of Beat and Jim

Joan Margaret Millward Farr, died in Clinton Road Shelter, aged 17. She has a plaque in Windmill Road Cemetery paid for by Mr. George Farr (father), 44 Benthall Road on the 8th July 1951. She was born on the 7th September, 1923 at Coventry and resided at 44, Benthall Road, Foleshill. Joan was employed at Courtaulds Ltd and buried in the Communal Grave. A family member was treated at a First Aid Post and sent home.

FARR In loving memory of dear mother, who passed away November 8th 1940 also daughter Joan who was killed November 14th 1940. Sadly missed by Dad and Lily.

James Ahessy, died as a result of enemy air action at 137, Sullivan Road, aged 32. He is buried in Grave Ref. A. 8/1. Communal Grave and was buried on the 23rd November 1940. Along the road at No. 143 was **James Robson**, aged 31 and the husband of Edna Robson. A plaque was paid for in Hearsall Common by Mrs. L. G. Graham. Arnuck Lodge, Irvine, Ayrshire on the 7th July 1951. No. 135 had four people treated at Barnsley Hall, Bromsgrove and at 143 two people detained in Warwick Hospital and one at Barnsley Hall, Bromsgrove.

Les Neale aged three years

I was in Elgar Road, the exploding bombs were deafening and shook the foundations of the house. I was wrapped in a blanket in the bogey hole under the stairs with my brother ,the fear of bogey man who lived there had long gone. Through the open door my father and uncle were lying on their stomachs under the bed in the front room under heavy blankets. Earlier that night they had donned their tin-hats and ladened with heavy buckets of sand and water, ran onto into the back field where a string of incendiaries had set alight to some hayricks. They were gone sometime but their giggling and laughter, on returning seemed out of context to the surrounding

178

danger. It unfolded that Mr. D... a neighbour, loaded with two buckets of sand, had the bottom of one fall out. The sudden change of weight unbalanced him and he ended up in a heap on the floor with the bucket on his head. A lull in the bombing prompted my uncle to slide out from under the bed to 'have a look'. He opened the front door and was immediately blown back against the stairs above our heads as a land-mine exploded some distance away.

News spread that two unexploded land-mines dropped into the back field so early next morning before the authorities had arrived, the local people were out cutting their souvenirs of silk from the parachute which was attached to the mines, oblivious it would seem to the danger. My uncle was one of those souvenir hunters and arrived back with a square of silk and a number of incendiary cases. For many years afterwards my grandmother had these standing on her piano like statuettes.

Soon afterwards, that morning we set off from our home in Elgar Road for Coventry Station. My parents had decided that Coventry was no place for children and so we were to be evacuated to our grandparents in Buckinghamshire. We were unable to get far along the Stoney Stanton Road with bricks and rubble blocking the way. We were informed that Broadgate had been flattened and that we wouldn't get through. However after several detours we eventually reached the Railway Hotel in Warwick Road only to see that the station was severely damaged and that their were no trains.

We set out for Leamington for a connecting train to take us to our destination. After walking for sometime we were given a lift in a posh car. Their were many other families on the road with the same idea of getting their children to safety and many were picked up by passing cars. Our good Samaritan loaded the pushchair into the back and took us to Leamington Station where we were ale to catch a train to Oxford and to the safety of Buckinghamshire countryside.

Coventry North Injuries

At 41 Browett Road one person Treated at First Aid Post and sent home and at 8 Beaumont Crescent one person treated at Hospital. Three injuries at Paxton Road, two at No. 50 (Treated at First Aid Post and sent home) and one at 35 (treated at First Aid Post and sent home). At No. 2 Lammas Road one person Detained in Hospital of St. Cross, Rugby and at No. 10 Lavender Avenue Detained in Stratford-on-Avon General Hospital and at No. 189 Detained in Barnsley Hall, Bromsgrove. Two people at No. 55 Cedars Avenue Treated at First Aid Post and sent home whilst No. 74 Detained in Stratford General Hospital.

Barkers Butts Lane, No. 87 was Detained in Stratford-on-Avon Emergency Hospital and at 66 Max Road one person Treated at First Aid Post and sent home. No. 40 Donnington Avenue had one person treated and another Detained in Warwick Hospital. Southbank Road at No. 61 a person was Treated at First Aid Post and sent home whilst No. 131 had a resident Detained in Warwick Hospital.

Nine casualties at Forfield Road 23 (two Detained in Warneford Hospital, Leamington Spa), 25a (Detained in Warneford Hospital, Leamington Spa and Treated at First Aid Post and sent home), 27 (Hospital, two Treated at First Aid Post and sent home), 50 (Treated at First Aid Post and sent home) and 56 (Treated at First Aid Post and sent home).

One injury at 6 Dallington Road (Treated at First Aid Post and sent home), 7 Welgarth Avenue (Treated at First Aid Post and sent home), 122 Moseley Avenue (treated Hospital), 62 Poole Road (Detained in hospital of St. Cross Rugby), 38 Engleton Road (Detained in Warwick Hospital), 70 Banks Road (Detained in Warneford Hospital, Leamington),90 Tomson Avenue (Detained in Rugby Emergency Hospital), 74 Fowler Road (Treated at First Aid Post and sent home), 85 Dugdale Road (Detained in Warwick Hospital), 4 Chelveston Road (Detained in Barnsley Hall Emergency Hospital, Bromsgrove), 66 Kingsbury Road (Detained in Warwick Hospital), 33 Brownshill Green Road (Detained in Warwick Hospital) 100 Duncroft Avenue (Detained in Hospital of St. Cross, Rugby) 1 Brackenhurst Road (Detained in Warwick Hospital), 34 Benson Road, (Detained in Stratford-on-Avon Emergency Hospital), 22 Farm Close (Detained in Stratford-on-Avon Emergency Hospital), 27 Keresley Road (Detained in Stratford-on-Avon Emergency Hospital), 19 Chesterton Road, (Detained in Hollymoor Emergency Hospital, Birmingham), Jubilee Crescent (Treated at First Aid Post and sent home) and 13 Ballantine Road (Detained in Alcester Emergency Hospital).

No. 38 Christchurch Road two persons injured (Detained in Warwick Hospital and Treated at First Aid Post and sent home) whilst at Norman Place Road, No 98 (Detained in the Hospital of St. Cross, Rugby and Treated at First Aid Post and sent home) and No. 158 (Treated at Gulson Road Hospital and sent home). Thurlestone Road had injuries at three different houses, 62 Detained in Warwick Hospital, 76 Hollymoor Hospital Birmingham and No. 78 Detained in Warwick Hospital.
At the far end of Sadler Road, 307 Treated at Works First Aid Post and sent home and at 313 Detained in Nuneaton Hospital. A similar number of injuries in Treherne Road 21 Detained in Stratford-on-Avon Emergency Hospital and at 130.

Bulwer Road at No. 23 one person detained in Stratford-on-Avon Emergency Hospital and at 31 Detained in Warwick Hospital. Beake Avenue No. 76 (Treated at First Aid Post and sent home), 78 (Detained in Warwick Hospital), 111 (Detained in Warwick Hospital), 123 (Detained in Hollymoor Hospital Birmingham) and 132 (Detained in Hollymoor Hospital, Birmingham).

Guardhouse Road No. 9 had two people treated at First Aid Post and sent home where as No 13 had one person. Cheveral Avenue had two injuries, No. 62 Detained in Hollymoor Hospital, Birmingham. No. 178 Treated at First Aid Post and sent home. No. 141 Capmartin Road had four injuries, one treated, 141 one Detained in Warneford Hospital, Leamington Spa, one Detained in Warwick Hospital and one Treated at First Aid Post and sent home.

Isolated injuries reported against the following Radford Road 188 Detained in Warwick Hospital, Gregory Avenue 9 Treated at First Aid Post and sent home, Links Road 100 Detained Hollymoor Hospital, Birmingham, Treherne Road 66 Treated at First Aid Post and sent home, Lanchester Road 19 Treated at First Aid Post and sent home, Grangemouth Road 185 Treated at First Aid Post and sent home, Owenford Road 26 Treated at First Aid Post and sent home Blackwatch Road 19 Detained in Stratford-on-Avon Emergency Hospital, Outermarch Road 31 Detained in Warwick Hospital, Parkgate Road, Parkgate Hotel Detained in Alcester Emergency Hospital, Kirkdale Avenue 44 Detained in Stratford-on Avon Emergency Hospital, Hen Lane 63 Detained in Warwick Hospital, Glaisdale Avenue 44 Detained in Stratford-on-Avon Emergency Hospital, Farndale Avenue 16 Detained in Warwick Hospital, Whitmore Park Road 64 Detained in Stratford-on-Avon Emergency Hospital, Holmsdale Road 73 Detained in Hospital of St. Cross, Rugby , Fisher Road 45 Barnsley Hall, Bromsgrove, Victory Road 39 Detained in Stratford-on-Avon General Hospital, Stoney Stanton Road 352 Detained in Warneford Hospital, Leamington, Bright Street 22, Pridmore Road 34 Detained in Alcester Emergency Hospital, Maycock Road 4, Kingfield Road 111 Detained in Emergency Hospital, Nuneaton, Marion Road, 9, Grange Road 344 Detained in Stratford-on Avon Emergency Hospital, Vinecote Road 1 Treated at First Aid Post and sent home, Longford Road 143 Detained in Nuneaton Emergency Hospital,

Evelyn Avenue 25 Detained in Warneford Hospital, Leamington, King George's Avenue 9 Treated at First Aid Post and sent home, Bartlett Close 9 Detained in Alcester Emergency Hospital, Dovedale Avenue 60 Treated at Works First Aid Post and sent home, St. Thomas Road 15 Detained in Warwick Hospital, Proffitt Avenue 13 Treated at First Aid Post and sent home, Mason Road 36 Treated at First Aid Post and sent home and Johnson Road 46 Detained in hospital of St. Cross, Rugby.

Four injuries at Middlemarch Road, 6 (Treated at First Aid Post and sent home), 128 (Detained in Warwick Hospital), 152 (Detained in Warwick Hospital) and 341 (Treated at First Aid Post and sent home). At three addresses in Burnaby Road, 57 (Treated at First Aid Post and sent home), 95 (Detained in Warwick Hospital) and 309 Detained in Warwick Hospital. At four addresses in Rollason Road 64 (Detained in Warneford Hospital, Leamington Spa), 79 (Detained in Warwick Hospital) 91 Detained in Warwick Hospital and 130 (Detained in Stratford-on-Avon General Hospital).

Across Holbrook Lane two injuries at 56 one detained in Hollymoor Hospital, Birmingham and 246 one Treated at First Aid Post and sent home. Yelverton Road had five casualties 13, (Detained in Hollymoor Emergency Hospital, Birmingham), 24, (Detained in Hollymoor Hospital, Birmingham), 89 (Hospital), 117 (Detained Barnsley Hall Emergency Hall Bromsgrove) and 73 (Detained in Stratford-on-Avon General Hospital). The same number of injuries in Rotherham Road 13, 23 (Detained Barnsley Hall, Bromsgrove), 46 (Detained in Hospital of St. Cross Rugby), 55 (Treated at First Aid Post and sent home) and 105 (Detained in Nuneaton Emergency Hospital).

Two injuries were recorded at a number of streets; Nunts Lane 46 Treated at First Aid Post and sent home, Princess Street 34 (one treated and one Detained in Evesham Emergency Hospital), Cobden Street 46 (Detained in Evesham Emergency Hospital) and 75 (Detained in Alcester Emergency Hospital), Oliver Street 82 (Detained in Warneford Hospital, Leamington Spa) and 129 (Detained in Warwick Hospital), Beresford Avenue 14 (Detained in Warwick Hospital and Treated at First Aid Post and sent home), Ransom Road 80 (Detained in Hollymoor Hospital, Birmingham) and 84 (Treated at First Aid Post and sent home), Curzon Avenue 2 (Treated at First Aid Post and sent home) and 46 (Treated at First Aid Post and sent home), Eden Street 32 (Detained in Hospital of St. Cross, Rugby) and 50 treated), Hall Green Road 41 (Detained in Hollymoor Hospital Birmingham) and 73 (Detained in Warwick Hospital), Windmill Road 17 (Detained in Stratford-on-Avon Emergency Hospital) and 99 (Detained in Barnsley Hall Emergency Hospital, Bromsgrove), Dame Agnes Grove unknown address and No. 11 (treated), Nuffield Road 40 (Treated at First Aid Post and sent home and Detained in Alcester Emergency Hospital), Blackwell Road 33 and 47 received treatment.

Residents of Webster Street 26, 32 Detained in Hollymoor Hospital, Birmingham and 60 Detained in Shuckburgh Park Convalescent Hospital, Daventry. At Peel Street three people at No. 26 were Detained in Nuneaton Hospital and one at No. 7 Detained in Stratford-on-Avon General Hospital.

Injuries at Hampton Road split across different addresses, 15 Detained in Stratford-on Avon Emergency Hospital, 58 Detained Barnsley Hall, Bromsgrove and 66 Detained in Stratford-on-Avon Emergency Hospital. Five casualties at Canal Road No. 11 Treated at Works First Aid Post and sent home, 29 Treated at Works First Aid Post and sent home, 31 Detained in Warwick Hospital and one Treated at First Aid Post and sent home and 45 Treated at Works First Aid Post and sent home. No. 5 Delhi Avenue Treated at First Aid Post and sent home.

Crabmill Lane received injuries at 126, 128 and 134 (Detained in Hospital of St. Cross Rugby) whilst at Churchill Avenue 27 (Detained in Warwick Hospital), 89 (Treated at First Aid Post and sent home), 122 (Treated at First Aid Post and sent home) and 127. Durbar Avenue 15, 18, 30 Barnsley Hall, Bromsgrove, two at No. 42 and No. 53 Detained in Shuckburgh Park Convalescent Hospital, Daventry

Four injuries at Lockhurst Lane 191, 198 Treated at Gulson Road Hospital and sent home, 199 Detained in Warwick Hospital and 201 one person treated at Barnsley Hall, Bromsgrove. Benthall Road Treated at First Aid Post and sent home and at No. 15 one person Detained in Stratford-on-Avon Emergency Hospital. The final injuries were Edgewick Road 2, (detained in Warwick Hospital), Kingfield Road 160 (treated at First Aid Post and sent home), Newlands Farm, Keresley thee persons detained in Warwick Hospital and Elm Cottage, Hawkesbury detained in Emergency Hospital, Nuneaton.

Remaining Areas

Outside Wootton House, Coventry Road, Longford, **George Walter Boyles** died aged 15. He was the son of Mr. and Mrs. G. A. Boyles, of 60, Lentons Lane, Hawkesbury and born on the 14th March, 1925 at Coventry. George was employed with Riley Motors Ltd and is buried in Bulkington Parish Churchyard. One person from 251 detained in Stratford-on-Avon General Hospital.

BOYLES – Treasured memories of our dear son, George who left us suddenly. A day of remembrance sad to recall. Ever in the thoughts of mother and dad, Leah, Gladys, Jack and Jim.

Brian Kelsey, 185 Coventry Road, Exhall – Aged 8½

We had experienced a number of air raids in 1940, prior to the big raid on the 14th November. With these raids we were nearly always in bed asleep when they started. We would stagger out of bed and get dressed. If the sirens sounded during the day, and we were at school, we went in the school air raid shelter, but I don't remember having lessons there.

For the air raid on the 14th November, my parents and my sister took shelter under the stairs as we didn't have an Anderson Shelter. We were told that this was the safest place to be. We did get an Anderson Shelter eventually. I can't remember the exact date, some time in 1941 I believe. I can remember helping to dig the excavation in preparation for it.

The big raid started early, about 7.00 p.m., and we hadn't even been to bed. This was the first indication that something was going to be different that night. A land mine dropped about 50 yards from the house across the road and we had to evacuate. About 1.30 a.m. an ARP Warden shouted "get out" and we had to get out fast. We didn't even lock the door. Luckily, we were all dressed, and when someone tells you to get out fast, even at eight years of age, you realise that you had better get going.

We walked to my grandparents' house in Bulkington, all four of us. I don't know where everyone else in the street went, but all the houses far down the street were evacuated. We set off carrying our gas masks. It was a brilliant moonlit night and you can never forget that you couldn't have disguised anything that night. We walked passed Bulkington Army Camp with the heavy anti-aircraft guns firing. The shells being fired up at the German aircraft made a different sound to the bombs falling down on us. With so much muck in the air, our faces had got all dirty. We arrived at Grandmother's house about 6.00 a.m. Grandmother was saying to us that we all needed a wash, and my face was scrubbed using cold water. I remember protesting, "that's cold". We stayed at Grandmothers, for three to four days whilst the bomb was defused by the a Royal Naval Bomb Disposal Squad and I went back to Exhall School

184

after about five or six days. There were only about three or four pupils who had turned up. I managed to get some parachute chord from the defused land mine. It was a lovely pale green colour. There was a rumour that it had Courtaulds Coventry written on it, but it didn't. I later used the cord to swap items with other children as I could cut bits of it off.

I remember that the trams in Coventry never ran again after the November raid because of the damage to the lines and overhead cabling. You could hear the blacked out trams coming prior to the big raid but, of course, after the raid, trams were replaced, eventually with blacked out buses, which you could not hear coming so well.

Remains of houses on Gas Street

Six employees of the Coventry Corporation, Gas Department died on duty and are buried in the Communal Grave. **Harold Cain** died at Coventry Gas Fitting Dept., Gas Street whilst on raid repair duty, aged 52. He was the husband of Mabel Cain, of 3, Clark Street, Bell Green.

Harold Goodwin and he died as a result of enemy action age 35 at the Gas Works, Gas Street. He was also a member of the Air Raid Patrol and is named on the Corporation Memorial in the Council House. Harold resided with his wife, Winifred Edith Goodwin at 286, Grangemouth Road. He was born in 1905 at Derby. A plaque in the War Memorial Park was paid for by his wife in September 1948. His son, John reveals that his mother never got a chance to attend the burial as she was informed off his burial after the event.

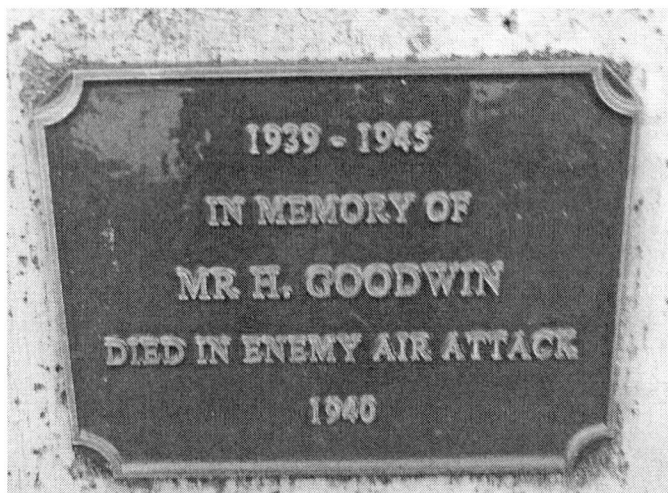

Reginald Johnstone died at Gas Works, Gas Street, aged 47. He was the husband of Ada Johnstone, of 22, Wyken Way, Stoke Heath and born on the 28th November, 1893 at Birmingham. Records indicate he died on admission to hospital and a plaque was taken out in Stoke Heath by A. Johnstone of 22 Wyken Way on the 23rd August 1949. Age 62, **Jeremiah Law**, died at the Corporation Gas Works. He was the husband of Elizabeth Anna Law, of 2, Cobden Terrace, Bradford Street.

LAW In loving memory of my dear Husband Jerry. Always remembered by his wife and children, daughters in law and son-in-law also Ray

Husband of Annie Pargetor, of 112, Clifford Bridge Road, Binley, **Ernest Victor** also died at the Gas Works, aged 42. He was born on the 4th February, 1899 at Kineton to John Pargetor an Agricultural Labourer and Mary E. Pargetor. Ernest was married to Annie and employed with Coventry Corporation, Gas Department.

PARGETOR (Ern) Loving memories of my dear, husband – Dearly loved and missed by his wife and children

Husband of Annie Prosser and from 10, Roundhouse Road, **Henry Prosser** died at Gas Street, aged 36. He was employed by Gas Department, Coventry Corporation.

PROSSER (Harry) Fondest memories of one we loved. Sadly missed by wife and children.

At Clarke, Cluley and Co., Gas Street, Coventry, aged 34. Air Raid Patrol, (Works). **William Edward Ludford** died as a result of enemy action. He was the son of William and Martha Ludford, of 7 Court, 1 House, Thomas Street and the husband of Gladys Mary Ludford. William was born on the 13th December, 1905 at Coventry and an employee of Clarke, Cluley & Co. Ltd. His Grave Reference is Coventry County Borough.

At No. 4 Gas Street one person was detained in Chadsnut Hall Auxiliary Hospital, Kineton, No. 5 treated at First Aid Post and sent home and from No. 42 one detained in Warwick Hospital and two people treated at First Aid Post and sent home. In the vicinity a person was injured at No. 33 Malvern Road, one person detained in Alcester Emergency Hospital and at No. 40 one person detained in Warneford Hospital, Leamington. Further afield at 1 Stretton Road, Wolston one person was detained in Stratford-on-Avon Emergency Hospital and at 26, Leamington Road one person detained in Hollymoor Hospital, Birmingham.

Hospitals

Birmingham

Two hospitals have casualties recorded; Queen Elizabeth Hospital and Hollymoor Hospital. **Florence Annie Lake**, died at Queen Elizabeth Hospital. Birmingham on the 4th January, 1941, aged 33. She resided at 23, Forfield Road, Coventry and was injured in Coventry on the night of the 14th November 1940. She was the wife of William Lake. Florence was initially admitted to Warneford Hospital, Leamington Spa along with another family member and has a Grave Reference of Coventry, County Borough, Warwickshire.

On the 20th November, 1940 at Hollymoor Emergency Hospital, Birmingham, **Mary Turner**, died aged 89. She was injured as a result of enemy action, and resided at 79, Bulwer Road, Radford, Coventry. Mary was the widow of Joseph Turner and has a Grave Reference of Birmingham County Borough.

Bromsgrove

On the 16th December 1940, **James White**, died age 41 at Bromsgrove Emergency Hospital, Birmingham Road as a result of enemy action in Coventry on the 14th November 1940. He was the husband of Lillian White, of 159 Radford Road, Coventry although he was a native of Sunderland and born on the 9th December, 1899. He was employed as a carpenter at SS Cars Ltd and buried in Stoke Churchyard, Coventry and the Commonwealth War Grave Commission state he is remembered in Bromsgrove Urban District and he has a commemorative plaque in the War Memorial Park paid for by wife and reads *'Mr James White Died from injuries received in air raid 16th December 1940'*.

Evesham

On the 7th December 1940, **Leslie George King,** AFS died at Evesham Emergency Hospital from wounds received as a result of enemy action whilst on duty on the 14th November 1940, he was buried in London Road Cemetery. A native of Coventry, he was born on the 18th March 1907 to Mr. and Mrs. J. King, of 24 Weston Street, Hillfields, Coventry and resided at 87 Marlborough Road. Leslie was employed at Savages Bakery, married to Frances May King. With his allocation of a plaque at the War Memorial Park an application for Stoke Heath by G. J. King of Weston Street was withdrawn.

A plaque in Radford Fire Station to the lost Fireman

Leamington
Joseph Seltzer died as a result of enemy action on the 24th November, 1940 at Warneford Hospital, Leamington as a result of injuries received at Coventry. He was aged 45 and resided at 133, Moseley Avenue, Coventry. He has a Grave Reference of Leamington, Municipal Borough.

Newport
Injured as a result of enemy action, November,1940 at Coventry and dying at the Royal Gwent Hospital, Newport, on the 28th January, 1942 was **Enid Annorah Waite**, aged 28. She was the daughter of Mr. and Mrs. A. Fisher, of 52, Tredegar Street, Cross Keys, Risca and the wife of Thomas Waite, of the same address. Enid has a Grave Reference County Borough, Monmouthshire.

Nuneaton

On the 15th November, 1940 at Nuneaton Emergency Hospital, **Leonard Ward** injured at Coventry died. She resided at 149, Lenton's Lane and is buried in the Communal Grave. **Emily Trevitt**, was injured at Coventry and detained in Nuneaton, Hospital, Chilvers Coton and died on the 10th January 1941. He resided at 107, King Edward Road and has a Grave Reference of Nuneaton Borough. A resident of No. 4 was detained in Alcester Emergency Hospital.

Rugby

At the Hospital of St. Cross Hospital, Rugby three casualties were recorded. Fireman, City of Nottingham Auxiliary Fire Service, **Clifford Richard Farndon**, was injured as a result of enemy action, on the 15th November, 1940 and died aged 31. He resided at 30, Cloister Street, Old Lenton, Nottingham and has a Grave Reference, Rugby Municipal Borough.

Clifton Road Cemetery Grave H111, holds **John Roberts**, He died as a result of enemy action on the 26th November, 1940, aged 74. He resided at Coach and Horses, White Friar Street, Coventry. Also on the 26th November, 1940 **Sara Jane Williams** died aged 78. She resided at 242, Foleshill Road, Coventry and has a Grave Reference Rugby Municipal Borough.

Stratford Upon Avon

On the 18th November, 1940 **James Brown,** died at Stratford Emergency Hospital as a result of enemy action in Coventry. He resided at 7, Hartlepool Road and has a Grave Reference of Stratford Municipal Borough. The following day, **Edith Mailey,** died at Emergency Hospital Stratford-on-Avon on the 19th November, 1940. She resided at 16 Rodney Place, Nelson Grove Row, Wimbledon and is buried in Evesham Road Cemetery in Grave 4855. The Reverend Mercer performed the service on the 26th November 1940. A widow, Edith was 46 years old.

Florence Helene Angus, died as a result of enemy air action, injured 14th/15th November 1940 at the Emergency Hospital, Stratford upon Avon, on the 23rd November, 1940 aged 46. Her husband was George. N. Angus, of 188, Radford Road, Radford, Coventry and from the incident a family member was detained at Warwick Hospital. At Evesham Road Cemetery, Stratford, Florence is buried in Grave no 4853, the service was held by Minister Reverend Harrison on the 28th November 1940.

From 57, Spon Street, Coventry **A. Hopkins** died as a result of enemy action at Stratford Upon Avon, Emergency Hospital, on the 23rd December, 1940. They were buried in Coventry at the London Road Cemetery. With an unknown date of death, **Ruth Wykes** died at Stratford Emergency Hospital. She resided at 151, Hawkins Road and has a Grave Reference Coventry Borough.

Warwick

Ten casualties are recorded at Warwick Hospital, they are in chronological order. Three persons died on the 16th November 1940.

Edwin James Booth, aged 38 was an Officer with Stoke on Trent, AFS Brigade. His address was given as 163, Gilman Street, Hanley, Stoke-on-Trent and he has the Grave Reference Warwick Municipal Borough. **John Grady**, was Injured as a result of enemy action, 14th November, 1940 at 20, Brook Street, died at Warwick Hospital on the 16th November, 1940, aged 83. He also resided at 20, Brook Street and is buried in the Communal Grave. Aged 50, **Bertie John Knighton,** resided at 73, Belgrave Road, Coventry and was married to Marjorie and was possibly injured at 28, Gorseway. He was returned to Coventry for burial in the London Road Cemetery.

KNIGHTON (Bertie John) In loving memory of a dear husband and father – From his loving wife and family

The following day, **W. H. Sanders** who was injured as a result of enemy action in Coventry, died at Warwick Hospital. He resided 64, Stoney Stanton Road and has a grave reference of Coventry Borough. On the 18th November, **Emma Martha Knutton,** died as a result of enemy action, at Warwick Hospital, aged 74. She was the wife of J. Knutton, of 63, Woodside Avenue, Coventry and buried in Coventry (London Road) Cemetery.

On the 23rd November, 1940, two citizens succumbed to wounds. Aged 78 the life of **Alfred Higgins** was lost. In Coventry he resided at 7, Brookville Terrace, Linden Road and he is buried in Warwick, Municipal Borough, Warwickshire. Little details are available on **J. L Holmes**, he was Injured as a result of enemy action at Coventry, died at Warwick Hospital, 23rd November, 1940. and is buried in Coventry (London Road) Cemetery.

On the 28th November, 1940, resident of 27, Pridmore Road, **Moses Barnett,** died at Warwick Hospital. He has a burial reference as Coventry Borough. Into December and **Richard Cottam** died on the 31st December, 1940, aged 67. He was the husband of Emma Cottam and resided at 25, Kenpas Highway. Richard is buried in Coventry (London Road) Cemetery.

In 1941 **George Bird**, died as a result of enemy action in November 1940 on the 8th January, 1941 at Warwick Hospital, aged 70. He resided at 28, Lythalls Lane, Foleshill, Coventry and his burial is listed as Warwick, Municipal Borough.

Unknown Address

The following have records that indicate they were killed as a result of the air raid and are listed alphabetically

Aircraftman 1st Class, **Charles Henry Baker,**, 852052, 917 Balloon Squadron, Royal Air Force (Auxiliary Air Force) died on the 22nd December, 1940, aged 41. He was the son of Fred and Ellen Baker, of Coventry and the husband of Olive Mary Baker, of Stoke, Coventry. He is buried in Block D. Row 3. Grave 28. Coventry (Stoke, St. Michael) Churchyard. Two casualties were simply buried in the Communal Grave, **Mr. Clarke** and **V. Cooper.**

Member of the Auxiliary Fire Services **Sidney Finlay**, died as a result of enemy action age 28 on the 7th January 1941. He was the son of A. and E. Finlay, of 45 St. Vincent Street, South Shields, Co. Durham and died at 108 Eastcotes, Coventry. He was employed at Coventry Swaging Co. Ltd and resided at 46 Glencoe Road.

Lance Corporal **Frances Clifford Gould,** 1881243, 232 Field Coy, Royal Engineers died on the 19th November, 1940 aged 22. He was the son of James Francis and Mabel Annie Gould of Nuneaton, born in Warwickshire and resided in Coventry. Frances is buried in Grave Ref. Sec Q. Grave 21. Nuneaton (Oaston Road) Cemetery.

Aircraftman 1st Class, **Franciszek Krzeminski,=**. 308 Polish Squadron, Polish Air Force died as a result of enemy action, in Coventry, on the 14th November, 1940. He was born on the 4th October, 1908. He is buried in Baginton Cemetery and may have died along with his colleagues at Crampers Field.

Sergeant **Thomas Landles**, 2745846, Aux. Mil., Pioneer Corps death was registered locally on the 14th November, 1940 – 15th November, 1940, aged 39. He was the son of Peter and Jemima Landles, of Edinburgh and the husband of Sarah Jane Landles, of Edinburgh. Thomas is commemorated on Panel 2. Edinburgh (Warriston) Crematorium. Records from the crematorium show he was cremated on the 21st November 1940 and his address was listed as Leamington Spa, his ashes were dispersed in garden of remembrance. Sarah's address was listed as 12 Dunbar Close, Edinburgh.

Aircraftman 1st Class **Thomas Roberts,** 8520453, Royal Air Force, (Auxiliary Air Force), 917 Balloon Squadron died on admission to hospital aged 30. He received the King's Commendation for Valuable Services in the air. His parents were Thomas and Harriet Roberts of Lincoln where Thomas was buried in Sec. A. Grave 1710, (Lincoln Canwick Road) Cemetery.

From 348 Battery, 110 Heavy Anti-Aircraft Regiment, Royal Artillery, **Sergeant George Robinson**, 832544 death was registered locally on the 14th November, 1940, aged 29. He was the son of Ellen Robinson, of York and buried in Section D. Grave 35. 11639. York Cemetery, Yorkshire.

Age 73, **James Henry Rutter**, died at 29, Bloomfield Avenue. He resided at 101, Bushbury Lane, Wolverhampton, Staffordshire. He was the husband of Mary Ann Rutter and born on the 16th November, 1867 at Wolverhampton. He resided at Malvern View, Burton Green, Kenilworth and was a retired Railway Driver. He lies in the Communal Grave.

Albert. Simpson, died as a result of enemy action, 14th November, 1940. He was the husband of Jane Elizabeth Simpson and had a Grave Reference of Coventry, County Borough. The 8th Bn., Royal Warwickshire Regiment lost Private **Maurice Sorrell** 5097830, whose death was registered locally on the 14th November, 1940. With no known grave he is commemorated on Panel 9. Column 1. Brookwood Memorial, Surrey.

Buried in Wolverhampton Cemetery is **Emma Amelia Spencer,** died as a result of enemy action on the 14th November, 1940. He resided at 99, Dorset Road. Listed in the City of Coventry Roll of the Fallen 1947 Edition was Police Inspector Edward Cyril Ward, who died as a result of enemy action on the 14th November, 1940. Local paper reports how he was promoted through the ranks and survived the war. A plaque application was received for Hugh Watkins but no further information obtained

Sergeant, **Charles William Welch**, 3239934, Aux. Mil., Pioneer Corps death was registered locally on the 14th November, 1940 – 15th November, 1940, aged 31. He was the husband of Sarah Welch and buried in Grave Ref. Sec. 109. Grave 224. Leamington (Whitnash Road) Cemetery.

Deaths Attributed to 14ᵗʰ/15ᵗʰ November 1940

Several deaths occurred in Leamington (due to the bombing in Coventry from an early released or misguided bomb) and these are listed alphabetically and burial associated with Leamington Municipal Borough. *Edward Gream Antrobus* was aged 80. He died and resided at 15, York Road. His parents were Reverend George Antrobus MA and Henrietta Antrobus of Beighton Vicarage, Derbyshire. Edward was married to Agnes Minnie Antrobus. Thier son *George Pollock Antrobus,* aged 48 was also killed.

Frederick Bray, aged 26 was a member of the Home Guard. He resided and died at 7, Dormer Place. Tom and Getrude Bray were his parents. *Annie Lousise Freeman*, aged 60 died and resided at 117 Kinross Road. She was the daughter of Mrs. Denton of Kettering and the wife of Thomas Freeman.

Works ARP *Stafford James Gordon Hammond* was also killed in Dormer Place and Dormer House. He was the son of Grace Isabel Hammond of 18, Castlegate, Richmond Surry and George William Chatterton Hammond. His wife Florence Howison Hammond also came from Richmond at 17, Stanmore Gardens.

The death of general labourer John Bavington, (65) lodging at 24, Bryn Road, Coventry who was injured in the air raid on November 14th 1940 was investigated by the County Coroner (Mr. C. W. Iliffe) who returned a verdict (that death was from pulmonarty embolism following a fracture of the pelvis, received during enemy action. Sarah Elizabeth Whatley the mans landlady said Bavington was injured about the hip in the November raid and was in hospital for three months. On Sunday night he went out and was brought home unconsciuos. He died almost immediately. A next door neighbour said she heard Bavington fall over on some loose bricks on the pavement outside his home. He was found lying on his back, unconsciuos and was taken into lodgings. Medical evidence was to the effect that Bavington pelvis was fractured and it failed to unite. Reported on the 9th January 1942.

Citations and Awards

Akhurst, A. V. Fireman, Central Zone, AFS. 192 Godiva Street. Ministry of Home Security commending him for gallant conduct. (Refer to Sheffield).

Alcock, Albert Edward. Head Warden. British Empire Medal (Civil Division). He played a part in the incident in which PC Moss won the George Cross. Alcock has attended every major incident in his section and has supervised and taken an active part in rescue work. He has worked untiringly in very dangerous and difficult conditions and on one occasion helped to rescue four civilians who were trapped. On another night he rescued an elderly man from a bed in a badly damaged house and whilst bombs were falling nearby removed him to safety. He also supervised the rescue of a number of people who were trapped in a private shelter and it was chiefly due to him that they were all rescued alive. His courage and inspiration was to his colleagues. 7th July 1941.

Barham, Peter Mr. George Medal. Aged 32 of 1 Lutterworth Road. Deputy Head Warden a coach finisher employed at the Armstrong-Whitworth.

Barnes, Alfred Wilfred. Member, ARP Rescue Party Coventry Commendations of 53 St. Lukes Road Showed daring and cunning in rescuing people who had been trapped beneath fallen debris, although bombs were falling and buildings were collapsing around them. London Gazette 7th February 1941

Barnes, William Harold. Member, ARP Rescue Party Coventry Commendations of Burnaby Road. (refer to Barnes, Alfred Wilfred) London Gazette 7th February 1941

Bawden, Albert Ernest. (deceased), Special Constable, Coventry Special Constabulary. 25th February 1941. National Commendation for work prior to this death in an air raid. Married man, member of the mobile section, B Division, Special Constabulary. He went out time after time, returning from incidents under the most hazardous conditions of danger. He was a gallant man and set a high example to others by complete disregard for himself. A partner in a firm of decorators, Special Constable Bawden is believed to have net with his death when the car he was driving crashed in a bomb crater and another bomb fell alongside.

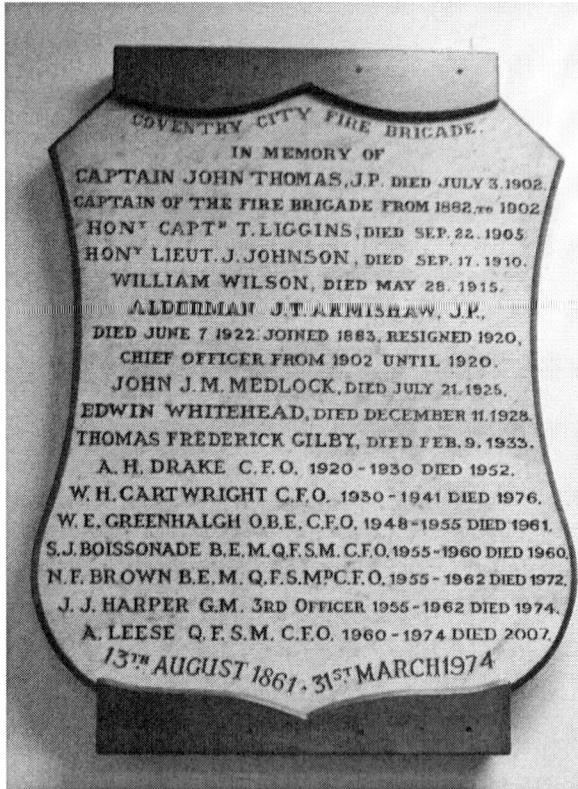

Boissonade, Sidney John. Station Officer, Coventry Fire Brigade. Awarded the Medal of the Civil Division of the Most Excellent Order of the British Empire for Meritorious Service. During the heavy raid on Coventry these officers undertook a tremendous task and carried it out in a most commendable manner. They were responsible for an extremely efficient and intricate system for relaying water in the centre of the City, as a result of which the spread of fire in this highly congested area was checked at many points. Between them they rallied and encouraged crews whose endurance was severely taxed. In movements of men and appliances they employed skill and resource for which previous experience had set no standard to use as a guide.

There cheerfulness and total disregard of personal safety were outstanding. 1, Chauntry Place. Aged 33. 28th March 1941

Bowdler, Sidney. Messenger, Coventry Auxiliary Fire Service. Livery Stables, Cox Street. National Commendation. Refer to Stainton. 28th March 1941

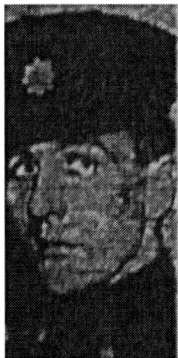

Brown, Joseph Horace Leading Fireman Coventry AFS
Awarded the Medal of the Civil Division of the Most Excellent Order of the British Empire for Meritorious Service. Brown showed conspicuous courage by remaining with his appliance when bombs dropped close by. He was rendered unconscious by blast in Broadgate but on recovery continued his job. When an incendiary bomb fell on the petrol tank of a towing vehicle he drove it to a jet to be extinguished. The car although slightly damaged was saved. Brown displayed a devotion to duty throughout the night. Married man lives at 23 Oldfield Road. Been in service 20 months. 4th April 1941.

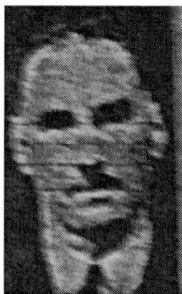

Brown, Norman Frederick Third Officer, Coventry Fire Brigade see Boissonade. British Empire Medal. 19, Chauntry Place. 37 years of age. Member of the fire brigade for 11 years

Butler, Edward Sydney. Postman, Post Office, Coventry. 14th February 1941 Commendation

Cassidy, Elizabeth. Commendation. Refused to take cover and continued to serve refreshments to all that required them. Lythalls Lane. 28th January 1941

Codling, Charles Murray. Gas Holder and Governor Control Attendant, Coventry Corporation Gas Department. Awarded the Medal of the Civil Division of the Most Excellent Order of the British Empire for Meritorious Service.

During an intensive air raid on Coventry Codling proceeded to inspect a gas holder. An incendiary had pierced the crown, igniting the escaping gas, which flamed to a height of approximately 20 feet. He ascended the vertical iron ladder attached to the frame of the holder to a height of 40 feet. Whilst walking across the crown of the holder, with wet clay blankets in bags he was knocked off his feet by the blast of a bomb which exploded near by. He got up and dropped a clay blanket over the aperture in the crown, which momentarily extinguished the flame at this point. The pressure in the holder, however lifted the clay bag and the gas ignited from the flame overhead. He descended from the holder and reported. With two other men Codling then proceeded to make another attempt to extinguish the flame on the gas holder crown with clay, and they were within 12 feet when it collapsed into its water sealing tank in a sheet of flame. 14th February 1941

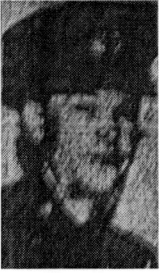

Collier. Fireman Collier in charge of a Coventry Works fire brigade has been awarded the George Medal for 'showing great zeal and gallantry' when Coventry was subjected to heavy raid. Chief Fire Officer Collier a works Chief Fire Officer of Coventry although blown off a roof and injured during an air raid he carried on until he collapsed. 6th January 1941

Coombes, Enoch Thomas. Scout, Silver Cross for gallantry. He was acting as a Wardens Messenger and made several hazardous and dangerous journeys through the City when the bombing was at it's highest. Employed Alfred Herbert.

Cormack, J. L. Silver medal of the RSPCA. Veterinary Surgeon.

Corn, Raymond Thomas. ARP Messenger, Coventry. British Empire Medal. This messenger rendered yeoman service during the whole of a sustained and exceedingly heavy attack on Coventry. Early in the evening telephonic communication ceased and Corn volunteered to carry vital messages. During extremely heavy enemy action Corn made his way to Central Control despite the fact that most of the route of his length was obstructed by fire and debris. He handed in his messages and afterwards he made at least three journeys to a first aid post with casualties and also to call for first aid and assistance. Throughout the whole of the night Corn without any though of personal danger gave unstinting help wherever it was needed. Resided 37 Kingston Road. 7th February 1941.

Costigan, Aileen Jean, Mrs. ARP Warden, Coventry. Awarded the Medal of the Civil Division of the Most Excellent Order of the British Empire for Meritorious Service.
Mrs. Costigan was on duty for the whole of the time that Coventry was subjected to a severe enemy air attack. Many bombs were dropped in the district where she worked, but throughout the whole of the raid, and in spite of falling HE bombs and falling shrapnel, she assisted in extricating people who were buried underneath demolished houses. With the uttermost indifference for her own safety she gave first aid to the

victims and repeatedly went to her home to obtain hot water, dressing and so forth. Her coolness under such trying conditions gave confidence. As the First Aid Post in her district had become demolished and Rest Centre nearby had been burned out , she attended to the needs of many people throughout the night , going from through the streets time and time again for this purpose. 14th February 1941

Craig, Allan. Royal Observer Corps. British Empire Medal. Awarded for his work with Coventry Centre of the Royal Observer Corps on the night of the 14th November 1940 air raid. He was duty controller of the centre on the night of the raid. His crew would have normally been relieved at midnight but his members carried on until after the raid was over, and it had been stated that they worked in the most trying circumstances. Compliments for the work of the crew on duty on this occasion were received from high official quarters. Head of a building firm. 6th May 1942

Duffield, Clarence. Commendation. Showed considerable daring and skill in driving his vehicles to various incidents, although bombs were falling so that his rescue party could get quickly to people who had been trapped beneath fallen debris. 84 Uplands. 7th February 1941

Duggan, John. British Empire Medal. 12, Prince of Wales Road. Full time member of a first-aid party. Duggan took his squad during a raid to a shelter which had received a direct hit. It was a mass of wreckage and burning fiercely. While bombs were exploding all around. Duggan worked desperately under the most hazardous conditions in an attempt to reach people who had been trapped in the shelter. He then proceeded to another incident where with his squad he succeeded at great risk of rescuing several injured people. He constantly exposed himself to danger in order to reach casualties and bring them to safety. Duggan seemed regardless of his own personal safety, and his courage was a source of inspiration to the members of his squad. His initiative undoubtedly saved many lives.

Durbridge Derek A. Awarded the Medal of the Civil Division of the Most Excellent Order of the British Empire for Meritorious Service. 16 year old AFS messenger he was acting as guide to a crew when a bomb exploded nearby. He was blown across the street. When he regained consciousness he was lying within a few feet of a blazing building and was covered with debris. It was sometime before he could extricate himself. Later in the night he was again caught by the blast of an exploding bomb. Despite his experiences he carried out his duties during the remainder of the night. 108 Fir Tree Avenue. 28th March 1941

Edmonston, Albert Alexanda. Auxiliary Fireman, Coventry Auxiliary Fire Service. Commendations for brave conduct in Civil Defence. Holmsdale Road. (Refer to Henney). 1st April 1941.

Ford, Ernest Hone Esq., M.Inst.C.E., City Engineer and Surveyor of Coventry. For services in connection with 'Civil Defence. 1st January 1941

Frost, Joseph William. Chief Mains Inspector, Coventry Corporation Gas Department. Commendations 14th February 1941

Gregg, Henry Norman M.B., Ch. B., MRCS, LRCP, Medical Officer, Emergency Medical Service, Coventry. Awarded George Medal. When the City of Coventry was heavily bombed by enemy aircraft. Dr. Gregg showed a high degree of courage and resource which contributed to the saving of a number of lives. While fires were raging and bombs falling, he coolly continued to go, partly on foot and partly on bicycle, from one incident to another admitting morphia to those trapped in wreckage, and applying first aid under conditions of extreme difficulty, with complete disregard for the intense bombardment and for the very personal danger entailed. 1 Evenlode Crescent. 32 year old medical officer attached to the First Aid Post at Barker Butts School and is also in private practice in the city. He has a distinguished record, in 1931 he gained distinction in medical hygiene and public health and in the same year achieved the senior clinical prize, the Foxwell Medal in Medicine and the Richards Memorial Prize. 17th January 1941

Griffin, Charles. Sergeant, South Staffordshire Regiment. George Medal.
A building was hit by high explosive bombs, causing much material damage and many fires and a detachment was asked to send a party to assist in rescue work. Sergeant Griffin and Corporal Williams together with a number of other soldiers, immediately volunteered to extricate a number of other men who had been buried under debris. A large fire had started near the rescue scene and the enemy used this as a target, continuously dropping high explosive and incendiary bombs all around. In addition two unexploded bombs were lying within fifty yards from where the rescue party was working. In spite of extreme danger Sergeant Griffin and Corporal Williams displayed high courage and coolness in directing the work of the rescue party. They succeeded after twelve hours of continuous work in saving the lives of no less then eleven men. It is stated "Although these NCO's had very little Army service to their credit at the time they set an example of coolness and indifference to danger of the highest order". 11th February 1941

Griffin, Robert Charles. Home guard. Medal of the Military Division of the Most Excellent Order of the British Empire for Meritorious Service. 48 Queen Marys Road. Acting as a roof spotter at a factory remained at his post under hazardous conditions while bombs and shrapnel were falling, passing information to the fire service, thereby enabling them to combat incendiary bombs and prevent serious damage to the factory.22nd January 1941. Sir Alfred Herbert in his message to the Works and Offices has paid tribute.

Griffiths, J. H. (Mr) Assistant Engineer, Post Office, Coventry. George Medal. During the concentrated air raid on Coventry, Mr. Griffiths although not scheduled for duty, travelled from his home to his office, a distance of 1.5 miles, through the heaviest of the bombing. He remained there during the raid, directing and encouraging the two men on duty. Mr. W. J. Williams and Mr. J. W. Wilkins. Thanks to their combined efforts, communication were established and maintained after the normal channels had been interrupted. In this way the Civil Defence Services came into action without delay. During the night a fire reached the building from below. With great difficulty Mr. Griffiths and his two colleagues got it under control. During their efforts to control the fire, Williams was overcome by smoke and fumes and had to be rescued by Griffiths and Wilkins. Later it broke out again and after further efforts to check it had been made they succeeded in obtaining the services of the Fire Brigade. Thanks to these efforts, the office was saved from destruction and the local communications which were of vital concern to the Civil Defence Services continued to function both during and after the raid.

Despite his exertions during the raid, Mr. Griffiths played a conspicuous part in the restoration of the services during the days immediately following. 14th February 1941.

Hall, Leslie Frank. Commendation 58 Billing Road. Gallant conduct, directed operations at the scene of many incidents and set an example of courage and devotion to duty under very hazardous conditions, thereby being an inspiration to all other personnel with whom he came in contact. 7th February 1941

Hampton, Lilian Mary Mrs. Telephonist, Coventry Auxiliary Fire Service. National Commendation 16 Woodland Avenue. Refer to Sinnett. 28th March 1941.

Hanocks, Mr. Ernest Williams. Additional Member of the Civil Division of the Most Excellent Order of the British Empire. Immediately after an air raid started Mr. Hancock came into the works from outside the town and took charge of all operations. His conduct and leadership were an example to everyone and contributed in no small measure to the excellent work carried out by all concerned. The works suffered severely from a number of HE and incendiary bombs but in spite of shortage of water all fires when not extinguished were preventing from spreading to greater proportions. Towards the end of the raid he was injured when the ARP Central Control Shelter received a direct hit from a HE bomb. He assisted however in rescuing his colleagues and endeavoured to carry on with his duties but his injuries made this impossible. 31st December 1940. A Coventry Works Manger has been awarded the MBE for 'conduct and leadership' during an air raid to which his works was damaged by high explosives and incendiary bombs. 6th January 1941

Henney, Cecil Walter Leading Fireman Coventry AFS. Commendation brave conduct in Civil Defence. Henney and Edmonston during a heavy raid were engaged in fire-fighting throughout the whole of one night. Henney led his crew at one period in releasing trapped people in spite of the fact that a heavy bombardment was proceeding. The pump of which he was in charge received a direct hit and was put out of action, despite this he carried on with rescue work, in which Edmonston assisted him throughout. 62 Hen Lane. 4th April 1941

Hodson, Thomas. Commendation. After extinguishing several incendiary bombs endeavoured to put out one which had fallen on the roof of the cathedral, by climbing a 40ft ladder in spite of the fact that HE bombs were then falling on the cathedral. Local Authority, Employee. 97 Belgrave Road. 7th February 1941.

Hope, Harold Bernard Leading Fireman Coventry AFS Commendation for brave conduct in Civil Defence. Although injured through a roof falling on him, continued to work from the top of a fire escape until he collapsed. He was given first aid but insisted on going back to his crew. He remained at his post throughout the whole of the night. 126 Lincroft Crescent. 4th April 1941

Hughes, William Albert. Commendation. Led his rescue party to many incidents with high explosive bombs were dropping and rescued many people who had been trapped beneath fallen masonry. Leader, ARP Rescue Party. 148 Windmill Rod. 7th February 1941

Huntley, John B. Lance Corporal Home Guard. 31 Wyken Way, Stoke Heath was blown from his motorcycle while on his way to duty and received leg and facial injuries. Machine out of action he nevertheless reported to headquarters and spent the night fighting incendiary bombs. Commended by the General Officer Commanding.

Hyde, Pearl Marguerite Councillor. Council House. Coventry WVS Chief. Most Excellent Order of the British Empire. Shepherded people to shelters and ministered their wants while bombing was in progress, and when during the days following she showed complete disregard of danger in organizing food distribution despite the danger off falling masonry, unexploded bombs and land mines. 4th February 1941

James, George Bryan. Deputy Commandant, Coventry Special Constabulary. Commendation. Mr. James is a member of the firm of Messrs Banks and James. 25th February 1941

Jones, Hubert Francis. George Medal. Head Warden. Age 48. 44, Lutterworth Road. Engineer, employed at Messrs. Armstrong Siddeley Ltd. The two men (Refer to Percy Barham) were associated together in an incident when three houses were completely demolished and several persons were buried beneath the debris. Jones and Barham (who had only recently been appointed Deputy Head Warden) immediately started a rescue effort. They worked furiously in spells of ten minutes each, so difficult and trying was the task, digging under the debris with their hands. The roof of one house was overhanging them, likely to collapse at any moment. The debris had to be propped up by timber and by crawling under this Jones and Barham were able to rescue a girl alive. Then another bomb exploded nearby causing the debris to collapse. Barham being buried and subsequently rescued by Jones at considerable risk.

Even then the two men were not beaten. Within a few minutes they returned to their own rescue work and later succeeded in getting another person out alive. In the course of these operations and in order to reach a cavity, Barham was suspended head downwards for a considerable period whilst Jones held his heels. The two men worked without a break under the most difficult and dangerous conditions and were exhausted by their efforts.

Kelly, Cambell Joseph Captain ARP Control officer and fire chief at a large Coventry factory, the award of the George Medal. He had already gained in the last war and Ireland – the OBE, MC, MM and Croix de Guerre with palm. Mr. Kelly's organization and personal bearing have been largely responsible for the building up of a highly efficient works air raid defence team. His personal activities on the night of an intensive raid were largely instrumental in saving his factory from destruction. He extinguished an incendiary bomb and immediately took 12 volunteers to help the City Fire Service deal with a serious fire, and on the way back helped to extricate the bodies of policeman who were trapped in debris left by a high explosive bomb. A large high explosive hit a workshop, but fire was avoided by prompt action under Kelly's guidance. Until 5 o'clock in the morning Kelly continued to give inspiring leadership to his men. There was no cover for any of the working parties and they all carried out what was asked off them with fortitude and courage. Served with the Royal Artillery, MM at Passchendaele, MC in 1918 26 Beaumont Crescent

Kirk, A. G. Leading Fireman, Central Zone, AFS. 19, St. Patricks Road. Ministry of Home Security commending him for gallant conduct. Refer to Sheffield.

Lake, William. Section Commander, Home Guard, Awarded British Empire Medal (Military Division) for gallantry during the raid in November. 29th April 1941

Lilley, W. Fireman. Bronze Medal of the RSPCA.

Lloyd, David. 38 year of first officer of the factory AFS who receives the Order of the British Empire. 2 Kenilworth Road, Cubbington

Maddocks, William Michael Divisional Officer, Coventry Auxiliary Fire Service, Central Division. Awarded the Medal of the Civil Division of the Most Excellent Order of the British Empire, for Meritorious Service:

During the heavy air raid on Coventry these officers undertook a tremendous task and carried it out in a most highly commendable manner. They were responsible for an extremely efficient and intricate system for relaying water in the centre of the City, as a result of which the spread of fire in this highly congested area was checked at many points. Between them they rallied and encouraged crews whose endurance was severely taxed.' In movements of men and appliances they employed skill and resource for which previous experience had set no standards toact as a guide. Their cheerfulness and absolute disregard of personal safety were outstanding. Manager Director of Messrs John Anslow Ltd, the Coventry House Furnishers 45 Woodland Avenue. 28th March 1941

Mann, William C.   Volunteer, Home Guard of 20 Moat Avenue. Employee of Courtaulds worked continuously for 20 hours under conditions of great danger. Commended by the General Officer Commanding.

Marshall, Elizabeth Mrs. Night sister, City Isolation Hospital, Coventry. Commendation. 11th February 1941.

Matts, Arthur Frederick Commandant, Coventry City Special .Constabulary. MBE (Civil Division) Commandant Matts has been on duty throughout the enemy air attacks on Coventry. He has shown complete indifference to his own safety, inspiring all under him by his leadership, initiative and devotion to duty.- The efficiency of the Coventry City Special Constabulary is due, very largely, to Commandant Matts' services. Associated with Coventry Special Constabulary for 21 years and since January 1939 has been the Commandant. Gallant conduct on the night of the 14th 15th November when you led a party of police officers in the salvage of important documents and records from the damaged and burned temporary offices of the Police Civil Defence Section. 7th March 1941

McGill, Samuel, Inspector, Coventry Police Force

Inspector McGill was on duty during a severe enemy attack on Coventry. He displayed exceptional gallantry and leadership in handling the men under him and in organising them for duty at air raid incidents. He went out repeatedly to establish contact whilst bombs were still dropping. Inspector McGill has on other occasions during air attacks on the city performed duties with utter disregard for his own safety. 28th February 1941

McNicholas, Michael, Night Telephonist and Call Office Attendant. Commendation 14th February 1941 (refer to Wilkinson)

Moore, Sam. Stretcher Bearer, Coventry. Commendation. 12th December 1940 Hostels, Holbrook Lane. Mr. Moore who is 43 is a first-aid post stretcher bearer and played a big part in the rescue of a number of persons trapped in an air raid shelter which was hit be a high explosive bomb. He is stated to have shown great courage because the whole of the work was being done during the actual raid, and several bombs fell quite close to him. He was in the state of almost exhaustion at the end.

Moss, Brandon. Special Constable, Coventry Special Constabulary. Awarded George Cross. Special Constable Moss was engaged on duty when a house was struck by a HE bomb and completely demolished, burying the three occupants. He led a rescue party in clearing an entry to the trapped victims under extreme dangerous conditions owing to collapsing debris and leaking gas. When conditions became critically dangerous he alone worked his way through a space he cleared and was responsible for the saving of the three persons alive. It was learned that other persons were alive in the adjoining premises and Moss once again led the rescue. The workers became exhausted after many hours off work but Moss laboured unceasingly and inspiringly through the complete night, again with falling debris and beams around him, and as a result of his superhuman effort and utter disregard for personal injury one person was rescued alive and four other bodies recovered. During the whole of the time of the rescue, bombs were dropping around and it was known that there was delayed action bomb in the doorway of a tavern only 20 yards away. Moss was working from 11pm to 6.30am without pause. Pictured PC Miss with his daughter on receipt of his medal.

Reported locally lives at 167, Siddeley Avenue, fitter employed by Armstrong Siddeley Ltd. Mr. Moss was on duty with another Special Constable (Refer to Alcock) in Clay Lane during the raid when they met two wardens whom they often contacted on that particular beat. There came the whistle of a bomb and Moss dropped in the roadway, while the wardens and his police colleague dashed for the shelter of passage between houses. The bomb struck the house adjoining the passage and the whole of the side of the wall collapsed on the men, killing them, it is believed instantly.

Bespattered by light debris and shocked by the blast. Moss's first thoughts were for his friends, and the people known to be still, in the demolished house. Single-handed he began rescue work on the house, and was feverishly engaged on the top of the debris when the rescue squad arrived. Right through the night he worked refusing to stop even for refreshment until 6.30 in the morning. By burrowing through the broken beams and mass of bricks he came ultimately upon the three people who occupied the house. A piano had saved them from being crushed and they were all rescued practically unhurt. The was still more work to do in the recovery of the bodies of his friends and by working through the house side and by cutting out a hole in the wall and crawling through to the point where he thought the wardens and his fellow 'special' were he eventually found them.

Oliver, C. S. Mr. General Manager and director of the Armstrong Co is nationally commended for Civil defence work.

Patstone, William Henry. Resident Caretaker, Barrs Hill Secondary School. Medal of the Civil Division, Order of the British Empire (OBE). Acting in a brave manner in conducting residents to safety whilst high explosive and incendiary bombs were still falling. He organised fire fighting parties and afterwards although affected by blast guided many of the homeless to shelter and inspired them by his coolness and courage. Formerly an Air Raid Patrol warden he gave this up to look after the school. The roof of the school was penetrated by a number of incendiary bombs but Mr. Patstone summoned aid and organised the work of putting them out. He was later engaged in cutting away a wooden roof that had been set on fire. He was blown of his feet by blast and severely shaken and continued with his work of rescue and fire-fighting all through the night. 4th March 1941

Perkins, Majorie Eileen Member of the British Empire. Works Nurse.

Miss Perkins who was employed as a Works nurse was in charge of the Works surgery. During the whole period of an intensive air raid she rendered excellent service to the casualties in the works in the nearby streets and at a public shelter a short distance away; this despite the fact that bombs were constantly falling all around. On two occasions Nurse Perkins was flung across the surgery by blast, the first time being injured internally and the second time rendered unconscious. After recovering consciousness and in considerable pain she carried on dealing with further casualties both at the works and outside, cheering and attending to those workpeople who could not be moved and visiting the shelter and encouraging everyone to remain calm. Throughout the night she did her work with utter disregard for her own personal safety. Her courage and outstanding devotion to the injured under the most trying circumstances was outstanding. Aged 25, underwent training as nurse at Coventry and Warwickshire Hospital. Full time member of the Livingstone Raid, first aid post 158 Norman Place Road 4th February 1941

Reference:-

HO 250/9

144049   Y INTER-DEPARTMENTAL COMMITTEE

ON CIVIL DEFENCE GALLANTRY AWARDS.

NAME:-

    (Rank)   (Christian Name)   AGE   CASE NO.
    Nurse   Marjorie Elizabeth Perkins   (Surname)   25

PRIVATE ADDRESS:-
          158, Norman Place Road, Coventry.   305

SERVICE:-   LOCAL AUTHORITY:-

TOTAL PERIOD OF SERVICE: Work's Nurse yrs. NORMAL CIVIL OCCUPATION: Coventry

PREVIOUS HONOURS OR AWARDS WITH DATES: Nurse to
                         Messrs. Pattison & Hobourn Ltd.

BRIEF SUMMARY OF GROUND OF RECOMMENDATION:
                               Administration to
  casualties at Works and nearby after severe injuries

DATE.   194 .   TIME:
        14/11   Night
RECOMMENDATION ORIGINATED BY

NO.   (   ) REGION Coventry C.C. & A.R.P. Controller
                   REGIONAL COMMISSIONER'S
   9   Birmingham   RECOMMENDATION.

DOCUMENTS APPENDED:- (1)   G.M.
               (2) Report by Controller
               (3)
               (4)
               (5)
               (6)
               (7)
               (8)

CASE CONSIDERED BY COMMITTEE: 194 ; RECOMMENDATION:

CASE CONSIDERED BY TREASURY COMMITTEE: 194 :

TREASURY RECOMMENDATION:

AWARD (IF ANY) GAZETTED: 194 .

ADDITIONAL NOTES:-

On the night of the 14th November, 1940, Miss Marjorie Eileen PERKINS, employed as a Works's Nurse by Messrs. Pattison & Hobourn Ltd., Cash's Lane, Coventry, was in charge of the Works Surgery. Normally she would have gone off duty at 10 p.m. but owing to the very intensive and sustained air attack which Coventry experienced that night, she remained on duty until 9.0 a.m. the following day.

During the whole period she rendered excellent service to casualties at the Works, in the nearby streets, and at the public Shelter at Messrs. O'Brien's Offices a short distance away, this despite the fact that bombs were constantly falling all around. On two occasions Nurse PERKINS was flung across the Surgery by blast, the first time being injured internally and the second time being rendered unconscious. After recovering consciousness, although in considerable pain, she carried on, dealing with further casualties both at the Works and outside, cheering and attending to those workpeople who could not be moved and visiting the Shelters and encouraging everyone to remain calm. Throughout the night she did her work with utter disregard for her own personal safety; her courage and devotion to the injured under the most trying circumstances were outstanding. Since that time she has had to remain under the care of her own doctor.

Controller's Remarks.
        The gallantry outlined above has been corroborated and I recommend the award of the George Medal.

                          (Sgd) S.A. HECTOR.
                Chief Constable & A.R.P. Controller.

        I recommend that Miss Marjorie Eileen Perkins should be considered for the award of the George Medal for her courage and devotion to duty during the Coventry Raid.

                          (Sgd.) DUDLEY.

Print, Herbert. Works Foreman. Commendation 37 year old roof spotter. Ex-artillery man 6 Purefoy Road. 28th January 1941

Probert, Arthur John Deputy Chief Officer Coventry Fire Brigade Those named below have been brought to notice for brave conduct in Civil Defence. He was responsible for the Fire Brigade control throughout the night and maintained the smooth running of the control under difficult working conditions and in face of circumstances outside all previous experience. 4th April 1941

Quinn, Betty Miss. St. Johns Ambulance Brigade, Coventry. George Medal. Miss Quinn was rendering voluntary service at an ARP Post when a shower of incendiary bombs fell on the district. Without waiting for assistance she ran outside. At this time AA batteries were putting up a heavy barrage and shrapnel was falling all around. Bombs began to fall and a man was injured by one. Miss Quinn assisted him to a public shelter. A report came in of an Anderson Shelter receiving a direct hit and although bombs were falling, Miss Quinn ran there and commenced digging in the crater with a spade.

She remained there and assisted to dig out seven persons who had been trapped and then attended to their injuries. She stayed there until the all had been removed by ambulance although shells were bursting overhead all of the time. She then returned to the post and carried on with assisting distressed persons there. 12th December 1940

Miss Quinn who lives at 39, Dymond Road was at her wardens post on the night of the raid. When many indemnity bombs dropped she was amongst the first to rush out and extinguish them. Clerk at Messrs Dunlop. Her Head Warden had told her to remain in her post shelter.

Richie, A. T. Silver medal of the RSPCA. Veterinary Surgeon.

Selby, Walter Ronald . Works fireman of Coventry in the list of Commendations. From Alfred Herbert gazetted for taking a rescue squad to save people who were trapped in burning buildings in Lythalls Lane. During these operations he was injured by a piece of flying wood, but although in great pain he insisted on being brought back t our control room. Later when all telephones were out of order, it became necessary to get a doctor to attend to some injured men, and also to advise the City Control of the situation at Alfred Herbert. Selby who overheard our Control trying to make contact with the City Control, Crawled to the nearest Police Station who were able to transmit the messages. 28th January 1941

Shanklyn, Jenkyn Member Works Rescue Squad, Coventry British Empire Medal. When Coventry experienced a very heavy enemy air attack Shanklyn's party was send to where a large bomb had exploded and caused heavy devastation to private dwelling houses. Shanklyn was the outstanding figure of the rescue party. He dug his way through the debris of two houses near the big bomb crater; after an arduous task found two bodies, which he dragged out and carried to ambulances. He searched further removing bricks from the stairway and rescued a female alive. She was conveyed to hospital in an ambulance. Shanklyn continued his work in other parts of the town and throughout showed no regard for his own safety or well being. Shanklyn, Jenkyn. 22 Lime Grove. Dug his way through debris in order to reach people who had been trapped. Continued his task off rescue without regard for his own personal safety. 7th February 1941

Sheffield, Charles Oliver. Patrol Office, AFS. Ministry of Home Security commending him for gallant conduct. Patrol Officers Sheffield's crew worked throughout the night fighting fires in the centre of the city. When another crew were buried in a building hit by a bomb they succeeded in rescuing one of the firemen. Later Patrol Officer Sheffield returned to the Central Fire Station and was responsible for extinguishing an outbreak of the roof. 26, Newland Road.

Shelton, J. B. Victoria Medal, RSPCA, Gallantry for saving five horses from blazing stables.

Shepard, Mr. Victoria Medal, RSPCA, Gallantry for saving five horses from blazing stables.

Shirley, Harry. Section Leader, Home Guard of 16 Hayes Lane. Employee of Courtaulds worked continuously for 20 hours under conditions of great danger. Commended by the General Officer Commanding.

Sinnett, John Edward. Chief Clerk, Coventry Auxiliary Fire Service. 570 Allesley Old Road. National Commendation. For remaining at posts in a fire control room that was extensively damaged and in an apparently exposed position. Throughout the raid, they endeavoured to maintain the smooth running of the control. 28th March 1941.

Skinner, Leonard. Cadet Corporal. Rescuing a woman and a baby from under the roof of a demolished house and for devotion to duty at great personal risk. Awarded the Meritorious Service Certificate of the St. John Ambulance Brigade. A heavy bomb dropped about 200 yards from Skinner's house, 87, Wheelwright Lane during the big raid and he hurried to help prepare the Ambulance Hall to receive casualties. Another bomb fell and brought in the roof of the hall so he made of to the scene of the first bombing to do what he could. Here he found many many badly damaged and demolished houses and from one rescued the woman and the baby. He administered first aid to them and awaited the arrival of the ambulance. In spite of the bombs that were falling around him he stopped at his post, ready to extinguish any fires that might start. Altogether a matter of 11 hours – nor at any time in his ordeal would he take shelter.

Stainton, Charles. National Commendation. Draughtsman. Performed a brave action and showed great initiative in laying out a hose and directing a jet with such success that in spite of their in experience of the work they extinguished one fire and prevented the spread of others. 60, Lawrence Sanders Road.

Vane, Dorothy Louise. ARP, Ambulance Driver, Coventry. Commendation. 12th December 1940. 38 Thomas Lansdail Street. Mrs. Vane was on duty as an ambulance driver at a local first aid post during the raid. A large number of incendiary bombs dropped around the post and realising the danger to the ambulance she removed them all to a safe place whilst the raid was still on.

Venables, John. AFS Messenger, Coventry. Commendation. 12th December 1940. 16 years old of 5, Eaton Road. Commended for voluntary work he put in assisting Coventry Police. During raids on the city. Venables has always insisted on being out, and has usually attached himself to the nearest Police Constable. On one occasion he helped an officer put out ten incendiary bombs of which may have well started serious fires.

Walker, Frederick Victor. 36 Fletchamstead Highway. Awarded George Medal for heroism when a time bomb became embedded in a Coventry factory workshop during an air raid.

Wallace, Matthew. 7 Buchanan Street, Johnstone, Renfrewshire. Member of Coventry Works rescue and demolition squad. Wallace was on duty during an intensive enemy attack and in its early stages, put out many incendiary bombs. He then went to another section of the works where three men were buried under debris. Special lifting gear had to obtained and Wallace went to fetch it though a district which was receiving heavy bombing. On his return he was primarily responsible for the rescue, almost uninjured of the trapped men. A call was then received for assistance at a large public shelter which had received a direct hit. Many people were trapped, and Wallace and a party of men assisted in the rescue work. He left the spot to drive a badly wounded man to hospital. On the journey the van he was driving was struck by bomb splinters and blown about by the blast, but he reached the destination. He then returned to the works and dealt with more incendiary bombs, and later led a party in the rescue of four persons trapped in a demolished house. Throughout the night, Wallace's leadership was outstanding and he displayed complete fearlessness.

Ward, A. Alfred Herbert. Commended by Lord Dudley for taking a rescue squad to Lythalls Lane. By your example and courage you were a source of inspiration to your squad which was thereby successful in its effort even though bombs were falling at the time.

Ward, Edward Cyril. Inspector, Coventry Police. George Medal. For outstanding courage, initiative and devotion to duty. During the raid an incendiary bomb fell on a Police Station, Inspector Ward climbed onto the roof and successfully dealt with the bomb. This action was performed while high explosive and incendiaries were falling around the building and probably prevented a very serious fire. Inspector Ward also led a rescue party to the basement of a shop where several persons were trapped by debris. After he had been working with the party for two hours with complete disregard for his own safety another HE bomb fell on the spot, killing the other four men of the rescue party and the occupants of the basement. Inspector Ward was thrown some distance by the blast, but he returned to make his report and during the whole incident displayed outstanding courage, initiative and devotion to duty. Born Wasperton near Warwick in 1902 went to Warwick School. There he passed the Oxford Junior and Oxford Senior local examinations before leaving in 1920. he joined the Police Force of February 5th 1923. His promotion was rapid, in six years he was promoted to the rank of Inspector. 4th March 1941

Warner, Arthur Henry Messenger, Coventry AFS

During an air raid, messenger Warner acting in the capacity of a fireman worked a pump until it ran short of petrol. He then went to his station for supplies and with these he cycled back to the fire and once more carried on, helping the firemen. Warner performed his duties of messenger during heavy bombing and showed great courage and determination. 22nd August 1941. Private Warner was killed in action 6th June 1944.

Westerby, Miss Joan. Emergency Medical Services, Coventry. British Empire Medal.

During an air raid on Coventry Miss Jean Westerby made no less then eleven separate journeys from the depot to different bombed areas. Her coolness and courage and the masterly way in which she drove her ambulance to and from the hospital evoked the highest praise. She was on duty for over 24 hours and only with the greatest difficulty was she persuaded to take a rest. She returned to duty shortly afterwards. Westerby, Joan 20 year old ambulance driver of 248 Binley Road. 17th January 1941

Wilkins, John William. Skilled Workman, Class 1 (Temporarily acting as Inspector) Medal of the Civil Division of the Most Excellent Order of the British Empire for Meritorious Service. (Refer to Griffiths)

Wilkinson, Thomas John Night Supervisor (Telephones) Michael McNicholas Night Officer and Call Office Attendant, Coventry.

During the whole period of the concentrated air raid on Coventry Mr. Wilkinson and Mr. McNicholas remained on duty on the top floor of a Post Office building, the roof of which was partly of glass. Buildings all around were demolished or set on fire, and there was continual risk of danger not only from bombs, but from falling debris. Mr. Wilkinson and Mr. McNicholas devotion to duty ensured throughout the night the communications upon which the successful functioning of the Civil Defence services so largely depended. 14th February 1941

Williams, Edward William. Corporal, South Staffordshire Regiment. George Medal. (Refer to Sergeant Charles Griffin)

Williams, William John. Unestablished Draughtsman Post Office. Medal of the Civil Division of the Most Excellent Order of the British Empire for Meritorious Service. (Refer to Griffiths)

Wilson, James Henry Divisional Commander, Coventry Special Constabulary. B Division. Commendation a principal of the firm of Messrs Wilsons Gas Meters Ltd. 7th February 1941

Wilson, William Charles. Commendation. 47 Grafton Street. For gallant conduct climbed 30 feet up a fall pipe and endeavoured to distinguish an incendiary bombs on the roof of the Gulson road Hospital , and being unsuccessful in this event picked up the lighted bombs with his bare hands and threw it to the ground. 7th February 1941.

Young Mrs. Manageress of the works canteen Refused to take cover and continued to serve refreshments to all that required them. Lythalls Lane. Commendation

The Enemy Attack on Coventry

The air raid on Coventry on the night of the 14th/15th made all the National Newspaper and those abroad also picture featured the air raid and the loss of life. *'War Illustrated'* on the 27th November 1940 has the headline *'Ferociously Mauled by The Bestial Nazis Coventry Head was bloody but unbowed'* and the article went onto describe *'From dusk to dawn on November 14 –15th Coventry ancient town of the Midlands which in recent days has won fresh fame and prosperity as the city cycle and motor cars, sewing machines, rayon and aircraft was bombed by wave after wave of German planes some 500 tonnes of high explosive bombs and 30000 incendiaries were dropped and the casualties were reported to be over a 1000'.*

Headlines from local papers headlined *'Wanton brutality of Coventry'; An outstanding feature of the German attacks on Britain during the week was the change of tactics seen on Thursday night raid on Coventry. The Nazis claimed that this was the biggest raid in the history of warfare. The raiders flew to high to discriminate and in fact the damage was almost entirely confined to churches (including the Cathedral), cinemas, large hotels, stores, business premises and dwelling houses generally. Over 250 people were killed and about 800 wounded. While the Nazis were bombing Coventry and other British towns our RAF bombers delivered a further heavy attack on Berlin.*

The minutes from the City of Coventry Council Meeting of the 3rd December 1940 at 10.30 o'clock in the forenoon captured:-

The Mayor made a statement in regard to the above attack and the events which followed it; and the Council, at his invitation rose as a mark of sympathy with the injured, and with the relatives of those killed. The Mayor said that, in the fortnight following the attack, the pressures of the emergency work was so great that it was impossible to hold the regular meetings of Committees and Sub-Committee but the National Emergency Committee met daily to discharge their civil defence functions and the Chairman and the Vice-Chairman of other Committees, in constitutional manner, acted on behalf of their Committees. With the return of more normal conditions, the routine meetings can be resumed, and the present meeting of the Council is being held on the day fixed for the meeting. He expressed the opinion, that under a very severe test, the Council's emergency organisation has withstood the strain. He spoke of messages of sympathy and of admiration, and of generous donations to the relief fund from Great Britain and the Empire. He also expressed appreciation of the visit of His Majesty the King and of Members of the Cabinet, and of the assistance given by the Military, the Regional Commissioner and his staff, and hosts of voluntary helpers. The relations between the Council and the Regional Commissioner were those of collaborators in a common purpose. The heroism and fortitude of the citizens had gained the respect of the world, and had enriched the traditions of the City.

It was moved by Councillor Mrs. Corrie, seconded by the Deputy Mayor, and resolved unanimously that having heard the Mayor's statement on the events since the Great Raid, the Council approve of the action which has been taken on behalf of the City by the Mayor, the National Emergency Committee, the members of the Council, and the officials, and express their thanks for the assistance rendered by the Civil Defence and other volunteers, the military and many other local authorities, and that the Mayor's statement be received with thanks.

Present were the Mayor (Alderman J. A. Moseley), the Deputy Mayor (Councillor A. R. Grindlay) and fourteen Alderman along with forty one councillors.

Further notes from the Chief Constable Report stated that the following were killed whilst on duty during a recent air raid attack:-

P. C. 25 K. Rollins
P. C. 82 W. H. Timms
Police War Reservist 20, F. S. Strong
Special Constable H. Berry
Special Constable W. R. Lambe
Special Constable F. Barratt
Special Constable A. Bawden
Police Messenger R. Lowrie (aged 16)
Police Messenger B. West (aged 17)

Notes on the 24th December 1940 added *'that the committee express their sorrow and their deep sympathy with the relatives of those who have given their lives; and record their admiration of the heroism and self-sacrifice which the officers displayed under desperate and trying conditions'*.

News After the Raid

On the 23rd November 1940 some of the victims of The Blitz were revealed and an appeal made for the provision of deep shelters, extension to the communal feeding scheme and appeals for coal so that water could be heated and sterilized to prevent the spread of diseases. News by the end of the moth was that six soldiers were sent to prison for looting in Coventry. Two soldiers stole cigarettes, lighters etc to the value of £5 from a shop in Earl Street, one also admitted to taking jewellery worth £34 from house in Spon Street. One received 12 months the other six with hard labour.

Two further young soldiers sent to six months hard labour for stealing from a pre-payment meter. Last two also charged with stealing medals, pencils and coins worth 14s, the owner returned home and found them in the premises. *'This sort of thing has to stop you will go to prison for 28 days'* said the Chairman to a 21 year old, shop assistant who pleaded guilty to the theft of cigarettes vale £1 8s from outside a tobacconist in Bulwer Road, wardens had removed the cigarettes and placed them on the footpath, she stated in the report she was sorry for her action and stated; *'other people were taking them'.*

Into the New Year and two soldiers who decided to sleep in a bombed building were charged with looting and sentenced to six months hard labour. During the night they were hungry and helped themselves to a dozen eggs, a tin of sardines, two tins of peas, three tins of fruit and some ham. It was reported as they *'did not like to drink water they took 11 bottles of champagne, nine bottles of mineral water and a bottle of port'.* Justifying their action they said they *'were hungry and thirsty'.* The owner returned home as was his daily check up and the men escaped through a rear window they were later caught and arrested.

Also in January, Coventry had started to rebuild as good progress was being made with 26 temporary shops in Corporation Street which were of timber and asbestos construction with concrete floors. An article in 'Life' magazine written by Dr. Harry Winters, explained *"'British patients showed no fear of panic or hysteria the only complaint came from a wounded German pilot who had been in hospital from a previous raid, the orderlies found him saying "too much bomb – too long – too much bomb".*

Mr. W. Maddocks, Divisional Officer of Coventry Central Zone addressed the Coventry Round Table at it's luncheon, and on the night of the blitz stated *"a number of buildings that were burnt out would still be standing if their were adequate numbers of watcher parties. Had it not been for the previous experience gained by the fire service, no-one knew what might have happened in Coventry. After the raid had been in progress for an hour or more no-one had any reason to believe that the raid would go on with its intensity for the amount of time it did"*

A Letter to the Editor from H. E. Mattock, Crampers Field in *'The Midland Daily Telegraph'* stated *'Sir I am pleased that Councillor Latham has performed such a vital duty by calling the attention of the city Council to the condition of many of the surface shelters in the city. Many of these shelters as councillor Latham stated falling down of their violation, and I can assert quire safely that the confidence of the people in the Radford district has been completely destroyed as to their efficiency'*.

Different news items appeared in February 1941 the fixing of bunks in domestic communal shelters was now considered premises owners must ensure that a adequate number of persons for the purpose of discharging fire prevention duties. The state of a bomb debris near the graveyard at Whitley Common was considered only temporary and a promise the common will eventually be stored to it's original beauty. The response was given by Mr. E. H. Ford in complaint to comment on the reckless dumping from the fringe of Coventry Cemetery to the common. Tons of wreckage and rumble were strewn with clothes and shattered furniture. Shortage of transport and the clearing by the military led to the situation. Mr. Ford stated *'the rubble would be reused for building operations and the common returned to its attractiveness'*. Mr. E. H. Ford was again called to comment and warned against advice from a London journalist to take timbers from bombed houses to use in air raid shelters, *'this was classed as theft'*.

In March 1941 a carpenter was sent to prison for the theft of cutlery, glasses, a jug and an ash tray from the Craven Arms Hotel, Coventry and sentenced to three months hard labour. The party said *'I saw them being thrown away and I didn't think it was stealing'*. Four men were charged with trying to obtain money from the Public Assistance board by false pretences. Three sent to prison for four months and one sent to prison for six months; *'The men had suffered no loss and used identity cards and change of clothing'*, the latter man had been around on the night of the big raid and stole jewels.

On the 10th March 1941 Coventry had 30,489 fire watchers and another supply of stirrup pumps had arrived for disposal at £1 each to fire watcher parties at the rate of one per party. On the same day, Professor J. B. S. Haldane an authority on the subject of air raid shelters and Chairman of the National ARP Coordinating Committee stated *"I came to Coventry today and I have seen something of what happened to the city during the bombing – the centre of the city is, I think worse than anything in London, except perhaps a few areas around the docks"*. Your brick shelters are definitely worse then the ones we have in London in his address to the Coventry Trade Union and Labour Organisation Emergency Committee held at Sydenham Palace Hotel. Instructions were send from London and had to be followed to the letter. In Coventry they had brick shelters that Lord Horder had condemned and with had previously been condemned by the Co-Coordinating Committee. People in Coventry should not be satisfied with brick shelters even if they were strengthened, councils should build bomb proof shelters, can stand the weight of a bomb proof roof. Fire watchers should have the opportunity of taking cover whilst incendiaries were falling the same time as HE's.

Reverend R. T. Howard stated the new Cathedral will be *'rectified by men not money'*. He believed the destruction of the cathedral would be regarded as marking the turning point of the war for it focussed he attention of the world on the forces of evil against which we were arrayed. On the 20th March 1941, it was reported The Special Committee to inquire into the scandal of Coventry's surface shelters has not yet completed its work.

In June 1941 it was reported further on the opportunity offered by the basement of Messrs Owen Owen Store for which at one point excavations were sunk to a depth of between 25 to 30 feet is being investigated by the City Engineer. The basement of the store was largely carved out of natural stone. *"The possibilities of the position and off driving tunnels making use of the basement has been considered. We may have to go a great deal deeper the ground required for a deep shelter is 50ft and 60ft.* The City Engineer has already reported to the Emergency Committee his opinion that a site near Trinity Street might be appropriate.

On the 30th January 1942 in *'The Coventry Telegraph' What time was the raiders passed signal sounded in Coventry on the morning of the November 15th 1940? Officially the signal was sounded at 6.16am, in fact very few people heard it. Most of the sirens were out of commission. Those of the electric type still functioning emitted what has been described a 'defiant wheese' and only the steam sirens were operate to operate with full force. Amid so much falling masonry the regular explosion of delayed action bombs and the crackling of burning debris, it is scarcely surprising that the remaining sirens were inconspicuous. Another and even more positive reason is that many thousands of people eleven hours of constant bombardment had taken advantage of the lull to get some sleep.*

German Propaganda

Shortly after the raid the German Press produced on booklet translated into *'Bombs on Coventry'*. The front page is shown:

War Books of the German Youth

Volume 84 Price 20 Pfennig

Experiences of the crew of a 'Junkers 88'
in operation against England

by Carl G. P. Henze

By order of the Youth Leader of the German Reich
and in conjunction with
the High Command so of the Army and Navy and the
Commander in Chief of the Air Force
and published by the
Regional Leader Gunter Kaufmann of the British Youth Organisation
Major Kaether of the High Command of the Army
Commander Nahrath of the High Command of the Navy and
Dr. Peter Supf for the Reich Air Ministry

The books started with and is translated:

End of November 1940. An unpleasant damp and dark late Autumn night hangs over the blacked-out Reich Capital, Berlin. Rain and snow fall on the ground from the low flying clouds; the cold damp air pierces the thick clothing of the few people who for one reason or another are still on their way or hastily striving to reach home.

In the snug warm room which serves as the living room of foreman Herbert Handorf's family nothing is to be seen of the unpleasant weather outside. Only now and then does the night wind strike against the drawn Persian-blinds, interrupting the monotonous drip of rain on the window-flashing. The well blacked out windows muffle the bluster of the rough weather so that little can be felt of it inside. The big tall clock in the corner points to eleven. Usually at this hour the stillness of night already reigns throughout the house, for father, daughter, and son of the foremans family of four must be out early every day – father Herbert to his factory, Erika, his daughter, to her office three quarters of an hour travelling time away in the West End, and the thirteen year old, Horst, the youngest, to the Litzmann School in the Mittelward Strasse. All have a pretty good distance to go from their flat in the pleasant house on the New Tempelhof Estate so father Herbert strictly observes that everybody is between the blankets by 10pm.

But today, for two reasons relaxations of the paternal admonition is permitted; first, it is Saturday and they can only stay in bed tomorrow morning, and secondly, there is yet another special reason – their eldest son is home on leave.

Warner Hendorf their 24 year old son, served as a mechanic with the German Lufthansa till 1935 and then went into the Luftwaffe as a volunteer. He soon became a pilot and flew with his squadron in the war against Poland. As a corporal his distinguished himself through courage and joy in action. In the further course of the War he was send to the West, flew over Paris, became a sergeant and took part in the battles in Holland and Belgium. Just recently he was promoted to Flight-Sergeant for his soldierly conduct in most critical situations over England, Now after a successful operation against Coventry, and slightly wounded, he has been given leave in order to get his wounded arm completely better.

He came in unexpectedly at noon today after not being at home for almost a year. The reunion must be celebrated! Marielies, the daughter of the grocer in the Berlin Strase, has been engaged to Werner for a year. She and her brother, Horst's school and classmate, complete the Hamdorf family circle for tonight. Both of them ought really to have been at home long ago, but Werner, animated by the pleasant company and good glowing punch, whose main ingredients Marielies had brought from her parents' shop, began to relate his experiences after supper. And father, who had been a first fitter in Richthofen's fighter squadron in the Great War, spurred him to further description of his experiences by his constant interrogations. This was, of course, a rare treat for the two youngsters, both cubs in the Youth Movement and also zealous members of the model aeroplane club, who with their fathers' consent, want later to enter the preliminary air-training technical school. And with so much air-mindedness about, neither mother nor the two girls can let themselves be outdone. Erika attends to the necessary drinks and is just bringing a fresh jug of steaming punch into the room.

The glasses clink once more. Father Handorf lights a fresh cigar, casts a glance at the clock and looks at his wife who can hardly suppress a slight yawn. Then, he says to his son, who is just filling his pipe, 'we ought really to be off to bed, but we shall not be together for a long time. So of you feel like it, carry on with your tale. If it's weather like this out there in the morning, we can stay in bed for a while. You had just got to where the electric wiring had failed over Coventry'.

And even Marielies, who is a short-hand typist at the Berlin branch of the Junkers Works, and is particularly proud that her Werner flies in one of the new Junkers 88, suggests with a pleading glance at Mrs. Handorf, who is busy knitting a pullover for Horst, "Yes, Werner, you must finish the story of your operation against Coventry".

The book continues….

There lies the target; a large factory block spared by the comrades who were here before us. The giant chimney stands dark and rigid in the blood cloud of the neighbourhood; the plant down below stands out as bright as day in the light of the flares, muzzle-flashes show up on a few roofs, but the shells from the flak of them burst wide above. Schmidfeder pulls the bomb lever. The racks under the aircraft open releasing their destruction-bringing load. The Oberleutnant sees clearly in the last flicker of the flickering flare the heavy bombs whistling downwards as Handorf banks the aircraft on its wing tips and makes a sharp curve. A few seconds later bright flames shoot up from the dark building; blazing columns of smoke and flares grow mushroom like to cover the battered workshops and serpent up almost to the height of the Ju88, A faint smell of burning penetrates through the cracks in the thick glass plating of the rear turret. Both bombs have found their mark!

Everything has collapsed. Part of the flak seems to have gone to the devil as well, for a few moments before, muzzle flashes were spitting out from broken roofs. Bright fire are springing up in the vicinity as well. The comrades are at work with equal success. The fire from the defences grows weaker and weaker.

Handorf has brought the aircraft back over the target in a wide sweep; two heavy still wait in the racks to complete their mission. This time there is no need for the Oberleutnant to drop a flare; the fire marks the target as light as day. The still undamaged buildings stand out dark against the red glare of fire. Once more the aircraft storms against these objectives – two giant workshops still remain. A tug of the bomb lever, a sharp turn of the aircraft and the second load whistles earthwards. The Oberleutnant sees the effect at once. These tow have found their mark as well!

Official Reports

Two reports were submitted after the war and published in *'The London Gazette'* that gave some insight into the strategies being deployed with regards to Civil Defence in Coventry.

The Anti-Aircraft Defence of the United Kingdom from the 28th July 1939 to the 15th April 1945. The following dispatch was submitted to the Secretary of State for War on the 21st October 1946 by Sir Frederick A. Pile, Bt, GCB, DSO, MC General Officer Commanding-in-Chief, Anti Aircraft Command.

In September 1939 the Anti-Aircraft Defences of the country were organized in a Command Headquarters and seven Divisional Headquarters. Coventry came under the 4th North West England, the West Midlands and North Wales. The total number of Heavy Anti-Aircraft guns was 695 many off which were obsolete and a number on loan from the Royal Navy, the total requirement was 2,232 guns. With light Anti Aircraft guns there were 253 out of requirement of 1,200 and searchlights faired better with 2,700 against a requirement of 4,700. By July 1940 when enemy attacks had started in full the totals had risen sharply to 1,200 Heavy Guns, 549 light guns (includes 273 40mm Bofors guns) and 3,932 searchlights with a manpower of 157,319.

In October 1940 it was considered that in order to produce more effective results guns should produce a volume of fire from many guns at once. Evidence was also presented that search lights were illuminate attacking fighters and thus providing a target for the enemy's rear gunners. To give the fighter a chance a technique known as 'Fighter Nights' was introduced, fighters would engage the bombers over the target area and once contact was made they should have a chance of shooting down the enemy. The disadvantage of this scheme meant that the anti aircraft guns could not fire or had to be restricted to heights at which the fighters had instructions to operate. The scheme was not popular although some successes were achieved on moonlit nights. The lack of gunfire incensed the civilian population who though the gunners were being negligent and resulted in a great loss of civilian morale. The enemy aircraft free from all anxiety were able to bomb their targets accurately.

After the preliminary raids on the West and Midlands, the first phase opened on the 7th/8th September 1940 the raids were continuously on London night after night. supplementary and diversional raids were scattered across the country so it was never possible to pull into London all the guns I wanted. On the 14th/15th November the Second phase, opened up with the main weight of attack was shifted from London to industrial centres and ports, although London continued to receive a succession of smaller raids. The concentration on industry and other objectives in the smaller town and cities was far greater then London and the dropping of a similar weight of bombs could therefore cause greater damage and dislocation than had been achieved in most of the London raids. Coventry was the first town to be singled out and others which in the course of the phase received particular attention were Liverpool, Bristol, Plymouth, Cardiff and Portsmouth. The guns defended London were at once reduced from 239 to 192, and another 36 taken from the Thames Estuary. By May 1941 developments in technique were considerable.

It was envisaged that the enemies main objective would be aircraft factories, cities and particularly London and the main purpose of defence was to prevent the enemy from reaching their objectives. To deal with aircraft that penetrated the searchlight corridor, important cities were made Gun Defended Areas with search lights to enable to heavy guns to fire by night. Static guns were produced more efficiently than mobile guns so efforts to move guns around were hampered.

At the end of 1940 a re-organisation was required for closer co-operation with Fighter Command and five new divisions were created with the West Midlands and Central Wales coming under the 11th Division. Three Anti-Aircraft corps were also created at this time.

This report was submitted by Marshal Sholto Douglas GCM, MC, DFC former Air Officer, Commanding in Chief Fighter Command. 16th September 1948. On September 7th the Luftwaffe London became it's main target and the night offensive gathered momentum, its scale of attack increased once more. By the end of October the night offensive had in many respects become a bigger threat to the kingdom than the day offensive, which had for the moment been successfully beaten off. At that stage London had been raided every night for the last eight weeks apart from one. One every night apart from four at least 100 tonnes of bombs had fallen in or around the capital.

Coventry, Birmingham and Liverpool had all suffered attacks of some weight. So far no intolerable harm had been done to industry or the public temper, although many people had been killed and much material loss and hardship had been caused. There was every reason to expect that the attacks would continue and perhaps grow heavier; for the past two months the defences had only claimed the destruction of only 79 bombers a number believed to be about half of one percent of the number of sorties the Germans had flown in that time. Obviously losses of this order were not likely to act as a deterrent.

Review

The bombers of the Luftwaffe came to Coventry on the night of the 14th/15th November 1940 with the objective of destroying the City of Coventry and demoralising it's citizens and the heart of England. By the end of the raid and subsequent days almost six hundred people were killed and over 1,000 injured to varying degrees. These were ordinary citizens taking shelter, in hurriedly build Anderson Shelters, Morrison Shelters, Works Shelters or as in many cases under the stairs.

For those who did not experience the night of the blitz in November 1940 will we never know what it was like, to discover your house bombed , friends or relatives missing and then have to deal with the consequences of a mass air raid in your own City, the current generation will never understand in it's entirety. No communication, no mobile phones, no cameras, no Internet and leaving school to go straight to work combined with loss of electricity, gas and blackouts, it was a world where those who did not experience it will never know.

I have to thank again those who survived the raid and provided me with the memories of the night, however I have only touched on one aspect of a country and a city at war. In order to give some perception, I have ordered streets in an approximate postcode order to equate to today's society so an appreciation can be understood of what happened in a street or district on that fateful night of the 14th/15th November 1940.

I have not dwelled on the strategies used by the Luftwaffe; nor the tonnage of bombs or the number of Incendiary Bombs that started the fires which ultimately acted as a guide for wave after wave of the squadrons of the Luftwaffe. I have concentrated on the people who lost their lives, those injured and those who performed acts which were recognised and awarded. Although not all the heroes from the night were decorated and some refused awards as in their words, 'they were just doing their job'.

No amount of preparation by the various Ministries could have prepared Coventry for the attack that was unleashed, an no-one can doubt the performance of those involved in Civil Defence, men and women who were called into action in addition to their normal employment. The legacy of the bombing in Coventry remains, by those who experienced the raid and by the shape of the skyline that runs across the City. As with The Great War there will soon be a time when nobody is left to tell first hand accounts of the night of the 14th/ 15th November 1940, and for researchers and family historians now is the time too ask.

Appendix A ARP Warden Injuries

501A	1613 Lacerated right foot. Treated by Private Doctor
502A	2518 Severe bruising hip and right leg. Trapped in shelter. Treated by Doctor
405E	223 Wounded by bomb explosion. Injured by HE proceeding to incident.
407C	101 Injury to back. Flying masonry
407C	1616 Dislocation of shoulder. Fighting IB
404C	713 Burns and shock. Fighting IB.
404C	2953 Burns. Fighting IB.
	Squashed ankle and burns. Injured whilst completing form.
	3158 Burns to face and eyes.
	900 Fractured leg
	544 Broken toe
	2648 Injured pelvis
	1738 Burns to face.
	2281 Injured chest and leg
	4043/M Bruised arms and legs. Buried Foleshill Div. HQ
100	2748 Fracture of the spine. Explosive IB
101	4268 Injury to eye. Flying debris.
102	2372 Fractured leg and other injuries. HE Bomb
102	4272 Injuries to chest and stomach. IB
104	4644 Injuries to eye IB.
106	659 Injuries to stomach. HE Bomb
106	4039/M -----. IB
100	4211 Injuries to face. IB
108	3173 Injuries to eyes. IB
107	884 Shock and facial injuries. IB
602	2955 Fractured rib and collar bone. HE Bomb

Appendix B Date Found

Casualties not listed were found on the 14th/15th November 1940.

Records did not cover all casualties

16th November 1940
Richard John Richardson
James Robson
Doris Scott
Ernest Harold Beadle
Corbett Egginton
Sylvia Mary Bott

17th November 1940
Harry John Collier
Norman Allton
William Henry Bowers

18th November 1940
William Mallard

19th November 1940
Agnes Ince
Raymond Henry Bell
Betty Bell
Ernest Leslie Hollingsworth
Lilian Hollingsworth
Rose Smith
Joan Tipson
William Hughes

20th November 1940
Ann Rose

21st November 1940
Florence Lavinia Ruddick
Malcolm George Ruddick
Frederick Arthur Cooke

23rd November 1940
Elizabeth Collingridge
John Tansey
Isabella Steel

27th November 1940
William Henry Guest

30th November 1940
Majorie Stubbs
Elizabeth White
Arthur John Stubbs

1st December 1940
Emily Carn

10th December 1940
George Fox Barker

4th February 1941
Mary Ann Williams

Appendix C Relative/Friend and Date Buried

Adams, Charles.		
Adams, Mary Brand	Daughter	23rd/ 29th November 1940
Adams, William Thomas	Daughter	21st /23rd November 1940
Ager, Ann Marie.	Husband	
Ager, John Lovell.	Daughter	20th November 1940
Ager, Kathleen Alice	Husband	Outside Burial
Ahessy, James.	Friend	23rd November 1940
Allitt, Jane.	Brother	23rd November 1940
Allport, Clara	Sister	23rd November 1940
Allport, Phyllis Marguerite.	Aunt	23rd November 1940
Allton, Norman	Father	Outside Burial
Angus, Florence Helene		
Archer, Charles.	Wife	23rd November 1940
Ashby, David	Wife	23rd November 1940
Atkins, Frederick.	Wife	20th/ 23rd November 1940
Baker, Charles Henry		
Ball, Ada Lillian	Father	23rd November 1940
Ball, Clara Beatrice	Husband	23rd November 1940
Ball, Florence May	Father	23rd November 1940
Ball, Raymond	Father	23rd November 1940
Ball, Thomas Edward	Father	29th November 1940
Ball, William Henry	Father	23rd November 1940
Banyard, William Joseph	Father	20th November 1940
Barker, Edith Mary	Son-in-law	23rd November 1940
Barker, George Fox.	Wife	17th December 1940
Barker, James.	Brother	23rd November 1940
Barker, Joan.	Brother	23rd November 1940
Barker, Mary Grace.	Uncle	23rd November 1940
Barnett, Moses		
Barratt, Frederick.	Widow	Outside Burial/ Cremated
Barrell, Bertram.	Wife	23rd November 1940
Barritt, Catherine	Husband	23rd November 1940
Barron, Alfred	Wife	23rd November 1940
Baseley, Agnes	Son	21st /23rd November 1940
Bass, Annie Elizabeth	Son	23rd November 1940
Bass, Clement Alfred Gordon	Father	23rd November 1940
Bass, Doris Hilda	Husband	23rd November 1940
Bass, George Arthur	Brother	23rd November 1940
Bass, Joan Mary	Brother	23rd November 1940
Bass, Leonard James	Brother	23rd November 1940

Bass, Thomas William	Son	20th November 1940
Bausor, Herbert.	Wife	
Bavington, John.		
Bawden, Albert Ernest	Wife	20th November 1940
Baxter, John	Mother	Outside Burial
Baylis William Charles.		20th November 1940
BAYLISS, EDGAR 608		21st November 1940
Beadle, Ernest Harold	Father-in-law	20th November 1940
Beadle, Irene May Edith.	Father	23rd November 1940
Beasley, Arthur Leonard	Father	23rd November 1940
Beasley, Barbara.	Father	23rd November 1940
Beasley, Dorothy	Husband	21st/23rd November 1940
Beck, Alfred John		
Bee, David		
Behan, Thomas		
Bell, Doreen Betty	Brother	23rd November 1940
Bell, Malvina.	Father	23rd November 1940
Bell, Raymond Henry	Brother	23rd November 1940
Bennett, Christopher	Wife	23rd November 1940
Bennett, Elsie.	Brother	23rd November/ 17th December 1940
Bennett, Florence May.	Brother	23rd November 1940
Bennett, Jack	Friend	23rd November 1940
Bennett, Walter.	Son	23rd November 1940
Berry, Harry	Wife	
Billings, Aubrey John.	Grandmother	17th December 1940
Billings, Eva	Mother	20th November 1940
Billings, Leonard John.	Mother-in-law	23rd November 1940
Billings, Marion Grace.		
Bird, Alfred	Wife	23rd November 1940
Bird, Edna Elsie May	Mother	23rd November 1940
Bird, George.		
Blagburn, James Cecil.	Wife	Private Burial
Blockley, Mary Jane	Sister	
Booth, Edwin James.		
Bott, Sylvia Mary.	Father	23rd November 1940
Bowers, William Henry	Wife	Outside Burial
Bown, Arthur William	Father	Outside Burial
Boyles, George Walter	Father	Private Burial
Bradford, Bert	Wife	Private Burial
Briers, Alan	Father	Outside Burial Leicester
Briers, Doris Jean	Father	Outside Burial Leicester
Briers, Jessie	Husband	Outside Burial Leicester
Briers, Sheila Lillian.	Father	Outside Burial Leicester
Britt, Alfred Eli	Brother	23rd November 1940

Brown, Arthur William		
Brown, Dennis.	Father	23rd November 1940
Brown, Edward George	Father	20th November 1940
Brown, James		
Brown, James.		
Brown, John Edwin.		Cremated Outside Burial
Brown, Joseph Palmer.	Wife	17th/ 9th December 1940
Brown, Walter Henry Edwin.		Cremated Outside Burial
Buckenham, George	Son	23rd November 1940
Buckley, Lizzie Lewis	Sister	Outside Burial/Blackburn
Buckley, Richard.	Brother	Outside Burial/Blackburn
Bullock, Harold	Wife	
Burns, Dennis Patrick	Father	23rd November 1940
Burrows, David Wilson		
Burton, Annie Louisa	Husband	20th November 1940
Butterfield, Alfred Friend		23rd November 1940
Butterfield, Dorothy Elizabeth.	Friend	21st /23rd November 1940
Cain, Harold.	Wife	20th November 1940
Carn, Emily	Daughter	4th December 1940
Carvell, Rosina	Son	23rd November 1940
Chinn, Agnes Maud.	Husband	23rd November 1940
Chinn, Eric	Father	23rd November 1940
Chinn, Vera Maud	Father	20th November 1940
Clarke, Eileen Mary.		
Clarke, Harry	Wife	28th November 1940
Clarke, Mr.		
Clarke, Philip Henry.		21st /23rd November 1940
Clarke, William Thomas	Wife	20th November 1940
Claypole, Ernest Leslie.	Father	20th November 1940
Clutterbuck, Frank	Wife	20th November 1940
Collett, Agnes Elizabeth	Brother	23rd November 1940
Collett, Cyril Ernest	Brother	20th November 1940
Collett, Hugh Wilfred	Son	23rd November 1940
Collett, Sidney Albert.	Brother	20th November 1940
Collier, Harry John		Outside Burial
Collingridge, Elizabeth	Husband	23rd November 1940
Congrave, Edith Husband		23rd November 1940
Congrave, Lewis		23rd November 1940
Cooke, Frederick Arthur	Wife	23rd November 1940
Cooke, George Edmund	Son	23rd November 1940
Cooke, George Frederick	Brother	23rd November 1940
Cooke, Louisa	Son	23rd November 1940
Cooper, Florence Lillian	Son	3rd/ 4th December 1940
Cooper, Henry	Brother	29th November 1940

Cooper, Joseph	Son	23rd November 1940
Cooper, Norah	Husband	23rd November 1940
Cooper, V.		
Cottam, Richard		
Courts, Albert Earl	Daughter	23rd November 1940
Cramp, Nellie	Father	20th November 1940
Crawford, Robert John	Mother	20th November 1940
Cronan, James	Son	23rd November 1940
Cronan, Sarah Lavinia	Dghter-in-law	29th November 1940
Cronin, Michael Joseph	Brother	Outside Burial
Cuthbertson, George	Mother-in-law	29th Nov 1940, 3rd Dec 1940
Cuthbertson, Joyce	Grandmother	23rd /29th November 1940
Cuthbertson, Mabel	Mother	29th November 1940
Daines, Ada.	Brother	23rd November 1940
Daines, Walter	Son	23rd November 1940
Daly, Louis James	Sister	23rd November 1940
Danes, Gordon David	Father	Outside Burial
Danes, Robert John	Father	Outside Burial
Davis, John Matthew	Father	23rd November 1940
Davis, Mary Ann	Husband	
Dawson, Kate.	Husband	20th November 1940
Dawson, Christopher Patrick		
Deacon, Ida Henrietta	Brother-in-law	23rd November 1940
Deacon, Walter Alfred	Son-in-law	23rd November 1940
Dennis, William James Albert.	Brother-in-law	23rd November 1940
Dingley, Colin Arthur	Father	23rd November 1940
Doyle, Edna May	Husband	
Doyle, Kevin Anthony		
Duncalf, Daisy Violet		
Eaton, Alfred		
Eaves, Joan Marjorie	Mother	23rd November 1940
Eaves, John	Wife	20th November 1940
Edmunds, Wesley Allen	Mother	Outside Burial
Edmunds, William Frederick		
Edwards, Gordon	Father	Outside Burial
Egginton, Corbett	Wife	23rd November 1940
Elliott, Annie		23rd November 1940
Elliott, Greta Edwina	Father	20th November 1940
Elliott, Margaret Rose	Father	23rd November 1940
Elliott, Ronald	Father	20th/23rd November 1940
Elson, Thomas Richard	Brother-in-law	23rd November 1940
Endersby, Stanley David	Wife	20th November 1940
Evans, Edna May	Father	
Evans, George Sidney James	Wife	23rd November 1940

Farndon, Clifford Richard		
Farr, Joan Margaret Millward	Father	20th November 1940
Faulkner, Elizabeth	Stepson	9th December 1940
Faulkner, William Joseph	Stepson	9th December 1940
Felgate, Reginald	Son	23rd November 1940
Fern, Wilfred Harold	Mother	20th November 1940
Florence, Martin	Son	23rd November 1940
Foley, Patrick		
Freeman, Thomas Muscott	Son	23rd November 1940
French, William		
Frost, Ethel	Husband	23rd November 1940
Frost, Leonard	Father	23rd November 1940
Garside, Eliza	Husband	21st/23rd November 1940
Gaskine, Harry	Wife	29th November 1940
Golby, Frederick	Sister	23rd November 1940
Golby, L.		
Golby, Leonard		
Goodwin, Harold	Wife	23rd November 1940
Gough, Walter	Wife	23rd November 1940
Gould, Frances		
Gould, James Henry		
Grady, John		29th November 1940
Graham, Mary	Husband	23rd November 1940
Green, Brenda Alice	Mother	23rd November 1940
Grinham, Dolly	Husband	23rd November 1940
Guest, William Henry		29th November 1940
Hadingham, Arthur Edward	Father	23rd November 1940
Hadingham, Winifred Blanche	Husband	23rd November 1940
Hands, Anthony Peter	Father	23rd November 1940
Harbourne, Bernard	Father	23rd November 1940
Harris, William Henry	Step Mother	
Harrison, Barbara Joyce	Father	23rd November 1940
Harrison, David	Son	20th November 1940
Harrison, Harold Frederick	Wife	20th November 1940
Hartell, William Edward	Wife	Outside Burial
Hartopp, Sydney	Mother	20th November 1940
Haynes, Catherine Elizabeth	Mother	23rd November 1940
HEATH, JOHN 546 62 THE BUTTS		20th November 1940
Heath, John	Wife	20th November 1940
Henly, Ada Elizabeth		21st November 1940
Heynes, Simon William	Father	Outside Burial
Higgins, Alfred		
Hill, Douglas	Father	23rd November 1940
Hill, May	Husband	23rd November 1940

Hipkiss, John Henry	Sister	23rd November 1940
Hiscocks, Alan	Mother	
Hoare, Hilda May	Mother-in-law	23rd November 1940
Hoare, John Denham	Grandmother	
Hoare, Margaret	Grandmother	23rd November 1940
Hoare, Walter James Denham	Mother	23rd November 1940
Hobbs, Albert.	Wife	23rd November 1940
Hobday, Daisy	Brother	23rd November 1940
Hobday, Eliza	Son	23rd November 1940
Hobday, George William	Son	23rd November 1940
Hobday, May	Brother	23rd November 1940
Holder, Brenda	Mother	20th November 1940
Holland, Almina	Father	23rd November 1940
Holland, Dennis Howard	Father	21st /23rd November 1940
Holland, Raymond	Father	23rd November 1940
Hollingsworth, Ernest Leslie	Brother-in-law	
Hollingsworth, Lillian	Mother	21st November 1940
Holmes, J. L.		
Holt, Frederick		
Hopkins, A		
Howells, Keith Desmond		
Howells, Royston Charles		
Howells, Winifred May		
Hughes, Harold Benjamin	Friend	29th November 1940
Hughes, William James	Wife	23rd/ 29th November 1940
Humphreys, Violet May	Mother	21st /23rd November 1940
Hydon, Ernest William	Brother-in-law	23rd November 1940
Ince, Agnes Harriett	Husband	OB/ 29th November 1940
Inman, Edgar	Wife	23rd November 1940
Isitt, Mary Hannah	Husband	23rd November 1940
Jackson, Charles Edward	Friend	3rd/4th December 1940
Jackson, William Alfred Edward	Wife	23rd November 1940
James, John Alfred	Wife	23rd November 1940
Jeffery, Constance Mary	Mother	Outside Burial
Jennings, Charles		
Johnstone, Reginald	Wife	20th November 1940
Jones, Beatrice Ada Mansfield	Brother	23rd November 1940
Jones, Clement Horace	Mother	21st /23rd November 1940
Jones, Edward	Father	23rd November 1940
Jones, John	Brother-in-law	
Jones, Thomas Digby	Wife	20th November 1940
Jones, William Arthur	Brother	
Jones, William Henry	Mother	23rd November 1940
Jowett, Frederick	Wife	

Judd, Cyril Wyatt Stockton	Wife	
Keay, William Thomas	Daughter	Outside Burial
Kemble, Robert	Mother	23rd November 1940
Kendrick, Mary Ann	Daughter	23rd November 1940
Kenney, James	Wife	20th November 1940
Kilbuern, Frederick	Father	20th November 1940
Kimberley, Maria Sarah		
Kimberley, William Henry	Wife	20th November 1940
King, Leslie George		
Kinzett, Stephanie	Father	Coventry Cemetery
Knighton, Bertie John		
Knutton, Emma Martha		
Krzeminski, Franciszek		
Laing, Agnes	Daughter	23rd November 1940
Laing, Elizabeth Margaret	Sister	23rd November 1940
Lake, Florence Annie		
Lambe, William Robert	Father	
Lampitt, Doris	Brother in law	Outside Burial
Landles, Thomas		
Lapworth, Dennis		
Lapworth, Joseph Thomas.	Father	
Law, Jeremiah.	Wife	20th/23rd November 1940
Layton, George.	Father	23rd November 1940
Leedham, John Harry Wood	Father	23rd November 1940
Leeson, Jane.	Friend	23rd November 1940
Leeson, Raymond.	Friend	23rd November 1940
Lenton, Doris May	Mother	20th /23rd November 1940
Letford, Gwen Ivy	Father	OB/29th November 1940
Lewin, Alec Edward	Brother	
Lewin, Charles John		23rd November 1940
Lewin, Gertrude Emily	Brother	
Leworthy, David Geoffrey	Mother	23rd November 1940
Leworthy, John Herbert.	Wife	23rd November 1940
Liggins, Christina Mary.	Husband	23rd November 1940
Littlehales, Pamela Mary	Father	
Livesey, Bertha	Husband	29th November 1940
Lockett, Ada		
Lockett, Albert Victor	Son	20th November 1940
LOGAN J. P. 474 14 Lucknow Street, Belfast		20th November 1940
Lovell, Ethel Mary	Father	Outside Burial
Lovell, Maurice William	Father	Outside Burial
Lowe, Arthur Henry		
Lowry, Thomas Roland	Mother	
Ludford, William Edward		

Mailey, Edith.		
Mallard, William		23rd November 1940
Marley, Herbert.		20th November 1940
Marley, Iris		20th November 1940
Marley, Olive Lily		20th November 1940
Marsden, Frederick Thomas	Wife	23rd November 1940
Mason, Violet	Mother	20th November 1940
Masser, Clifford David	Step-father	Outside Burial
Masters, Henrietta	Mother	23rd November 1940
Matthews, Leonard Lucien	Father	20th November 1940
Mcarthur, Alexander Thomas	Mother	
Mccormack, Arthur	Wife	Outside Burial
Mcgarrity, Michael	Mother	23rd November 1940
Mcinerney, John	Wife	Private Burial
Mcmurdie, David Arthur		
Miles, Horace William	Brother-in-law	23rd November 1940
Miles, Lillian Olive	Brother	23rd November 1940
Miller, Marjorie Elaine	Mother	23rd November 1940
Mills, William	Father	20th November 1940
Moody, Ethel	Mother	Outside Burial
Moody, Percival Clement	Mother-in-law	
Morrell, Maureen Patricia	Brother	23rd November 1940
Morris, Frederick Arthur	Father	23rd November 1940
Moss, Raymond	Wife	23rd November 1940
Murphy, Edith	Friend	23rd November 1940
Murphy, John Irvine	Friend	23rd November 1940
Needle, John George	Mother	20th November 1940
Nelson, Thomas Richard		
Neville, Fred	Sister	20th November 1940
Newall, Richard Arthur	Wife	21st /23rd November 1940
Newson, Mavis Evelyn	Brother	23rd November 1940
Newson, William	Son	23rd November 1940
Nightingale, Susannah	Daughter	
Nolan, Timothy		20th November 1940
Norman, John Cooper	Sister	20th November 1940
Norman, Lavinia	Husband	23rd November 1940
Oliver, Edith Evelyn	Father-in-law	21st November 1940
Oliver, Jack	Father	20th November 1940
Orton, Colin	Aunt	23rd November 1940
Orton, Olive Ida	Sister-in-law	23rd November 1940
Orton, Percy Lionel	Sister	23rd November 1940
Orton, Thelma	Aunt	21st /23rd November 1940
Osborne, Emily	Husband	23rd November 1940
Overbury, Arthur	Daughter	20th November 1940

Page, James.	Father	Private Burial
Pargetor, Ernest Victor	Brother-in-law	23rd November 1940
Parncutt, George Thomas	Wife	23rd November 1940
Parr, Edith Annie	Son	Outside Burial
Parr, Nancy May	Brother	Outside Burial
Parsons, Alfred Hendry	Brother	23rd November 1940
Partington, Hilda May	Husband	23rd November 1940
Payne, George Francis	Son	20th November 1940
Phillips, Walter	Wife	23rd November 1940
Piggon, Brenda May		
Podesta, Reschotti	Sister	20th November 1940
Pointon, Edith Emily	Husband	21st /23rd November 1940
Porter, Mary	Son	23rd November 1940
Preston, Albert	Son	9th December 1940
Preston, Florence Annie	Son	29th November 1940
Price, Dulise	Son	23rd November 1940
Price, Graham Charles	Father	Outside Burial
Price, Harold Ewart Jayne	Son	23rd November 1940
Price, June Patricia	Father	Outside Burial
Price, Ruth Ann	Father	Outside Burial
Print, Arthur	Wife	23rd November 1940
Proctor, Doris Kate	Mother-in-law	23rd November 1940
Proctor, Reginald	Mother	23rd November 1940
Prosser, Henry	Wife	23rd November 1940
Pugh, Sarah	Daughter	29th November 1940
Pugh, William Thomas	Daughter	29th November 1940
Purchase, Thomas John	Wife	23rd November 1940
Pyett, Percy William		
Randall, Charles William	Wife	23rd November 1940
Randall, Elsie Marjorie	Husband	23rd November 1940
Redgate, Harriet	Husband	23rd November 1940
Redgate, Hilda May	Father	23rd November 1940
Rees, Eveline	Father	23rd November 1940
Richardson, Frank	Father	23rd November 1940
Richardson, Gordon John		23rd November 1940
Richardson, Richard John	Wife	Outside Burial
Riley, Ethel	Husband	20th November 1940
Ring, Daisy Millicent	Son	20th November 1940
Ring, John Thomas	Stepson	20th November 1940
Robbins, Peter Edgar Arthur	Father	Outside Burial
Roberts, Audrey Annie	Husband	23rd November 1940
Roberts, Audrey Patricia	Father	23rd November 1940
Roberts, Christina May	Sister	20th November 1940
Roberts, Ernest David	Daughter	20th November 1940

Roberts, Ernest Eric	Sister	23rd November 1940
Roberts, Frederick		23rd November 1940
Roberts, Herbert William	Friend	
Roberts, John		20th November 1940
Roberts, Leslie Arthur.	Sister	23rd November 1940
Roberts, Rose May	Daughter	21st /23rd November 1940
Roberts, Thomas		OB/Lincoln
Robinson, Frances Nelly	Brother-in-law	23rd November 1940
Robinson, Frederick	Brother	
Robinson, George		
Robinson, Peter	Brother	23rd November 1940
Robson, James		23rd November 1940
Rogers, Dorothy May	Mother	23rd November 1940
Rogers, Ernest	Brother	23rd November 1940
Rollason, Agnes	Friend	20th November 1940
Rollins, John Donald	Uncle	23rd November 1940
Rollins, Kenneth Charles	Wife	Outside Burial
Rollins, Marion	Brother	
Ronan, John		20th November 1940
Rooke, Alice Elizabeth.	Sister	17th December 1940
Rooms, Charles Arthur	Father	23rd November 1940
Roper, William Robert Loudon	Father	23rd November 1940
Rose, Ann	Daughter	23rd November 1940
Roughton, Alfred Ernest		23rd November 1940
Roughton, Ernest John		23rd November 1940
Rowson, Emma Amelia		
Ruddick, Florence Lavinia	Husband	23rd November 1940
Ruddick, Malcolm George	Father	23rd November 1940
Rutter, James, Henry		23rd November 1940
Sanders, W. H.		
Satcwell, Victor Alexander	Wife	23rd November 1940
Scarrott, Donald Albert		23rd November 1940
Scott, Doris	Mother	
Scott, Frank		
Scott, Lionel	Wife	20th November 1940
Sear, Stanley Arthur	Father	
Seltzer, Joseph		
Sharrocks, Eveline	Brother	23rd November 1940
Shillcock, Harriet	Husband	
Shore, Garnet	Wife	Outside Burial
Simpson, Albert		
Simpson, Joseph Samuel	Father	23rd November 1940
Simpson, Muriel Gwendoline	Father	23rd November 1940
Sims, Owen Francis	Wife	23rd November 1940

Sinclair, Ada	Brother-in-law	Outside Burial
Sinclair, William Malcolm	Brother	23rd November 1940
Smith, Arthur	Brother-in-law	20th November 1940
Smith, Arthur Edward	Son	23rd November 1940
Smith, Dennis John	Mother	23rd November 1940
Smith, James William	Wife	23rd November 1940
Smith, Josephine Ann	Father	23rd November 1940
Smith, Margaret Ettie	Brother	20th November 1940
Smith, Phyllis Cicily	Mother	23rd /29th November 1940
Smith, Robert		
Smith, Rose	Husband	20th November 1940
Smith, Walter Edward	Wife	23rd November 1940
Smyth, Joan Margaret	Mother	
Sorrell, Maurice		
Spalding, Elsie Rebecca	Husband	20th November 1940
Spencer, Emma Amelia	Husband	
Steele, Isabella	Daughter	3rd/4th December 1940
Steele, Stephen	Friend	29th November 1940
Stephens, Gertrude Annie	Sister	23rd November 1940
Stephens, Horace	Wife	OB/29rd November 1940
Stephens, William Joseph	Son	23rd November 1940
Stokes, Minnie	Mother-in-law	21st /23rd November 1940
Storer, Alice Marjorie	Sister	20th November 1940
Storer, Walter Charles	Daughter	20th November 1940
Strong, Frederick Soloman		
Stubbs, Arthur John	Brother	9th December 1940
Stubbs, Dorothy	Father	3rd/ 4th December 1940
Stubbs, Irene	Father	3rd/ 4th December 1940
Stubbs, Marjorie	Uncle	9th December 1940
Sutton, Edith Mary	Husband	20th November 1940
Sutton, Kenneth	Father	23rd November 1940
Tallis, Edward	Sister	23rd November 1940
Tanner, Elizabeth	Niece	17th December 1940
Tansey, John	Sister	23rd November 1940
Tarver, Doris	Mother	23rd November 1940
Tarver, Harold Asa	Mother	23rd November 1940
Taylor, Harry		23rd November 1940
THOMAS, ALBERT 444		21st November 1940
Thomas, Phyllis	Husband	
Thompsell, Roger William	Wife	20th November 1940
Thompson, Florence	Brother-in-law	23rd November 1940
Thompson, Walter	Brother	23rd November 1940
Thorpe, Winifred Joan	Father	23rd November 1940
Timms, William Alfred Henry	Mother	Outside Burial

Tipson, Patricia Ann	Father	20th November 1940
Tipson, Alan Roy	Father	20th November 1940
Tipson, Ellen Sarah	Husband	20th November 1940
Tipson, Joan Alice	Father	20th November 1940
Tipson, Pamela Elizabeth	Father	20th November 1940
Toney, Sarah Ann		20th November 1940
Tong, Wilfred Henry	Wife	Outside Burial
Tovey, Daisy Dot	Brother	23rd November 1940
Tovey, Daisy Millicent.		
Tovey, Doris	Brother	3rd December 1940
Trevitt, Emily		
Turner, Mary		
Twamley, Oliver	Brother-in-law	23rd November 1940
VANE, Mr.		23rd November 1940
Villiers, Esther	Son	20th November 1940
Villiers, Harry	Brother	23rd November 1940
Waite, Enid Annorah		
Walford, Edwin	Brother	23rd November 1940
Walford, Edwin	Uncle	
Walford, Esther	Uncle	21st November 1940
Walford, Norman	Uncle	23rd November 1940
Walsh, Elsie	Solicitor	20th November 1940
Walters, Ethel May	Brother	23rd November 1940
Walters, Richard	Brother-in-law	20th November 1940
Walters, Richard Derrick	Uncle	20th November 1940
Ward, Clara	Son	29th November 1940
Ward, Leonard		23rd November 1940
Ward, Patricia	Mother	23rd November 1940
Warren, Margaret	Father	23rd November 1940
Watkins, Bertha Ellen		
Watkins, Hugh. Plaque application		
Watson, Alice	Son	23rd November 1940
Watson, George Henry	Son	23rd November 1940
Watson, Walter William	Daughter	Outside Burial
Welch, Charles William		
West, Bertram Whyatt	Father	20th November 1940
White, Elizabeth		9th December 1940
White, James		
White, Thomas	Brother-in-law	3rd December 1940
Whitehouse, Christine Mary	Brother	23rd November 1940
Whitehouse, Herbert Alec	Son	23rd November 1940
Whitehouse, Olive Annie	Son	23rd November 1940
WHITFIELD 221		23rd November 1940
WHITFIELD 222		23rd November 1940

Williams, Catherine Nora	Husband	23rd November 1940
Williams, John Emlyn	Son	29th November 1940
Williams, Mary Ann	Son	
Williams, Sara Jane		
Wilson, Mary Alice	Sister	23rd November 1940
WILSON, T. 225 Dame Agnes Grove		20th November 1940
Winterburn, Joan	Mother	23rd November 1940
Wiseman, Annie	Husband	23rd November 1940
Witcomb, Christine	Uncle	9th December 1940
Witcomb, Ethel	Brother-in-law	
Witcomb, Joan	Uncle	9th December 1940
Witcomb, John Gregory	Brother	9th December 1940
Witcomb, Sylvia	Uncle	9th December 1940
Wood, Kenneth John	Wife	23rd November 1940
Wood, Robert Wilton	Brother-in-law	Outside Burial
Woodfield, Albert Thomas	Father-in-law	Outside Burial
Woodfield, Frances Zena	Father	Outside Burial
Wright, Anne Elizabeth	Husband	
Wright, Francis John	Wife	27th November 1940
Wykes, Ruth		
Yardley, Ann	Daughter	20th November 1940
Yarrow, James Harold	Wife	
Yates, Elizabeth	Brother	23rd November 1940
Yates, Florence	Son	23rd November 1940
Yeomans, Frederick Samuel	Brother	20th November 1940
260 Unidentified female		23rd November 1940
261 Unidentified child		23rd November 1940
286 Unidentified female		23rd November 1940
301 Unidentified Baby girl 56 21st November 1940		
313 Unidentified person		23rd November 1940
320 Unidentified		
326 Unidentified		
331 Unidentified		
333 Unidentified Person Foleshill Union Shelter 23rd November 1940		
347 Unidentified Person		23rd November 1940
355 Unidentified Soldier from Hillman Humber 23rd November 1940		
370a Unidentified female 35 Burlington Road		23rd November 1940
424 Unidentified Person		23rd November 1940
434 Unidentified Male		21st November 1940
467 Unidentified		23rd November 1940
535 Unidentified Male		23rd November 1940
582 Unidentified person		23rd November 1940
612 Unidentified female		21st November 1940
618 Storer Female Frederick Bird School		23rd November 1940

646 Unidentified Male 111 Beechwood Avenue   9th December 1940
654 Female   23rd November 1940
681 Unidentified   17th December 1940
682 Unidentified   17th December 1940
694 Unidentified found 30 St. Christians Road 27th February 1941
710 Unidentified Male Bablake School Shelter   29th November 1940
728 Unidentified   4th December 1940

Appendix D Communal Grave Map and References

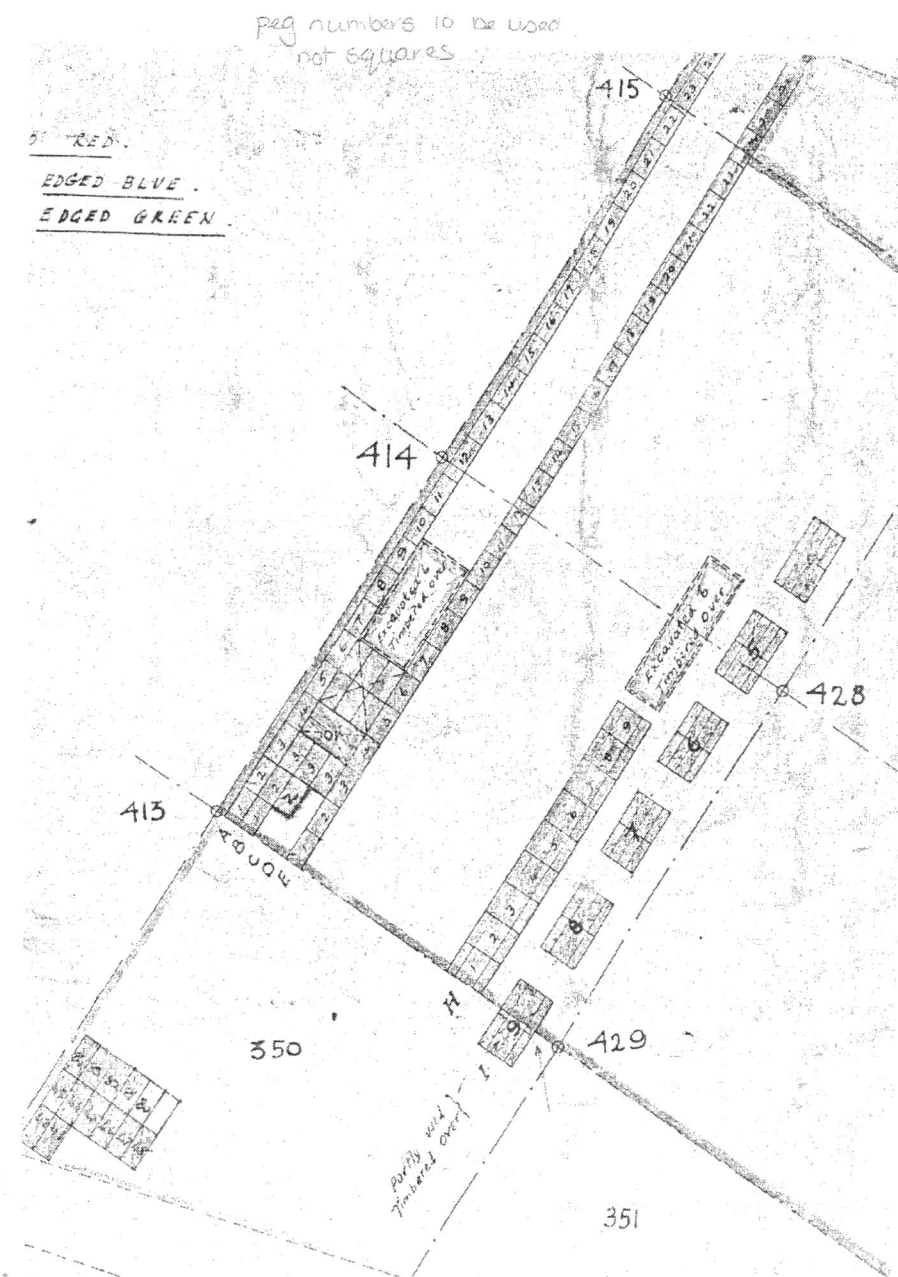

A. 2/3 Tansey, John
A. 7/2 Hoare, Walter James Denham
A. 10/1 Jones, Clement Horace
A. 10/2 Garside, Eliza
A. 10/3 Archer, Charles.
A. 11/1 Yates, Elizabeth
A. 11/5 Parncutt, George Thomas
A. 119/3 Randall, Elsie Marjorie
A. 12/2 Thompson, Walter
A. 12/4 Rollins, John Donald
A. 12/5 Deacon, Ida Henrietta
A. 13/1 Roberts, Ernest Eric
A. 13/2 Egginton, Corbett
A. 13/4 Bell, Doreen Betty
A. 13/4 Leeson, Jane.
A. 13/5 Morris, Frederick Arthur
A. 13/5 Wiseman, Annie
A. 14/1 Stokes, Minnie
A. 14/3 Hadingham, Winifred Blanche
A. 14/4 Proctor, Reginald
A. 14/5 Hobday, May
A. 15/1 Bass, George Arthur
A. 15/3 Kendrick, Mary Ann
A. 15/5 Bennett, Christopher
A. 16/1 Wood, Kenneth John
A. 16/2 Leworthy, David Geoffrey Harwood
A. 16/2 Leworthy, John Herbert.
A. 16/4 Ball, Florence May
A. 16/5 Newall, Richard Arthur
A. 17/1 Robson, James
A. 17/2 Whitehouse, Christine Mary
A. 17/3 Allitt, Jane.
A. 17/4 Parsons, Alfred Hendry Edward.
A. 17/5 Ball, Clara Beatrice
A. 17/5 Evans, George Sidney James
A. 18/1 Barker, Joan.
A. 18/2 Butterfield, Dorothy Elizabeth.
A. 18/2 Holland, Almina
A. 18/2 Holland, Raymond
A. 18/3 Phillips, Walter

A. 18/4 Rooms, Charles Arthur

A. 19/1 Masters, Henrietta
A. 19/2 Richardson, Frank
A. 19/4 Roberts, Frederick
A. 20/1 Thompsell, Roger William
A. 20/2 Courts, Albert Earl
A. 20/4 Porter, Mary
A. 20/4 Smith, James William
A. 21/1 Bennett, Jack
A. 21/2 Allport, Phyllis Marguerite.
A. 21/3 Moss, Raymond
A. 21/4 Taylor, Harry
A. 21/5 Cooke, Frederick Arthur
A. 22/1 Jones, Beatrice Ada Mansfield
A. 22/2 Burns, Dennis Patrick
A. 22/3 James, John Alfred
A. 22/4 Hughes, William James
A. 23/1 Wilson, Mary Alice
A. 23/2 Florence, Martin
A. 24/1 Roper, William Robert Loudon
A. 24/2 Cronan, James
A. 24/3 Harbourne, Bernard
A. 24/4 Hill, Douglas
A. 4/1 Hobday, Daisy
A. 4/2 Gough, Walter
A. 4/3 Bennett, Florence May.
A. 4/5 Baseley, Agnes
A. 4/6 Yates, Florence
A. 4/10 Miles, Horace William
A. 5/1 Robinson, Frances Nelly
A. 5/2 Pargetor, Ernest Victor
A. 5/3 Tarver, Doris
A. 5/4 Holland, Dennis Howard
A. 5/5 Collingridge, Elizabeth
A. 6/1 Bass, Annie Elizabeth
A. 6/2 Bass, Leonard James
A. 6/3 Lenton, Doris May
A. 6/4 Barker, Edith Mary
A. 6/5 Hoare, Hilda May
A. 7/1 Hill, May
A. 7/3 Hydon, Ernest William
A. 7/4 Print, Arthur
A. 7/5 Humphreys, Violet May
A. 8/1 Ahessy, James.
A. 8/2 Murphy, John Irvine

A. 8/3 Randall, Charles William
A. 8/4 Smith, Dennis John
A. 8/5 Jackson, William Alfred Edward
A. 9/1 Bird, Edna Elsie May
A. 9/2 Mallard, William
A. 9/3 Rees, Eveline
A. 9/4 Oliver, Edith Evelyn
A. 9 3/4 Walters, Ethel May
B. 12/1 Freeman, Thomas Muscott
B. 4/1 Cooper, Florence Lillian
B. 4/1 Cuthbertson, George
B. 4/2 Stubbs, Arthur John
B. 4/2 Stubbs, Marjorie
B. 4/2 White, Elizabeth
B. 4/2 Witcomb, Christine
B. 4/2 Witcomb, Joan
B. 4/2 Witcomb, John Gregory
B. 4/2 Witcomb, Sylvia
B. 4/3 Faulkner, Elizabeth
C. 4/1 Jackson, Charles Edward
C. 4/2 Faulkner, William Joseph
D. 4/1 Steele, Isabella
D. 4/1 Stubbs, Dorothy
D. 4/1 Stubbs, Irene
D. 4/1 Tovey, Doris
D. 4/1 White, Thomas
D. 4/2 Preston, Albert
D3. 3/5 Behan, Thomas
E. 10/1 Mills, William
E. 10/2 Tipson, Alan Roy
E. 10/2 Tipson, Joan Alice
E. 10/3 Collett, Sidney Albert.
E. 10/4 Spalding, Elsie Rebecca
E. 11/1 Roberts, Ernest David
E. 11/2 Endersby, Stanley David
E. 11/3 Collett, Cyril Ernest
E. 11/4 Eaves, John
E. 11/5 Dawson, Kate.
E. 11/6 Miles, Lillian Olive
E. 12/1 Yeomans, Frederick Samuel
E. 12/3 Cain, Harold.
E. 12/4 Ronan, John
E. 12/5 Scott, Lionel
E. 12/6 Barker, James.

E. 13/2 Cramp, Nellie
E. 13/2 Johnstone, Reginald
E. 13/3 Nolan, Timothy
E. 13/4 Daines, Walter
E. 13/5 Rose, Ann
E. 13/6 Whitehouse, Olive Annie
E. 14/1 Mason, Violet
E. 14/2 Elliott, Ronald
E. 14/3 Proctor, Doris Kate
E. 14/5 Roberts, Rose May
E. 14/6 Whitehouse, Herbert Alec
E. 15/1 Clarke, William Thomas
E. 15/2 Chinn, Vera Maud
E. 15/4 Henly, Ada Elizabeth
E. 15/5 Beadle, Ernest Harold
E. 15/5 Lewin, Charles John
E. 15/6 Richardson, Gordon John
E. 16/1 Farr, Joan Margaret Millward
E. 16/2 Villiers, Esther
E. 16/3 Green, Brenda Alice
E. 16/4 Daines, Ada.
E. 17/1 Baylis William Charles.
E. 17/2 Roberts, Christina May
E. 17/3 Elliott, Margaret Rose
E. 17/5 Hollingsworth, Lillian
E. 17/6 Redgate, Harriet
E. 18/1 Neville, Fred
E. 18/2 Clutterbuck, Frank
E. 18/3 Toney, Sarah Ann
E. 18/4 Partington, Hilda May
E. 18/5 Adams, Mary Brand
E. 18/6 Pointon, Edith Emily
E. 19/1 Oliver, Jack
E. 19/2 Matthews, Leonard Lucien
E. 19/3 Buckenham, George
E. 19/5 Sutton, Kenneth
E. 19/6 Billings, Leonard John.
E. 20/1 Harrison, David
E. 20/3 Ward, Leonard
E. 20/4 Walford, Edwin
E. 20/5 Prosser, Henry
E. 20/6 Watson, George Henry
E. 21/1 Brown, Edward George
E. 21/2 Burton, Annie Louisa

E. 21/3 Mcgarrity, Michael
E. 21/4 Liggins, Christina Mary.
E. 22/1 Kenney, James
E. 22/2 Kilbuern, Frederick
E. 22/4 Rutter, James, Henry
E. 22/5 Bott, Sylvia Mary.
E. 22/6 Villiers, Harry
E. 23/1 Riley, Ethel
E. 23/2 Banyard, William Joseph
E. 23/4 Stephens, William Joseph
E. 23/5 Collett, Hugh Wilfred
E. 24/2 West, Bertram Whyatt
E. 24/3 Barritt, Catherine
E. 24/4 Miller, Marjorie Elaine
E. 24/5 Tovey, Daisy Dot
E. 24/6 Laing, Elizabeth Margaret E.
25/1 Payne, George Francis
E. 25/2 Sutton, Edith Mary
E. 25/3 Goodwin, Harold
E. 25/4 Bass, Clement Alfred Gordon
E. 25/5 Bird, Alfred
E. 26/- Golby, Frederick
E. 26/1 Billings, Eva
E. 26/2 Podesta, Reschotti
E. 26/3 Walford, Norman
E. 26/5 Britt, Alfred Eli
E. 27/3 Smith, Josephine Ann
E. 3/4 Holder, Brenda
E. 3/5 Ager, John Lovell.
E. 4/1 Kimberley, William Henry
E. 4/2 Bawden, Albert Ernest
E. 4/3 Ring, Daisy Millicent
E. 4/4 Claypole, Ernest Leslie.
E. 4/5 Harrison, Harold Frederick
E. 5/2 Smith, Rose
E. 5/3 Crawford, Robert John
E. 5/4 Needle, John George
E. 5/5 Lockett, Albert Victor
E. 6/2 Smith, Arthur
E. 6/3 Storer, Alice Marjorie
E. 6/4 Yardley, Ann
E. 6/5 Fern, Wilfred Harold
E. 7/1 Jones, Thomas Digby
E. 7/2 Hartopp, Sydney

E. 7/3 Atkins, Frederick.
E. 7/4 Marley, Iris
E. 7/5 Smith, Margaret Ettie
E. 7/6 Marley, Herbert.
E. 8/1 Overbury, Arthur
E. 8/2 Norman, John Cooper
E. 8/3 Rollason, Agnes
E. 8/4 Walters, Richard
E. 8/4 Walters, Richard Derrick
E. 8/5 Law, Jeremiah.
E. 9/1 Tipson, Ellen Sarah
E. 9/1 Tipson, Pamela Elizabeth
E. 9/1 Tipson, Patricia Ann
E. 9/2 Storer, Walter Charles
E. 9/3 Walsh, Elsie
E. 9/4 Elliott, Greta Edwina
E. 9/5 Bass, Thomas William
E. 9/6 Marley, Olive Lily
E. 24/1 Heath, John
E. 26/4 Hoare, Margaret
E 12/2 Ring, John Thomas
E2. 1/6 Watson, Alice
E2. 6/7 Frost, Leonard
H. 12/3 Cooper, Norah
I4. 1/1 Twamley, Oliver
I4. 1/2 Leeson, Raymond.
I4. 1/3 Osborne, Emily
I4. 1/5 Carvell, Rosina
I4. 2/1 Redgate, Hilda May
I4. 2/1 Williams, John Emlyn
I4. 2/2 Beadle, Irene May Edith.
I4. 2/3 Price, Harold Ewart Jayne
I4. 2/4 Sims, Owen Francis
I4. 2/5 Bass, Joan Mary
I4. 3/1 Smith, Arthur Edward
I4. 3/2 Purchase, Thomas John
I4. 3/3 Roughton, Ernest John
I4. 3/4 Barrell, Bertram.
I4. 3/4 Orton, Percy Lionel
I4. 4/1 Hobbs, Albert.
I4. 4/2 Thorpe, Winifred Joan
I4. 4/3 Ruddick, Florence Lavinia
I4. 4/3 Ruddick, Malcolm George
I4. 4/4 Dennis, William James Albert.

O/4 Billings, Aubrey John.
O/4 Billings, Marion Grace.
O/4 Brown, Joseph Palmer.

O/4 Rooke, Alice Elizabeth.
O/4 Tanner, Elizabeth

Appendix E Injured on 14th/15th November 1940 and later killed

Elizabeth Hannah Allitt was injured on the night of the 14th/15th November 1940 treated at a first aid post and sent home. She was killed on the 10th April 1941 after being buried in an air raid shelter, Warwick Row, aged 66.

Eric Boardman was injured on the 14th November and sent home after being treated at a first aid post, aged 24. He joined the 2nd Battalion Royal Berkshire Regiment and was killed in action, Shwebo, Burma on the 7th January 1945, aged 28.

Leonard Clay was detained in Hollymoor Emergency Hospital in Birmingham and died on service on the 10th July 1943 at Bletchley with the 9th Bn., Royal Warwickshire Regiment. He is buried in London Road Cemetery.

Gunner Robert Henry Morrell, 880576, 4 Regt., Royal Horse Artillery died on active service, 19th General Hospital, Middle East Force on the 22nd December, 1941. Age 24. He was born on the 4th July, 1917 at Harold Green, Dublin. Employed by General Electric Co. Ltd and enlisted 12th May, 1938. Grave Ref. 1. F. 14. Fayid War Cemetery, Egypt. Records state he was treated at a first aid post.

Arthur Farthing was detained in Barnsley Hall Emergency Hospital, Bromsgrove on the 14th/ 15th November 1940. He resided at 67 Smith Street, aged 53 and was a Home Guard. He was killed at 67 Smith Street on the night of the 8th April 1941.

Appendix F Treated Home address outside Coventry

68th Bomb Disposal, Royal Engineers Detained in Chilvers Coton Emergency Hospital

916 Squadron RAF Detained in Hollymoor Emergency Hospital, Birmingham

917th B. B. Squadron Detained in Evesham Emergency Hospital

Allesley Detained in Warwick Hospital

Allesley, Peabody Cottages, Detained in Hospital of St. Cross, Rugby

Allesley, The Gables Detained in Stratford-on-Avon Emergency Hospital

Ansty RAF Treated at First Aid Posts and sent home

Ansty Village

Arley Ransom Road 6a Gun Hill Detained in Stratford-on-Avon General Hospital

Arley, Rectory Cottages 13 Detained in Warwick Hospital

Atherstone Coleshill Street 51 Detained in Barnsley Hall Emergency Hospital, Bromsgrove

Atherstone Kings Avenue 47

Atherstone, Stanley Road 14 Detained in Warneford Hospital, Leamington Spa

Baginton Airport Treated at First Aid Posts and sent home

Baginton RAF Station Detained in Hospital of St. Cross Rugby

Banbury Cope Street 26 Detained in Warwick Hospital

Barton-on-Humber Frerely Road 79 Detained in Warwick Hospital

Bedford Knightsbridge Avenue 19 Detained in Stratford-on-Avon Emergency Hospital

Bedworth Alexandra Road 17 Detained in Hospital of St. Cross Rugby

Bedworth Alexandra Road 17 Treated at First Aid Post and sent home

Bedworth Chapel House 3, Chapel Street, Detained in Barnsley Hall Emergency Hospital, Bromsgrove

Bedworth Coventry Road 56 Detained Barnsley Hall, Bromsgrove

Bedworth Evans Close 7 Treated at Works – Returned to duty

Bedworth Goodyers End Lane 10, Detained in emergency Hospital, Nuneaton

Bedworth Harbury Road 26 Detained in Warwick Hospital

Bedworth Margaret Avenue 54 Detained in Nuneaton Emergency Hospital

Bedworth Regent Street 16 Detained in Stratford-on-Avon General Hospital

Bedworth Regent Street 55 Treated at First Aid Post and sent home

Bedworth Saunders Avenue 1 Detained in Stratford-on-Avon Emergency Hospital

Bedworth Wood Street, Collycroft, Detained in Warwick Hospital

Bedworth Woodland Road, 39, Detained in Hollymoor Hospital, Birmingham

Belfast, Counay Street 32 Detained in Alcester Emergency Hospital

Birmingham Bernacre Street, 38.

Birmingham Detained in Hospital of St. Cross, Rugby

Birmingham Hampton Road 35 Detained in Hollymoor Hospital Birmingham

Birmingham Kingsway 97, Quinon, Treated at First Aid Post and sent home

Birmingham Parliament Street 44 Detained in Alcester Hospital

Birmingham Unett Street 6 Hockley Detained Barnsley Hall Emergency Hospital, Bromsgrove

Birmingham, Church Lane 10 Treated at First Aid Posts and sent home
Blackburn Dewhurst Street 8 Detained in Stratford-on-Avon Emergency Hospital
Brinklow, Heath Lane Detained in Stratford-on-Avon Emergency Hospital
Bulkington Wolsey Road, 28 Detained in Stratford-on-Avon General Hospital
Calham, Chuddeston Detained in Alcester Hospital
Dublin Hammand Street 3 Detained in Warwick Hospital **Durham,** Tenth Street 58 Barnsley Hall, Bromsgrove
Edgehill Hallsworth Avenue 32 Detained in Hospital of St. Cross Rugby
Erdington Marsh Lane 103
Fillongley, Wood End Lane Detained in Barnsley Hall Emergency Hospital, Bromsgrove
Hinckley Hinckley Street 44
Kenilworth, Spring Street 10 Detained in Warneford Hospital, Leamington
Kenilworth, Spring Street 10 Detained in Warneford Hospital, Leamington
Kenilworth Common Lane Treated at First Aid Posts and sent home
Kenilworth Clinton Lane 59 Detained in Warwick Hospital
Kenilworth Henry Street 5 Detained in Warwick Hospital
Kenilworth Red Lane 58 Detained in Barnsley Hall Emergency Hospital, Bromsgrove
Lancashire, 1 Wilkins Street, Glitheroe Detained in Warwick Hospital
Leamington Spa Regent Street 96 Detained at Shuckburgh Park Convalescent Hospital, Daventry
Leamington Spa Woodbine Street 27 Detained in Warwick Hospital
Leicester Glenn Gate 43 Treated at First Aid Posts and sent home
Leamington, Brunswick Street, 88 Treated at First Aid Post and sent home
Leicester, Westgate Treated at Gulson Road Hospital and sent home
Lichfield, Hovis Road 12
Littlethorpe near Leicester The Square 22, Detained in Stratford-on-Avon General Hospital
London, 17 Elmgrove Road, Dinas Powis, SW Barnsley Hall Bromsgrove
London Nightingale Road 283 Detained in Warwick Hospital
London, Rodney Place 16 Detained in Stratford Emergency Hospital
Loughborough Gladstone Street 75 Detained in Barnsley Hall Emergency Hospital, Bromsgrove
Meriden Village Farm Detained in Nuneaton Emergency Hospital
Meriden. Diddington Hall, Detained in Stratford-on-Avon Emergency Hospital
Northampton Boughton Green Road 114 Treated at First Aid Post and sent home
Northampton, Greenhills Road 89 Detained in Hospital of St. Cross, Rugby
Nottingham. 149, Allendale Avenue, Detained in Stratford-on-Avon Emergency Hospital
Nuneaton, Bracebridge Street, 34, Detained in Warwick Hospital
Nuneaton Fitton Street 50 Detained in Hollymoor Emergency Hospital, Birmingham
Nuneaton Leyland Road 3 Treated at First Aid Post and sent home
Nuneaton Litton Street 50 Detained in Warwick Hospital
Nuneaton Long Shoot 254 Treated at First Aid Post and sent home

Nuneaton Road 67 Detained in Stratford-on-Avon General Hospital
Nuneaton Ventnor Street, 24, Detained in Warwick Hospital
Nuneaton, Bermuda Road Barnsley Hall, Bromsgrove
Nuneaton, Oldbury Road 254 Detained in Warneford Hospital, Leamington
Rugby Little Church Street, 12 Detained in Shuckburgh Park Convalescent Hospital, Daventry.
Rugby Westfield Road 82 Treated at First Aid Posts and sent home
Scarborough Wykener Street 4
Stafford Romford Road 11 Detained in Stratford-on-Avon Emergency Hospital
Stoke Fire Service Treated at First Aid Post and sent home
Stoke on Trent Havelock Road 19 Treated at First Aid Posts and sent home
Stoke-on-Trent, Parkville Street 51 Detained in Barnsley Hall Emergency Hospital
Stretton under Fosse Detained at Hospital of St. Cross, Rugby
Sutton Coldfield Avenue Road Detained in Stratford-on-Avon Emergency Hospital
Sutton Coldfield Walmley Road 14   Detained in Warwick Hospital
Walsall, New Street 23 Hollymoor Hospital Birmingham
Warwick Cherry Street, 2 Detained in Stratford-on-Avon Emergency Hospital
Widnes, CLC Cottages, Farnworth, Lancs. Detained in Stratford-on-Avon Emergency Hospital
Wolverhampton Pinfold Lane 98 Treated at First Aid Post and sent home
Wolverhampton, Cannock Road 573 Treated at First Aid Posts and sent home
Wolverhampton, Castle Croft Road

Appendix G Treated with no known address

Nine people treated at First Aid Post and sent home
Four people detained in Alcester Emergency Hospital
Four people detained Barnsley Hall, Bromsgrove
Six people detained in Evesham Emergency Hospital
Four people treated at Gulson Road Hospital and sent home
Three people detained in Hollymoor Emergency Hospital, Birmingham
Two people treated at Works First Aid Post and sent home
Two people detained in Emergency Hospital Rugby
One person detained at Shuckburgh Park Convalescent Hospital, Daventry.
One person detained in Stratford Emergency Hospital
Three people detained in Warneford Emergency Hospital, Leamington
Eight people detained in Warwick Hospital

No. 9 First Aid Post Detained in Warneford Hospital, Leamington
Nuffield RAF School Treated at First Aid Post and sent home
Queens Hotel
RAF Ansty
RAF Baginton Detained in hospital of St. Cross, Rugby
RAF Detained in Hollymoor Hospital Birmingham
RAF Sandy Lane Treated at First Aid Post and sent home

Alveston Road 3 Detained in Hospital of St. Cross, Rugby
Ash Grove 6 Detained in Stratford-on-Avon General Hospital
Berkswell Street 51
Blackmore Road 47 Detained in Hollymoor Hospital, Birmingham
Bryan Road 33 Detained in Stratford-on-Avon Emergency Hospital
Chapel Street 12
Charlton Road 41 Detained in Stratford-on Avon Emergency Hospital
Cherry Street 12 Detained in Warneford Hospital, Leamington Spa
Cherry Street 9 Treated at First Aid Post and sent home
Covenden Terrace 4 Treated at Gulson Road Hospital and sent home
Denby Road 55 Detained in hospital of St. Cross, Rugby
Drill Hall Detained in Hollymoor Hospital, Birmingham
Drury Street 12 Detained in Warwick Hospital
Eva Road 2
Eva Road 2 Detained in Barnsley Hall Emergency Hospital, Bromsgrove
Geoffrey Woods Cross 34 Detained in Warwick Hospital
Gilbert Street Detained in Stratford-on-Avon Emergency Hospital
Grove Road 8 Detained in Stratford-on-Avon Emergency Hospital
Henry Street 46 Detained in Stratford-on-Avon General Hospital
Hill Cross 17 Treated at First Aid Posts and sent home

Hill Cross 17 Treated at First Aid Posts and sent home
Humber Motor Works Treated at First Aid Post and sent home
Humber Motor Works Treated at First Aid Posts and sent home
Lean Street 14 Treated at First Aid Post and sent home
Manchester Street 80 Detained in Alcester Emergency Hospital
Newfield School, Detained in Hollymoor Emergency Hospital, Birmingham
Perkins Street 12 Detained in Hollymoor Hospital Birmingham
Pinley Gardens, The Firs Detained in Hospital of St.Cross Rugby
Post Office, Longford Detained in Shuckburgh Park Convalescent Hospital, Daventry
Roehampton Drive 68 Detained in Hollymoor Hospital, Birmingham
Stanton Street 21 Treated at First Aid Posts and sent home
Stephen Street 11 Detained in Hospital of St.Cross Rugby
Technical College Treated at First Aid Posts and sent home
The Grange 17, Keresley Treated at Warneford Hospital, Leamington Spa and sent home

Index

Brown, Arthur William 95
Brown, Dennis. 172
Brown, Edward George 172
Brown, James 190
Brown, James. 97
Brown, John Edwin. 144
Brown, Joseph Palmer. 80
Brown, Walter Henry Edwin. 144
Buckenham, George 100
Buckley, Lizzie Lewis 100
Buckley, Richard. 100
Bullock, Harold 164
Burns, Dennis Patrick 59
Burrows, David Wilson 132
Burton, Annie Louisa 41
Butterfield, Alfred
Butterfield, Dorothy Elizabeth.
Cain, Harold. 185
Carn, Emily 80
Carvell, Rosina 156
Chinn, Agnes Maud. 64
Chinn, Eric 64
Chinn, Vera Maud 64
Clarke, Eileen Mary.169
Clarke, Harry 53
Clarke, Mr. 192
Clarke, Philip Henry. 102
Clarke, William Thomas 169
Claypole, Ernest Leslie. 77
Clutterbuck, Frank 102
Collett, Agnes Elizabeth 49
Collett, Cyril Ernest 49
Collett, Hugh Wilfred 49
Collett, Sidney Albert. 49
Collier, Harry John 50
Collingridge, Elizabeth 161
Congrave, Edith 50
Congrave, Lewis 50
Cooke, Frederick Arthur59
Cooke, George Edmund 83
Cooke, George Frederick 83
Cooke, Louisa 83
Cooper, Florence Lillian 70
Cooper, Henry 70

Cooper, Joseph 70
Cooper, Norah 50
Cooper, V. 192
Cottam, Richard
Courts, Albert Earl 110
Cramp, Nellie 161
Crawford, Robert John 50
Cronan, James 64
Cronan, Sarah Lavinia 64
Cronin, Michael Joseph 71
Cuthbertson, George 70
Cuthbertson, Joyce 70
Cuthbertson, Mabel 70
Daines, Ada. 148
Daines, Walter 148
Daly, Louis James 71
Danes, Gordon David 103
Danes, Robert John 103
Davis, John Matthew 124
Davis, Mary Ann 83
Dawson, Kate. 161
Dawson, Christopher Patrick 161
Deacon, Ida Henrietta 104
Deacon, Walter Alfred 104
Dennis, William James Albert. 149
Dingley, Colin Arthur 133
Doyle, Edna May 77
Doyle, Kevin Anthony 77
Duncalf, Daisy Violet 81
Eaton, Alfred 160
Eaves, Joan Marjorie 110
Eaves, John 42
Edmunds, Wesley Allen 148
Edmunds, William Frederick 160
Edwards, Gordon 152
Egginton, Corbett 94
Elliott, Annie 98
Elliott, Greta Edwina 98
Elliott, Margaret Rose 98
Elliott, Ronald 98
Elson, Thomas Richard 113
Endersby, Stanley David 84
Evans, Edna May 50
Evans, George Sidney James 103

Farndon, Clifford Richard 190
Farr, Joan Margaret Millward 178
Faulkner, Elizabeth 174
Faulkner, William Joseph 174
Felgate, Reginald 148
Fern, Wilfred Harold 81
Florence, Martin 75
Foley, Patrick 70
Freeman, Thomas Muscott 56
French, William 84
Frost, Ethel 173
Frost, Leonard 173
Garside, Eliza 72
Gaskine, Harry 55
Golby, Frederick 72
Golby, L. 85
Golby, Leonard 85
Goodwin, Harold 186
Gough, Walter 124
Gould, Frances 192
Gould, James Henry 86
Grady, John 191
Graham, Mary 50
Green, Brenda Alice 41
Grensill, Violet 156
Grinham, Dolly 75
Guest, William Henry 158
Hadingham, Arthur Edward 93
Hadingham, Winifred Blanche 93
Hands, Anthony Peter 97
Harbourne, Bernard 147
Harris, William Henry 46
Harrison, Barbara Joyce 77
Harrison, David 87
Harrison, Harold Frederick 126
Hartell, William Edward 153
Hartopp, Sydney 81
Haynes, Catherine Elizabeth 64
Heath John 67
Heynes, Simon William 130
Higgins, Alfred 191
Hill, Douglas 147
Hill, May 169
Hipkiss, John Henry 114

Hiscocks, Alan 145
Hoare, Hilda May 83
Hoare, John Denham 83
Hoare, Margaret 83
Hoare, Walter James Denham 83
Hobbs, Albert. 142
Hobday, Daisy 114
Hobday, Eliza 114
Hobday, George William 114
Hobday, May 114
Holder, Brenda 59
Holland, Almina 141
Holland, Dennis Howard 141
Holland, Raymond 141
Hollingsworth, Ernest Leslie 115
Hollingsworth, Lillian 115
Holmes, J. L. 191
Holt, Frederick 169
Hopkins, A 190
Howells, Keith Desmond 169
Howells, Royston Charles 169
Howells, Winifred May 169
Hughes, Harold Benjamin 158
Hughes, William James 158
Humphreys, Violet May 96
Hydon, Ernest William 113
Ince, Agnes Harriett 135
Inman, Edgar 124
Isitt, Mary Hannah 150
Jackson, Charles Edward 53
Jackson, William Alfred Edward 171
James, John Alfred 132
Jeffery, Constance Mary 51
Jennings, Charles 171
Johnstone, Reginald 186
Jones, Beatrice Ada Mansfield 130
Jones, Clement Horace 60
Jones, Edward 115
Jones, John 130
Jones, Thomas Digby 124
Jones, William Arthur 165
Jones, William Henry 179
Jowett, Frederick 103
Judd, Cyril Wyatt Stockton 118

Keay, William Thomas 60
Kemble, Robert 144
Kendrick, Mary Ann 60
Kenney, James 78
Kilbuern, Frederick 76
Kimberley, Maria Sarah 67
Kimberley, William Henry 141
King, Leslie George 188
Kinzett, Stephanie 77
Knighton, Bertie John 190
Knutton, Emma Martha 191
Krzeminski, Franciszek 192
Laing, Agnes 67
Laing, Elizabeth Margaret 67
Lake, Florence Annie 188
Lambe, William Robert 183
Lampitt, Doris 163
Landles, Thomas 192
Lapworth, Dennis 93
Lapworth, Joseph Thomas. 93
Law, Jeremiah. 186
Layton, George. 105
Leedham, John Harry Wood 153
Leeson, Jane. 171
Leeson, Raymond. 171
Lenton, Doris May 59
Letford, Gwen Ivy 78
Lewin, Alec Edward 159
Lewin, Charles John 159
Lewin, Gertrude Emily 159
Leworthy, David Geoffrey Harwood 63
Leworthy, John Herbert. 63
Liggins, Christina Mary. 106
Littlehales, Pamela Mary 80
Livesey, Bertha 73
Lockett, Ada 127
Lockett, Albert Victor 127
Lovell, Ethel Mary 95
Lovell, Maurice William 95
Lowe, Arthur Henry 87
Lowry, Thomas Roland 84
Ludford, William Edward 187
Mailey, Edith. 190
Mallard, William 66

Marley, Herbert. 129
Marley, Iris 129
Marley, Olive Lily 129
Marsden, Frederick Thomas 119
Mason, Violet 55
Masser, Clifford David 51
Masters, Henrietta 96
Matthews, Leonard Lucien 112
Mcarthur, Alexander Thomas 148
Mccormack, Arthur 51
Mcgarrity, Michael 170
Mcinerney, John 48
Mcmurdie, David Arthur 120
Miles, Horace William 51
Miles, Lillian Olive 72
Miller, Marjorie Elaine 81
Mills, William 51
Moody, Ethel 113
Moody, Percival Clement 113
Morrell, Maureen Patricia 167
Morris, Frederick Arthur 172
Moss, Raymond 152
Murphy, Edith 116
Murphy, John Irvine 116
Needle, John George 110
Nelson, Thomas Richard 115
Neville, Fred 171
Newall, Richard Arthur 119
Newson, Mavis Evelyn 163
Newson, William 163
Nightingale, Susannah 95
Nolan, Timothy 177
Norman, John Cooper 155
Norman, Lavinia 155
Oliver, Edith Evelyn 104
Oliver, Jack 104
Orton, Colin 104
Orton, Olive Ida 150
Orton, Percy Lionel 150
Orton, Thelma 150
Osborne, Emily 72
Overbury, Arthur 65
Page, James. 42
Pargetor, Ernest Victor 186

Parncutt, George Thomas 81
Parr, Edith Annie 103
Parr, Nancy May 103
Parsons, Alfred Hendry Edward. 87
Partington, Hilda May 169
Payne, George Francis
Phillips, Walter 102
Piggon, Brenda May 51
Podesta, Reschotti 141
Pointon, Edith Emily 72
Porter, Mary 170
Preston, Albert 73
Preston, Florence Annie 73
Price, Dulise 155
Price, Graham Charles 103
Price, Harold Ewart Jayne 155
Price, June Patricia 103
Price, Ruth Ann 103
Print, Arthur 154
Proctor, Doris Kate 101
Proctor, Reginald 101
Prosser, Henry 187
Pugh, Sarah 94
Pugh, William Thomas 94
Purchase, Thomas John 97
Pyett, Percy William 88
Randall, Charles William 153
Randall, Elsie Marjorie 150
Redgate, Harriet 150
Redgate, Hilda May 150
Rees, Eveline 46
Richardson, Frank 172
Richardson, Gordon John 78
Richardson, Richard John 173
Riley, Ethel 57
Ring, Daisy Mllicent 55
Ring, John Thomas 55
Robbins, Peter Edgar Arthur 173
Roberts, Audrey Annie 66
Roberts, Audrey Patricia 66
Roberts, Christina May106
Roberts, Ernest David 57
Roberts, Ernest Eric 52
Roberts, Frederick 48

Roberts, Herbert William 165
Roberts, John 106
Roberts, Leslie Arthur.
Roberts, Rose May 57
Roberts, Thomas 192
Robinson, Frances Nelly 131
Robinson, Frederick 158
Robinson, George 193
Robinson, Peter 131
Robson, James 178
Rogers, Dorothy May 105
Rogers, Ernest 105
Rollason, Agnes 97
Rollins, John Donald 113
Rollins, Kenneth Charles 84
Rollins, Marion 113
Ronan, John 77
Rooke, Alice Elizabeth. 157
Rooms, Charles Arthur 51
Roper, William Robert Loudon 52
Rose, Ann 107
Roughton, Alfred Ernest 119
Roughton, Ernest John 119
Rowson, Emma Amelia 72
Ruddick, Florence Lavinia 150
Ruddick, Malcolm George 150
Rutter, James, Henry 193
Sanders, W. H. 191
Satcwell, Victor Alexander 47
Scarrott, Donald Albert 110
Scott, Doris 168
Scott, Frank 168
Scott, Lionel 130
Sear, Stanley Arthur 166
Seltzer, Joseph 189
Sharrocks, Eveline 155
Shillcock, Harriet 151
Shore, Garnet 124
Simpson, Albert 193
Simpson, Joseph Samuel 46
Simpson, Muriel Gwendoline Gladys 46
Sims, Owen Francis 167
Sinclair, Ada 159
Sinclair, William Malcolm George 159